D0931270

In this reexamination of Canada's balance-of-payments experience under the gold standard, the authors develop and empirically test a new portfolio approach to the mechanism of balance-of-payments adjustment. This adjustment mechanism responded to massive inflows of foreign capital during a critical period of Canada's economic growth in the early years of the twentieth century. The authors show that the existence of international mobility of capital requires a fundamental revision of the price-specie-flow theory that has traditionally been used to explain adjustment when the balance of payments was more nearly dominated by the balance of trade. The approach taken by professors Dick and Floyd not only answers the critics of Jacob Viner, who first explored the Canadian case after 1900, but also offers a new perspective on how the gold standard in general actually worked.

This new interpretation of the Canadian experience is an extension of the monetary approach to balance-of-payments adjustment that realizes the full implications of international capital mobility. Interest-rate differentials do not drive capital flows, but instead reflect risk premiums set by the exchange of imperfectly substitutable securities of different countries in world-asset markets. Changes in domestic relative to foreign price levels equilibrate markets for goods, but do not satisfy purchasing-power parity. This innovative theory may apply to any fixed exchange-rate system when capital is internationally mobile.

The authors apply standard elementary economic principles to this working of the balance of payments under the gold standard, making this book useful reading for those studying intermediate- and upper-level economics, especially in the field of international finance.

Canada and
the gold standard

Studies in Monetary and Financial History

EDITORS: Michael Bordo and Forrest Capie

Barry Eichengreen, *Elusive Stability: Essays in the History of International Finance, 1919–1939*

Kenneth Mouré, *Managing the Franc Poincaré, 1928–1936: Economic Understanding and Political Constraint in French Monetary Policy*

Larry Neal, *The Rise of Financial Capitalism: International Capital Markets in the Age of Reason*

Aurel Schubert, *The Credit-Anstalt Crisis of 1931*

David C. Wheelock, *The Strategy and Consistency of Federal Reserve Monetary Policy, 1924–1933*

Canada and the gold standard

Balance-of-payments adjustment, 1871–1913

Trevor J. O. Dick
University of Lethbridge

John E. Floyd
University of Toronto

CAMBRIDGE
UNIVERSITY PRESS

Published by the Press Syndicate of the University of Cambridge
The Pitt Building, Trumpington Street, Cambridge CB2 1RP
40 West 20th Street, New York, NY 10011–4211, USA
10 Stamford Road, Oakleigh, Victoria 3166, Australia

© Cambridge University Press 1992

First published 1992

Printed in Canada

Library of Congress Cataloging-in-Publication Data
Dick, Trevor J. O.
Canada and the gold standard : balance of payments adjustment,
1871–1913 / Trevor J. O. Dick, John E. Floyd.
    p.   cm. – (Studies in monetary and financial history)
Includes bibliographical references and indexes.
ISBN 0–521–40408–8
1. Balance of payments – Canada – History.   2. Gold standard –
History.   I. Floyd, John E. (John Earl), 1937–   .   II. Title.
III. Series.
HG3883.C3D53   1992
382'.17'097109034–dc20
91-19222
CIP

A catalog record for this book is available from the British Library.

ISBN 0–521–40408–8 hardback

Contents

v

Tables and figures

Tables

Figures

Preface

The experience of exchange rate instability since 1971 has renewed interest in the workings of the classical gold standard before 1914, when fixed exchange-rate regimes were dominant and smooth balance-of-payments adjustments widespread. How and why did the gold standard work so well, and are there reasons to hope for a return to this regime? Such a hope lingered in the interwar period, but the abandonment of gold as a medium for settling international obligations in the early 1970s does not augur well for return to a gold standard. The intellectual appeal of fixed exchange rates, however, has never evaporated, nor has the curiosity about how the gold standard actually worked. The present study transcends the debate over fixed versus flexible rates to present a new perspective on the classical gold standard that highlights the role of international capital mobility in the adjustment process.

Although the ideas presented in this book have potentially wider applicability to other monetary regimes and historical contexts, the immediate testing ground is the Canadian pre–World War I experience – long considered a prime example of smooth balance-of-payments adjustment under the gold standard. We view these ideas as a natural and belated evolution of economic thought prompted by the increasing importance historically of capital movements in the balance of payments, a phenomenon that draws attention to distinctive and hitherto little recognized implications of the recently developed monetary approach to balance-of-payments adjustment. Our ongoing work is continuing to uncover evidence in other countries and regimes in support of the theory offered here when capital mobility is an important element in the story.

This study is the fruit of nearly a decade of collaboration between the authors, who have interacted to refine the theory and explore hidden depths of the empirical evidence. The result, we believe, is a theoretically consistent framework of analysis that is particularly revealing about the mechanism of adjustment that was at work in the Canadian balance of payments between 1871 and 1914.

In the course of our collaboration, we have accumulated many debts to past and present authors, to the organizers of numerous seminars and conferences, to funding agencies, and to many others who have both enlightened and lightened our task by helping us to find and understand the appropriate data and by assisting us in the necessary tasks of producing a tidy and readable manuscript.

We acknowledge, in particular, lively and provocative discussion with Gordon Anderson, Michael Bordo, Charles Calorimis, Forrest Capie, Jack Carr, Michael Devereux, Gerry Dwyer, Stephen Easton, Barry Eichengreen, Al Hynes, Greg Jump, Mervyn Lewis, Don McCloskey, Ronald McKinnon, Angelo Melino, Anna Schwartz, Ronald Shearer, and Rick Simes. We have also benefited from correspondence with Arthur Bloomfield, Alec Cairncross, Jacob Frankel, Charles Kindleberger, Georg Rich, Larry Neal, and Brinley Thomas, and from the comments of two anonymous referees.

Our ideas matured as various parts and versions of the argument were subjected to the critical scrutiny of seminar participants at the Australian National University, Northwestern University, La Trobe University, the University of Melbourne, the University of Tasmania, Stanford University, the University of Toronto, the 1981 Seminar on the Application of Quantitative Methods to Canadian Economic History, the 1988 Annual Cliometrics Conference, the Ninth World Congress of the International Economic Association at Athens, Greece, 1989, and the Tenth International Economic History Congress at Louvain, Belgium, 1990.

The work has been supported financially by the Social Sciences and Humanities Research Council of Canada and the universities of Lethbridge and Toronto. Some of the work was completed while Dick was a visiting scholar at Harvard University and a research associate at the University of California at Berkeley, and while Floyd was a visiting fellow at the Research School of Social Sciences at the Australian National University. We acknowledge the support of our home universities that made it possible to devote undisturbed time to the project and the host universities for providing stimulating environments in which to work. The computing staffs of all these institutions helped to keep us in contact by electronic mail without which collaboration would have been much slower and more difficult.

We also acknowledge the comments and suggestions of two anonymous referees who read earlier versions of the manuscript, and the painstaking attention to detail by the staff of Cambridge University Press, helping us at numerous points to better articulate and clarify our meaning.

The interest and enthusiasm of others to debate with us on controversial topics and to contribute to our thought as the work progressed in no way relieves the authors of full responsibility for the final product. While we have learned much in the process, our main thesis has changed little from its original conception, and the evidence in its favor has progressively mounted.

Finally, we acknowledge the forbearance of our families, who have borne with many of the sacrifices made along the way to turn ideas and evidence into a publishable manuscript.

University of California at Berkeley   T.J.O.D.
University of Toronto   J.E.F.
June 1991

1. Introduction

This monograph is more than a study in Canadian economic history – it refines and tests a modern portfolio theory of balance-of-payments adjustment under gold standard conditions. It is a study of how Canada's economy adjusted to the massive inflow of capital in the early years of the twentieth century and how her monetary system functioned within the international gold standard. It is also a test of a particular theory of gold standard adjustment, a theory built on the assumption of an integrated world market for capital assets. This theory implies a radically different balance-of-payments adjustment process than the traditional classical price-specie-flow mechanism. And we believe it explains the evidence better than does the traditional theory.

Our study follows a long and venerable tradition. In 1924, Jacob Viner published a celebrated study of Canada's balance of payments for the period 1900–13. His work was one of a number of empirical studies by students of F. W. Taussig at Harvard University.[1] Of these studies, Viner's attracted the most attention because it provided a vigorous defense of the traditional classical theory of balance-of-payments adjustment. This provoked strong criticism both at the time and over the years since publication and, despite continued scholarly efforts to rethink the theory and reexamine the data, the controversies have never been satisfactorily resolved. Neither have a number of related controversies about the operation of the gold standard, in particular, the sterilization of gold flows, the role of the Bank of England, and the importance of capital movements in the adjustment process. Although most scholars organize their thinking within the standard classical framework, there are dissident opinions.

---

[1] Other studies in the group include Williams (1920), Graham (1922), White (1933), and Beach (1935). Williams studies the adjustment mechanism for Argentina under depreciated paper. Graham focuses on the effects of British capital flows into the United States during the greenback period. White's study examines the effects of capital exports from France during the years 1880–1913. Beach studies capital outflows from Britain during the same period

The Canadian experience before the Great War is an ideal testing ground for theories of balance-of-payments adjustment – another reason why Viner's work attracted more attention than its companion studies. An enormous inflow of capital occurred during the first decade and a half of the twentieth century. Absorption of this capital necessitated very substantial real and monetary adjustments within the Canadian economy. The question was and still is: What form did these adjustments take?

This monograph reexamines the adjustment mechanism from a fresh theoretical perspective. We incorporate international capital mobility within a framework of joint intercountry portfolio equilibrium. Balance-of-payments adjustments are once-and-for-all exchanges of money and nonmonetary assets, with little if any change in the balance of trade. In the traditional classical price-specie-flow mechanism, balance-of-payments adjustments involve deficits and surpluses in the balance of trade brought about by changes in domestic relative to foreign price levels.

Our theoretical framework has roots going back over three decades. The classic papers of Fleming (1962) and Mundell (1963) established important fundamentals of the adjustment process under perfect capital mobility, but their analysis did not explicitly incorporate stocks and flows and therefore did not generalize easily to handle imperfect capital mobility. Much earlier, Johnson (1958a) outlined carefully the distinction between stock and flow balance-of-payments adjustments. He did not, however, properly integrate these concepts with the standard model and his work was ignored for over a decade.

In the late 1960s McKinnon and Oates (1966) again addressed the stock-flow problem and Floyd (1969a, 1969b) and Harkness (1969) developed explicit balance-of-payments stock-adjustment models.[2] These works drew attention to serious problems with the standard generalization of the Mundell–Fleming model to the analysis of imperfect capital mobility. In particular, the fallacy of treating capital flows as a function of international differences in interest rates became recognized. A simple integrated model of stocks and flows failed to emerge, however, because the analysis did not correctly integrate balance-of-payments flow adjustments. Early revisionist work was thus eclipsed by the newly emerging monetary approach to balance-of-payments theory developed in the early 1970s by Mundell and Johnson and their students at the University of Chicago.[3]

---

[2] See also Willett and Forte (1969) and Miller and Whitman (1970).
[3] Some of the early contributions to this literature are in Frenkel and Johnson (1976).

The monetary approach interpreted balance-of-payments adjustments as strictly monetary phenomena, rediscovering and reworking much of traditional classical balance-of-payments analysis. In the process, international stock adjustments and the analysis of international capital movements in general were again relegated to the back burner. Nevertheless, the old Mundell–Fleming model, which correctly handles monetary shocks when capital is perfectly mobile, remained integral, if often implicit, in many papers.

Capital movements and stock/flow equilibrium again receive explicit attention in a paper by Frenkel and Rodriguez (1975) and stock/flow equilibrium with perfect capital mobility forms a cornerstone of Mussa's (1982) analysis of exchange-rate dynamics under rational expectations. Following Floyd (1985), our theoretical formulation further extends the analysis of perfect and imperfect capital mobility, integrating much of the earlier literature in a simple straightforward stock/flow equilibrium framework.

As it applies to the gold standard, our theory has an important precedent in two recent papers by McCloskey and Zecher (1976, 1984). Their work follows the monetary approach, interpreting balance-of-payments adjustments and the associated gold movements as strictly monetary phenomena. International capital mobility is implicit in their model. They appear to have in mind an adjustment process similar to ours, although they do not rigorously develop the theoretical framework within which balance-of-payments adjustments operate. They argue instead that "purchasing power parity" was essential to the adjustment process.

Our analysis supports and extends McCloskey and Zecher's conclusions about balance-of-payments adjustment. We develop rigorously a portfolio equilibrium foundation for their position and test it empirically in ways suggested by our theory. We find no support for the purchasing-power parity doctrine as traditionally defined. We do find support for the view that the price levels of the individual countries are linked together under a gold standard when capital is internationally mobile. The link is not the rigid and direct one implied by the standard theory of purchasing-power parity, however.[4]

In our theory, interest rates in the various countries are linked together in a unified world market for assets. There is freedom of international exchange combined with differences in risk. An excess demand or supply

---

[4] A careful reading of McCloskey and Zecher's work, supplemented by correspondence and conversation with them, confirms that they in fact have this less rigid linkage among country price levels in mind when they are defending purchasing-power parity.

of money in one part of the world leads to a once-and-for-all exchange of money and assets. The result is a one-shot transfer of gold as world portfolio equilibrium is reestablished. This balance-of-payments adjustment is largely independent of the countries' relative price levels.

The ratio of each country's price level to the price level abroad is determined by the world (including home) demand for that country's goods relative to goods abroad. Gold flows between countries to satisfy changes in the demand for money that arise from changes in incomes and relative price levels. These are induced by exogenous real-sector developments such as shifts in the allocation of world investment among countries, changes in individual country's savings rates, and changes in technology and tastes with respect to various countries' goods. For individual countries, money holdings are determined by prices and not the other way around as the traditional classical theory implies.

For the world as a whole, however, money determines prices in accordance with the standard quantity theory. The situation is exactly analogous to regions within a country, as McCloskey and Zecher (1976) recognize. Given world monetary conditions, the price level in Illinois is determined by the demand and supply conditions for the goods produced in that state, with Illinois residents acquiring the necessary money balances by exchanging assets for them. Illinois residents can have an effect on the price level in Illinois only if they own a significant fraction of the U.S. (more correctly, world) money supply. On the other hand, a change in the world demand for money leads to a change in the price level everywhere, including Illinois.

Our analysis resolves anomalies that, as Bordo (1984) notes, begin to appear in the traditional gold standard theory after the turn of the century. The first of these is what Triffin called the "overall parallelism − rather than divergence − of price movements, expressed in the same unit of measurement, between the various trading countries maintaining a minimum degree of freedom of trade and exchange in their international transactions."[5] British balance-of-payments adjustments, for example, occurred remarkably smoothly with none of the wrenching relative price level divergences implied by the traditional theory.

A second major anomaly is the evidence that most central banks did not play by the rules of the gold standard game. Bloomfield notes that "central banks in general played the rules of the game just as badly before 1914

[5] Triffin (1964, p. 4).

as they did thereafter."[6] How could the gold standard have survived if this was in fact the case?

The third anomaly is the parallelism, again to use Triffin's term, in interest-rate movements among countries. The standard view is that discount-rate increases are undertaken by deficit countries to relieve a drain of their reserves to surplus countries. As Bloomfield notes, however, the discount rates of virtually all countries tend to rise and fall together over the course of the world business cycle. There is no evidence of the relationship between interest rates and gold flows implied by the traditional theory.[7]

In reacting to these anomalies, both Triffin (1964) and Williamson (1961, 1963) suggest viewing the adjustment process in a general equilibrium context. The price levels of the various countries should be closely linked with balance-of-payments adjustments, reflecting money-market disequilibria and their elimination. This is precisely the tack we take in the research presented here.

The anomalies are easily explained when the theory is formulated in general equilibrium terms, with capital mobility appropriately incorporated. The parallelism in prices arises because the mechanism of adjustment works through one-shot portfolio adjustments and not through relative price effects on the balance of trade. There is no reason to observe divergences of price levels in connection with balance-of-payments disequilibria.

Central banks do not appear to play according to the conventional rules because the rules are not what the traditional classical theorists thought them to be. Under a gold standard central banks face constraints, not rules. Apart from affecting the world demand for gold, not a practical option for even the largest countries, they have no control over their domestic money supplies in either the short or long runs. They cannot sterilize the effects of gold flows if they want to. On the other hand, changes in the reserve ratios of the commercial banks or in the public's desired ratio of gold to total money holdings in a particular country result in gold flows without money-supply changes. This makes it appear as though the country's central bank is sterilizing the effects of gold flows on the money supply.

Changes in central banks' desired ratios of gold holdings to money supply also result in gold flows without money-supply changes. Since these gold movements cannot affect the level of domestic economic activity, any

[6] Bloomfield (1959, p. 50).
[7] Bloomfield (1959, pp. 35–7).

attempt by the authorities to pursue monetary independence is unsuccessful. Yet changes in central bank reserve ratios may nevertheless occur because of changes in the opportunity costs of holding reserves and the perceived risk of a run on gold.

Our analysis also clarifies a number of issues relating to interest rates and international capital and gold flows. First, we establish that international capital flows in the aggregate do not "respond" to international differences in interest rates. The conditions of world portfolio equilibrium simultaneously determine interest-rate levels and the allocation of the ownership of each country's assets among all countries' residents. This accounts for the parallelism in interest rates. The steady-state flows of capital depend on savings rates and the allocation of world investment. One might observe on occasion a correlation (either positive or negative) between international capital flows and interest differentials. There is no reason, however, to expect a relationship of the sort postulated in the traditional classical approach.

Our analysis confirms the classical view that tightening domestic credit is an effective method of stimulating gold inflows and discouraging outflows, but such a policy is not likely to create an observable interest-rate differential when domestic and foreign assets are good substitutes in portfolios and gold flows are relatively small in relation to the outstanding stocks of every country's assets. In addition, changes in the rediscount rate do not affect domestic credit independently of the actual rediscounting and open-market operations by the central bank. Rediscount rates will thus be less related to capital and gold flows than are short-term rates generally. In any case, the validity of the classical theory turns on interest-rate differentials, not levels.

Our task in the chapters that follow is to develop the theory supporting the above claims and marshal the evidence to substantiate it. Our theoretical results are applicable to all countries, large and small. Because we restrict our empirical work to the Canadian experience, however, our efforts are necessarily less than a comprehensive analysis of the gold standard overall. We present a thorough analysis of Canada's role in the gold standard and of the financial and balance-of-payments implications of the remarkable growth of the Canadian economy during the study period. Our empirical findings for Canada lend strong support to our views about how the international gold standard functioned, but further tests, using data for other countries, are necessary to fully substantiate our theory.

The time period chosen for our study, 1871–1913, corresponds approximately to the period during which Canada continuously adhered to the gold standard. Canada had no formal central bank but the Canadian chartered banks and the Dominion government maintained convertibility of bank and Dominion notes, respectively, into gold. American and British coins also circulated as legal tender at fixed rates defined in terms of gold. Except for the greenback era in the United States (1862–79), our period is also a time when Canada's major trading partners adhered to the gold standard.

In terms of consistent data series, 1871 – the year of the first Dominion banking act – provides a convenient starting point for our analysis.[8] With the passage of the Finance Act in 1914, the Dominion government provided for commercial bank borrowing from the government in a way that broke the link between the money supply and gold maintained in the preceding gold-standard era. We therefore conclude our empirical study with 1913.

Our empirical evidence is more complete than that used by Viner, who restricted himself to the years 1900 to 1913. We take the same long-period historical perspective of most other gold standard scholars, notably Williams (1920), White (1933), Beach (1935), and Bloomfield (1959). All data we use are described and listed in the three appendixes.

In the next chapter we review the standard classical theory of adjustment as presented by Viner (1924, 1937) and outline the evidence uncovered in his classic study. Chapter 3 develops the modern portfolio theory of adjustment in its simplest form within the context of the pre-War Canadian institutional setting. We begin with a verbal statement of the model and then proceed to a more formal mathematical presentation of price-level and money-supply determination. The formal model is constructed on the working assumption that capital is perfectly mobile between Canada and the rest of the world.

Chapter 4 reviews the data and presents an empirical overview of developments in the Canadian economy during the study period. Chapters 5, 6, and 7 present our empirical tests. Chapter 5 states and empirically tests a group of hypotheses that parallel those tested by Viner. These tests deal with the question of whether the relationship between the net capital inflow and the balance of trade is consistent with the predictions of theory and whether there are stable relationships between the quantity of money demanded by the public and the quantities of primary and secondary re-

[8] Nova Scotia, New Brunswick, Quebec, and Ontario formed the Dominion of Canada at Confederation in 1867. Manitoba joined in 1870, British Columbia in 1871, and Prince Edward Island in 1873.

serves held by the banks and interest rates, real income, and the scale of the economy. The evidence here is fully consistent with our view of the adjustment mechanism. But it is also consistent with the classical interpretation. On the basis of these tests alone, only a few small pieces of evidence favor our theory over the traditional one.

Chapter 6 presents an empirical analysis of international reserve flows. First we test restrictions implied by the differing implications of our theory and the classical one with respect to the relationship between the balance of trade and the balance of payments under international capital mobility. Our theory is consistent with the evidence but the classical approach fails to explain it, largely because it cannot explain the capital account. Second, we conduct a series of nonnested hypotheses tests which further support our theory in preference to the traditional specie-flow mechanism. Finally, we examine the evidence on the responsiveness of net capital movements to international differences in interest rates. No strong empirical relationship between international capital flows and short-term interest-rate differentials is found. These results in Chapter 6 overwhelmingly support our theoretical interpretation and reject the standard view.

Chapter 7 focuses attention on two further empirical issues raised by the confrontation of our theory with the traditional classical one. The first is the question of timing and causality. On preliminary investigation it is found that insufficient lagged relationships are present in the data series to permit Granger–Sims causality tests.[9] This conclusion that no lags can be identified favors our theory, which does not require any lags. The second issue is the contemporaneous statistical relationship between Canadian money and the price level of the rest of the world, holding constant the foreign money supply and real income. Neither our theory nor the traditional one postulates a causal effect of Canadian money on foreign prices, but our theory can explain the observed contemporaneous correlation between these two variables while the traditional theory cannot.

We turn in Chapter 8 to a detailed analysis of Viner's work and the criticisms of it over the years. Our theory, we argue, provides a cleaner explanation of the causal and circumstantial evidence presented by Viner, and nullifies most of the criticisms of it. The major criticisms reflect, in our view, uneasiness over the seeming absence of a causal effect of the capital inflows on gold flows and hence domestic prices. Our contribution

---

[9] We are using only annual data series. Although some monthly and quarterly data exist, there are not enough series to permit a full testing of our model at this level. It would take another major project to remedy these data deficiencies, if indeed they could be remedied.

is to provide the model that articulates these criticisms and reinterprets the evidence in the light of them. This chapter also reviews the evidence uncovered in extensive recent work by Georg Rich. Rich gives this evidence the traditional interpretation but it is also consistent with our portfolio approach to the adjustment mechanism.

In Chapter 9 we shift direction and pose the theoretical question: Can one derive the classical adjustment mechanism from the principles of wealth maximization, subject to the usual constraints, when the assets of various countries differ in risk and therefore are not perfect substitutes in portfolios? In other words, can we construct the traditional adjustment mechanism from an assumption of imperfect mobility of capital? To answer this question, we undertake a further formal development of the theoretical model presented in Chapter 3. We conclude that the traditional classical theory is inconsistent with maximizing behavior of individual wealth-owners even when the assets of various countries are not perfect substitutes in portfolios and there are barriers to trade in individual assets. The traditional classical mechanism is consistent with maximizing behavior only when *no* international movements of capital are possible. Therefore, the fact that substantial freedom of international trade in assets exists under the international gold standard becomes in itself strong evidence in favor of our theory of the adjustment mechanism.

In Chapter 10 we review the main features of Canada's balance-of-payments history before 1914 and use the portfolio theory of adjustment to provide response scenarios for the principal episodes of external shock associated with capital inflow. Our reinterpretation shows how the gold-standard regime smoothly accommodated an important source of economic growth. We also observe how the growing relative historical importance of the capital account has drawn attention to the distinction between the balance of payments and the balance of trade, and undermined the usefulness of the price-specie-flow mechanism for understanding balance-of-payments adjustments.

Chapter 11, the final chapter, reviews our findings about the adjustment mechanism in the Canadian case and outlines what they imply about how the international gold standard must have worked. These implications represent a challenge for further empirical research.

2. The standard neoclassical specie-flow mechanism

The classical mechanism of international monetary adjustment can be traced back at least to David Hume. Perhaps the best modern statement is due to Jacob Viner.[1] The standard version states that gold flows automatically between countries to adjust their levels of money and prices to maintain balance-of-payments equilibrium. An excess supply of money in the domestic economy causes a rise in the domestic price level relative to the price level abroad. Domestic goods become relatively more expensive in world markets, causing exports to fall and imports to increase. The resulting deficit in the balance of payments leads to an outflow of gold, reversing the movement of domestic relative to foreign price levels. This process redistributes the world gold stock among countries until relative domestic and foreign price levels consistent with balance-of-payments equilibrium are reestablished.

The mechanism of adjustment operates essentially the same way for real shocks. Assume, for example, an exogenous increase in domestic exports. The balance of payments improves and gold flows in. The resulting increase in the money supply causes the domestic price level to increase relative to the foreign price level. Domestic goods become relatively more expensive in world markets, increasing imports and reducing exports until balance-of-payments equilibrium is reestablished. Gold movements act as a means of adjusting domestic and foreign prices to the increase in demand for domestic goods in world markets.

A minor refinement deals with the effects of exchange-rate movements on the balance of trade. When an increase in exports relative to imports is required, a part of the adjustment can be brought about by a devaluation of the domestic currency to the gold export point. If the cost of transporting gold is significant, this movement of the exchange rate can bring about an increase in exports relative to imports without a flow of gold. Similarly,

---

[1] See Viner (1937, chapters 6 and 7) and Hume (1752, pp. 330–41, and 343–5).

a balance-of-payments surplus is partially accommodated by an appreciation of the domestic currency to the gold import point.

A number of writers have introduced a further refinement of the mechanism by incorporating the effects of gold movements on income and, in turn, on imports.[2] An outflow of gold reduces the financial resources available for expenditure on goods in the deficit country and increases them in the surplus country. This reduces spending in the former and increases it in the latter. As a result, the deficit country's balance of payments improves even without the effect of relative price level adjustments. These "real balance effects," however, are only a small part of the adjustment process.[3] Relative price level adjustments are central to the operation of the price-specie-flow mechanism.

International capital movements are not rigorously analyzed by the classical writers. Such movements appear, however, in refined versions of the price/income-specie-flow mechanism and play a major role in discussions about what actually happened. Long-term capital movements are treated as exogenous in the adjustment mechanism; short-term movements are viewed as a response to international differentials in interest rates. Short-term capital movements moderate gold flows, permit seasonal movements in exports relative to imports, and smooth out the reaction of the system to sudden disturbances of international equilibrium. Suppose, for example, that gold flows out. This leads to a tightening of domestic credit and an increase in interest rates. Short-term capital is attracted, moderating both the deficit of payments over receipts and the gold outflow. The classical economists also lay some stress on short-term capital movements as a mechanism by which gold can be transferred without a shift in exports relative to imports. A central bank desiring to increase the national gold stock can tighten credit and raise the domestic interest rate, attracting short-term capital and inducing an inflow of gold. The possibility of perverse and destabilizing short-term capital movements is also recognized.

It is this view of the price-specie-flow mechanism that Viner attempts to test in his classic study of Canada for the period 1900–13.[4] Canada experiences a massive inflow of long-term capital. According to the classical adjustment mechanism, this results in an inflow of gold and a rise in Canadian prices relative to foreign prices sufficient to create an excess of

---

[2] See, for example, Meier (1953), Ingram (1957), Stovel (1959), and Williamson (1963).
[3] The reason becomes apparent in the discussion in chapter 3.
[4] Viner (1924) acknowledges (pp. 22–3) a similar line of argument developed earlier by Coats (1915).

imports over exports equal to the net inflow of capital. Viner (1924) finds that relative prices do indeed move as the classical theory predicts, but that the movement of gold seems rather small to have brought about the observed relative price movements. He writes

[T]he variations in Canadian gold stocks appear too small to have been the effective means of adjusting the Canadian balance of indebtedness to the borrowings abroad, especially when the size of these borrowings, and the lack of important co-operation in the adjustment of balances from variations in exchange rates are taken into consideration. . . . If variations in exchange rates and gold movements operating through their influence on relative prices, on the profitability of import and export, comprise the entire mechanism of adjustment of trade balances, should not the tremendous and irregular flow of capital into Canada have been accompanied by gold movements much more substantial and marked by much greater fluctuations than indicated . . . above? (pp. 161–2)

The chartered banks, it appears, had little control over their note and deposit holdings. He continues

The country's supply of currency could not be appreciably altered by the banks without drastic curtailment or expansion of loans and no appreciable shift from bank currency to other currency was possible. The banking system as a whole had little power of control, therefore, of the amount of its note issues, at least for short periods. The demand liabilities of the bank(s) on account of note circulation were . . . the result of general conditions largely independent of bank control. (p. 174)

Of the deposit liabilities, the volume . . . payable after notice or at a fixed date was equally clearly not subject to strict regulation by the banks. . . . The banks were always glad to accept a substantial savings account . . . [and] they paid the same rate of interest on such deposits throughout the period, so that variations in the rate of interest were not used as a means of regulating the volume of savings deposits. (pp. 174–5)

The amount of deposits payable on a fixed date, consisting chiefly of temporary surplus funds of business concerns, could perhaps be regulated to a slight extent by varying the amounts of loans and discounts. (p. 175)

A variation in the volume of loans granted by the banks, however, would operate primarily to bring about a corresponding variation in the volume of demand deposits. (p. 175)
But even the volume of loans granted by the banks, and consequently the volume of demand deposits, had only a very limited degree of flexibility. . . . [The banks] repeatedly claimed that no deserving request for an extension of credit was refused. There is no evidence that, at any time during the period under study, they used their power over the volume of loans to adjust their cash reserve ratios. (pp. 175–6)

Viner thus concludes that the banks

succeeded . . . in maintaining their cash (gold and Dominion notes backed by government gold stocks) reserve ratios constantly at the desired level through seasonal
fluctuations in demand liabilities and cyclical fluctuations in business conditions
only by deliberately adjusting their cash reserves to their total demand liabilities
and not vice versa. . . . Since the cash reserves of the banks closely represent the
amount of monetary gold in Canada, it follows that gold movements into and out
of Canada are directly dependent upon the total demand liabilities of the banks,
and are not directly dependent upon the state of the international balance of payments. (p. 177)

He then notes that the Canadian banks are able to maintain their cash
reserve ratios at a nearly uniform level because they hold substantial "secondary" or "outside" reserves in the form of bank balances and funds on
call in New York and London. These secondary reserves are a "call" on
gold. They also have an advantage over cash reserves, namely, the earning
of interest income.

By using the "outside" reserves as a fund to absorb temporary surpluses or to provide cash to meet foreign demands, the Canadian banks are able to extend credit in
Canada in the volume demanded by the state of business and at the same time to keep
the ratio of cash reserves to total liabilities close to what under the circumstances of
the moment seems to them to be the lowest safe point. If total liabilities expand or if
disturbed business conditions make a higher cash reserve ratio seem expedient, the
banks draw on their outside reserves. If total liabilities decline or if general business
confidence and prosperity make a smaller cash reserve ratio appear safe to banks,
they transfer their surplus cash to the outside reserve. (p. 178)

This leads Viner to conclude that the "fluctuations in the outside reserves
of the Canadian banks operate to adjust the Canadian balance of payments
to capital borrowings in the manner attributed to gold movements in the
generally accepted mechanism of international trade" (p. 178).

He then describes how the mechanism worked. He notes that a permanent
inflow of capital into Canada through, say, continuous annual sales of
securities in London, leads to an increase in chartered bank deposits,
accompanied by an increase in the banks' secondary reserves in New York
or London. The deposits are created, and the secondary reserves acquired,
when the chartered banks convert the sterling proceeds of loans into domestic currency. According to Viner's analysis, the increase in the money
supply associated with these newly created deposits causes domestic prices
to rise, creating a trade-balance deficit equal to the net capital inflow. As
this deficit rises, the conversion of Canadian into foreign currency to
purchase the excess goods abroad leads to a decline in deposits in Canada
and in the secondary reserves of the chartered banks. The conversions of

foreign into domestic currency deposits to transfer the assets match the conversions of domestic into foreign currency deposits to transfer the excess of imports over exports only after the stock of domestic and secondary reserves rises enough to produce the new equilibrium level of domestic relative to foreign prices. Throughout the process the chartered banks convert into gold whatever proportion of their secondary reserves they deem necessary for safe conduct of their business.

The Canadian process is as automatic as the process described in the generally accepted theory. It differs from the latter solely in that fluctuations in bank deposits and in outside reserves play the part in Canada which the classical theory attributes to gold movements. (p. 181)

The essential feature of Viner's modified classical adjustment mechanism relevant to the present investigation is the direction of causality. In this mechanism, an autonomous inflow of capital leads to an inflow of deposits and higher domestic money stock, which leads, in turn, to a rise in Canadian prices and a trade-balance deficit of the same size as the net capital inflow. The only difference between Viner's modified theory and the standard one is the substitution of an inflow of deposits backed by secondary reserves for an inflow of gold in the traditional price/income-specie-flow mechanism.

3. A new view of gold standard adjustment

International capital movements are not satisfactorily integrated into the classical theory of balance-of-payments adjustment. The apparent consistency of the classical approach with individual portfolio optimization has great superficial appeal. The view that short-term capital responds in the aggregate to international interest-rate differentials, however, involves a fallacy of composition. It is true that an individual wealth-owner with unchanged information and attitudes toward risk shifts his portfolio in the direction of those securities whose interest rates increase. But what is true for an individual is not true for the aggregate of all individuals.

When all wealth-owners shift their portfolios from lower to higher interest-yielding securities, there is an excess supply of those securities bearing lower interest rates and an excess demand for those bearing higher interest rates. The lower interest rates rise and the higher rates fall until wealth-owners are just willing to hold all the securities in existence. Higher interest rates for a particular country's securities are thus the *result* of an adverse evaluation by international investors. They are not an inducement to shift capital into the country.

The essential basis for capital flows in a properly formulated model is that the equilibrium allocation of world investment among countries is different from the allocation of world savings. Technological change and resource discoveries in different parts of the world create incentives for capital (and labor) to gravitate to particular countries. Each country's savings level depends on the incomes and tastes of its residents. It is not necessarily equal to the level of investment. Capital flows through time from those countries that have greater savings than investment to those with greater investment than savings.

An important factor determining the international allocation of capital is the risk differences associated with employing capital in various locations. At each point in time, world investors have a given desired allocation of their wealth to capital employed in various countries. If the desired allocation of wealth differs from the allocation of capital that actually

15

exists, interest rates are bid up in those countries having excess employed capital and down in those having insufficient capital. These interest-rate adjustments continue until world investors in the aggregate are just willing to hold each country's existing stock of employed capital. Higher interest rates signify a greater degree of risk and imply lower present values of capital than do lower interest rates.

The present value of capital also depends on the expected flow of future returns. It can be high in a particular country even if interest rates on capital in that country are also high. New investment is allocated to equalize the present value of capital across countries.[1] Thus, high real interest rates in a particular country may or may not be associated with high investment in that country.

The mix of short-term and long-term claims to the capital stock employed in a particular country and the interest rates on these claims are simultaneously established. The condition of equilibrium is that world wealth-holders be willing to hold the country's total capital stock. By a process of intermediation, the primary forms of capital such as physical plant and equipment come to be owned indirectly via a particular structure of intermediate assets. This structure depends on the tastes of world asset-holders. Intermediaries borrow long and lend short or vice versa as required by the market. The market interest rates on short-term and long-term intermediate assets in each country therefore depend on the willingness of world investors in the aggregate to create and hold these assets.

The interaction between gold flows and short-term interest rates, which occupies a large place in the gold-standard literature, must be interpreted in the light of the intermediation process just described. Excess demand for money in one country causes its residents to convert nonmonetary assets into cash by selling domestic and foreign securities to foreign residents. Given the existing levels of domestic and foreign prices and the balance of trade, this produces a balance-of-payments surplus. When the international value of the domestic currency has risen to the gold import point, gold flows in. During this process, the ratio of domestic to foreign securities that domestic residents are trying to sell exceeds the ratio of domestic to foreign securities foreigners are willing to buy at the old structure of world interest rates. This happens because each country's residents typically hold a portfolio mix skewed toward home securities.

---

[1] This does not rule out the possibility that, for some periods of time, the present value of capital in particular industries and countries can be below its cost of production. In this event, no new investment takes place in that industry or country.

Reestablishing world asset market equilibrium thus requires a bidding up of domestic interest rates relative to foreign interest rates. Similarly, excess supply of money in a country causes gold to flow out and domestic interest rates to fall relative to foreign interest rates. The magnitude of these interest-rate effects depends on how substitutable the assets of the two countries are in portfolios – the greater the substitutability, the smaller the effect on interest rates.

The central bank of a country can thus attract gold reserves quite easily by selling domestic bonds and withdrawing domestic money from circulation, inducing the public to sell assets abroad and causing gold to flow in. A consequence may be somewhat higher domestic relative to foreign interest rates. Similarly, a central bank with excess gold reserves can expand the money supply, causing gold to flow out. Alternatively, it can reduce gold reserves by selling gold directly to foreigners in return for foreign assets, or acquire gold reserves by selling assets to foreigners. The effects of these direct sales and purchases of gold on international interest-rate differentials depend on the mix of foreign and domestic assets bought or sold in return for the gold. They also depend on how substitutable these assets are for each other in portfolios.

Two things should be especially noted from this discussion: First, gold flows and interest-rate changes occur *simultaneously* as a result of changes in the demand and supply of money. Interest-rate changes do not cause gold flows. Second, no change in the balance of trade is necessary to transfer gold from one country to another. If the residents of a country, or its government, want to acquire gold they simply sell domestic and foreign assets in return for it. There is no reason for the domestic price level to be bid down in relation to prices abroad and cause increases in exports relative to imports as specified in the standard specie-flow mechanism.

Essentially the same conclusions follow when equilibrium is disturbed by exogenous changes in real factors affecting the balance of payments. Suppose, for example, there is an exogenous increase in a country's exports. The immediate implication is an excess demand for the country's output since there is no reason for consumption, investment, or other components of aggregate demand to have changed. Excess aggregate demand causes domestic prices to rise, leading to an expansion of imports and a contraction of exports until the trade balance returns to its former level, eliminating the excess aggregate demand. The rise in prices necessitates an increase in nominal money holdings that domestic residents acquire by selling assets to foreigners and gold flows into the country. The difference from the standard classical price-specie-flow mechanism is that gold inflows occur as a result of the increase in domestic prices and not the other way around.

This is a consequence of international capital mobility. If capital is *not* internationally mobile, no sale of assets abroad in return for money can take place. No increase in the money supply can occur via inflows of gold to finance the rise in the price level. The excess aggregate demand drives up domestic prices as in the case of capital mobility, reducing the real money supply and causing domestic interest rates to be bid up, an outcome prevented, when capital is mobile, by an induced sale of assets abroad in return for gold. Rising domestic interest rates reduce investment relative to saving, allowing a surplus of exports over imports to remain after equality of the aggregate demand for domestic goods with domestic output is re-established. The rise in the domestic price level and the appreciation of the domestic currency to the gold import point are thus insufficient to eliminate the surplus of exports over imports. This surplus is financed by an inflow of gold.

As time passes, the increase in the domestic gold stock increases the domestic money supply. Interest rates decline and prices are bid up further until the surplus of exports over imports and the gold flow are eliminated. This is the standard specie-flow mechanism. Its essential feature is that gold is transmitted between countries by a divergence of exports and imports. In the new view, presented here, gold is transmitted by an international capital market transaction. International immobility of capital acts like a constraint on the system. It diverts what would otherwise be a purely monetary nominal asset adjustment into a change in imports, exports, and other real variables.

What does the above theory tell us about how the Canadian monetary system must have operated in the institutional circumstances of the time? To answer this question, we first describe briefly the monetary system in Canada during the period under discussion. Then we discuss price level determination and the relationship between money and prices in Canada.

The Canadian monetary system before World War I

At Confederation, financial markets in Canada were primitive compared to those of London and New York. About twenty Canadian banks were operating, issuing money in the form of notes and deposits, making loans to finance trade, and holding reserves. Private banks provided all the note circulation before 1865. Provincial notes were issued after that year and were superseded by Dominion notes after 1871. It is useful first to visualize the system without government-note issue, incorporating Dominion notes later.

In addition to bank notes and deposits, the money supply consisted of a variety of coins. Some Canadian coinage existed in Upper Canada from 1858, but a large part of the coinage was composed of British shillings and American silver money. A fully Canadian coinage was established soon after Confederation.[2]

The banks backed their deposit and note issue with reserves of gold coin and bullion, much of which was held in New York, and with call loans and deposits in New York and London that could be converted to gold at any time. Although there was a call loan market in Montreal during the latter part of the study period, it was not a short-term-loan market comparable to the markets in New York and London. Canadian banks almost from the start carried on a substantial business in the major U.S. cities.[3] Despite the rudimentary Canadian capital market, capital mobility between Canada, the United States, and Great Britain was high. There were few if any restrictions on the international exchange of assets. Because Canada was a trading country, many major business deposit holders were fully involved in international trade and finance. The country was on a gold standard by virtue of three principal facts: the commercial banks were committed to redeem their notes and deposits in gold on demand by profit maximizing considerations (and also by law in the case of bank notes); Dominion notes, which made up the entire circulation of notes denominated under five dollars, were redeemable in gold by the government; and U.S. $10 pieces and British £1 coins were legal tender at $10 and $4.8666 respectively. Token coins were not redeemable in gold, but circulated at face value by law and convention. Any coins worth more than their face value were melted down.

Redeemability of notes and deposits in gold meant a fixed exchange rate with the British pound throughout the nineteenth century and until 1914.[4] It meant a fixed exchange rate with the U.S. dollar as well, except for

---

[2] The early history of the coinage is exhaustively treated in McCullough (1984b).
[3] The most extensive reconstruction of this foreign business activity is provided in Rich (1988).
[4] See McCullough (1983) for the nineteenth century background.

periods when the dollar was not convertible, such as the 1837–38 crisis and the greenback period from the beginning of the Civil War until 1879.[5] After the Civil War, the United States suffered substantial inflation and the dollar depreciated markedly with respect to the pound and the Canadian dollar. This was reversed after 1870 and the resumption of convertibility in 1879 was at the old gold parity.

Price level determination in Canada

It is necessary to think of Canada as a region in a common currency system – as Prince Edward Island is today with respect to the rest of the country. This region is producing a variety of products for export and domestic consumption, and importing other products. Prices are determined by supply and demand in a world context. For traded goods, prices are determined abroad. Where the goods are nontraded, prices are determined wholly by the demand and supply of domestic residents. Demand and supply are constrained on both the production and consumption sides, however, by the opportunity to produce and consume alternative substitute products at internationally determined prices.

It is helpful to think of a situation where foreigners are trying to spend more in Canada on goods, services, and securities than Canadians are trying to spend abroad. This implies excess aggregate demand for Canadian output. In the long run the price of Canadian output must therefore rise relative to the price of foreign output. Expenditure must be switched off Canadian and onto foreign goods until total expenditure on Canadian output equals the value of output produced. The prices of traded goods cannot rise in response to the increase in aggregate demand in Canada because they are determined in the world market and the exchange rate is fixed. The entire burden of adjustment, therefore, must fall on the prices of nontraded goods.

An exogenous switch of world expenditure onto Canadian goods thus leads to a rise in the prices of nontraded relative to traded goods and an increase in the price level. Expenditure can shift onto Canadian goods as a result of a shift in world demand on the part of consumers or an increase in real investment in Canada, part of which involves expenditure on domestic nontraded goods. Such an increase in investment – that is, a real-

[5] See Mitchell (1908).

location of world saving toward investment in Canada rather than somewhere else – is a major part of the phenomena to be explained.

To proceed more formally, note the identity of the total receipts of Canadian residents with their total payments.

$$P_U U + P_T T + DSB = P_U U_C + P_T T_C + S \tag{3.1}$$

P_U and P_T are the prices of nontraded and traded goods respectively, U and T are the domestic outputs of the respective goods, U_C and T_C are the quantities of them consumed, S is domestic savings, and DSB is net repatriated earnings (interest and dividend receipts from abroad minus the corresponding payments to foreigners), sometimes referred to as the debt service balance. Equation (3.1) says that total earnings from the production of traded and nontraded goods plus net earnings from abroad must be either saved or spent on the consumption of traded and nontraded goods.

Total investment expenditure in Canada is the sum of the quantities of the two goods absorbed into investment, U_I and T_I.

$$I = P_U U_I + P_T T_I \tag{3.2}$$

Add and subtract the level of investment on the right-hand side of (3.1).

$$P_U U + P_T T + DSB = P_U(U_C + U_I) + P_T(T_I + T_C) + S - I \tag{3.3}$$

Market clearing implies equality of the demand and supply of the nontraded good.

$$U = U_C + U_I \tag{3.4}$$

Substitute (3.4) into (3.3).

$$P_T(T - T_C - T_I) + DSB + I - S = 0 \tag{3.5}$$

Equation (3.5) says that, *ex ante*, the balance of trade plus the debt service balance plus the net capital flow must sum to zero – that is, a current account surplus must be counterbalanced by a capital account deficit as a real goods market equilibrium condition.

Equations (3.4) and (3.5) can be expanded by imposing some standard behavioral relations. Consumption depends on income, Y, with its division between traded and nontraded goods depending on the price ratio P_U/P_T.

$$U_C = C^U(P_U/P_T, Y) \tag{3.6}$$

$$T_C = C^T(P_U/P_T, Y) \tag{3.7}$$

The partial derivatives of consumption of the two goods with respect to income in the functions $C^U(P_U/P_T, Y)$ and $C^T(P_U/P_T, Y)$ are positive, whereas a rise in the relative price of the nontraded good increases consumption of the traded good and decreases consumption of the nontraded good.

Investment depends on the level of output in the economy and the rate of interest as well as a portmanteau variable, Ω incorporating technological change and natural resource discoveries. Again, the division between nontraded and traded goods depends on the relative prices.

$$U_I = I^U(P_U/P_T, r^*, X, \Omega) \tag{3.8}$$

$$T_I = I^T(P_U/P_T, r^*, X, \Omega) \tag{3.9}$$

X denotes the level of aggregate output and r^* is the real interest rate determined in world capital markets.[6]

Aggregate output depends on the stocks of domestically employed labor, N, and capital, K, as well as on the portmanteau variable Ω.

$$X = F(N, K, \Omega) \tag{3.10}$$

The allocation of output between nontraded and traded goods depends on relative prices and the nature of technology.

$$U = U(P_U/P_T, X, \Omega) \tag{3.11}$$

$$T = T(P_U/P_T, X, \Omega) \tag{3.12}$$

Finally, aggregate income depends on aggregate output, the real debt service balance, equal to the *DSB* deflated by the price level and denoted by Z, and the terms of trade, μ, exogenously determined by forces outside the Canadian economy.

$$Y = Y(X, Z, \mu) \tag{3.13}$$

A change in the terms of trade can be viewed as a change in the export relative to the import price component of the index of traded goods prices without a change in P_T itself.

The equilibrium relative price of nontraded in terms of traded goods can be obtained by substituting the relevant behavioral relations into either (3.4) or (3.5). Equivalent results follow from both substitutions, but it is easier to substitute into (3.4).

---

[6] It is analytically convenient here to assume that capital is perfectly mobile internationally, so that interest rates are the same in Canada and abroad. This assumption will be relaxed informally from time to time as the discussion proceeds and formally in the theoretical analysis of Chapter 9.

$$U[P_U/P_T, F(N, K, \Omega), \Omega] = C^U[P_U/P_T, Y(F(N, K, \Omega), Z, \mu)]$$
$$+ I^U[P_U/P_T, r^*, F(N, K, \Omega), \Omega] \qquad (3.14)$$

Equation (3.14) can be rearranged to express P_U/P_T as a function of the various exogenous variables.

$$P_U/P_T = q(N, K, Z, r^*, \mu, \Omega) \qquad (3.15)$$

The relative price of nontraded in terms of traded goods thus depends on a set of real factors exogenous to the Canadian economy.

It is easy to see that the effects of changes in N and K on the relative price variable are ambiguous – these variables affect both the demand for nontraded goods and the supply. A fall in r^* leads to an increase in investment in Canada. This has the effect of increasing the demand for the nontraded good, causing P_U/P_T to rise.[7] An improvement of the terms of trade raises income and consumption, again increasing the demand for and relative price of the nontraded good. The effects of the portmanteau variable Ω can be postulated by appropriately choosing the partial derivatives of $U(P_U/P_T, X, \Omega)$, $F(N, K, \Omega)$, $I^U(P_U/P_T, r^*, X, \Omega)$ and hence $q(N, K, Z, r^*, \mu, \Omega)$ with respect to it. The situation analyzed here requires that an increase in Ω represent technological change permitting the development of new land and leading to an increase in the demand for nontraded goods. This implies a positive effect of Ω on $q(N, K, Z, r^*, \mu, \Omega)$.

The domestic price level, defined in terms of the prices of goods produced, can be conveniently expressed as a geometrically weighted index of traded and nontraded goods prices. Combined with equation (3.15), this yields

$$P = P_U^{\alpha} P_T^{(1-\alpha)} = (P_U/P_T)^{\alpha} P_T$$
$$= [q(N, K, r^*, Z, \mu, \Omega)]^{\alpha} P_T \qquad (3.16)$$

where α is the share of the nontraded good in domestic output.

The price of traded goods, P_T, can be expressed in terms of the price index of goods produced abroad.

---

[7] It should be kept in mind that a fall in r^* is a fall in the world interest rate. This could occur as a result of changes in savings patterns, changes in the productivity of capital over a wide area of the world, or an increase in the world gold stock in the presence of short-term price level rigidity.

$$P_T = \frac{1}{(q^*)^{\alpha^*}} P^* \tag{3.17}$$

Here q^* is the ratio of nontraded to traded goods prices in the rest of the world, P^* is the index of output prices abroad, and α^* is the share of nontraded goods in the rest of the world's price index.[8]

Using the quantity theory equation, the price level in the rest of the world, P^*, can be expressed in terms of the money supply, output ($=$ income), and the (not necessarily constant) income velocity of money in the rest of the world, V^*. The rest of the world's money supply is, in turn, some multiple $1/\delta^*$ of the stock of gold held abroad, G^*. Since Canada is so small in relation to the rest of the world, none of these foreign variables is affected significantly by what happens in the Canadian economy.

$$P^* = (V^*G)/(\delta^*Y^*) \tag{3.18}$$

Velocity is treated as constant because the introduction of a more complex demand function for money contributes nothing to the analysis at this point in the discussion.

The Canadian price level can be fully determined using (3.16), (3.17), and (3.18).

$$P = \frac{q(N,\,K,\,r^*,\,Z,\,\mu,\,\Omega)^{\alpha} V^* G^*}{\delta^*(q^*)^{\alpha^*} Y^*} \tag{3.19}$$

The important thing to notice is that neither the money supply in Canada nor the demand for money by Canadian residents appears in this equation. The world price level depends on the world money supply (that is, on the gold stock and the money multiplier) and on the demand for money in the world as a whole. The latter depends on factors affecting world output and on the income velocity of money. Canadian goods are more or less expensive than world goods in accordance with the conditions of their production and the extent of the demand for them on the part of world (including Canadian) residents. If Canadian-produced goods are relatively valuable in world markets, the price level in Canada is high relative to the world price level. If Canadian goods happen to be relatively cheap, the

---

[8] This follows from the fact that

$$P^* = P_U^{*\,\alpha^*} P_T^{(1\,-\,\alpha^*)} = \left(\frac{P_U^*}{P_T}\right)^{\alpha^*} P_T = (q^*)^{\alpha^*} P_T$$

Canadian price level is low. Whether the price level in Canada is high or low relative to foreign prices depends therefore on real factors relating to production and consumption. The overall level of world prices depends on the world gold supply.

The Canadian money supply and Canadian prices

Where does the Canadian money supply fit into the picture? The demand for real money balances in Canada is dependent on income and interest rates. The demand for nominal money balances is then

$$M = P{\cdot}L(r^*, Y) \tag{3.20}$$

where the real interest rate in Canada equals the world real interest rate, given the assumption of perfect capital mobility. Expected inflation is ignored at this point. Since P, r^*, and Y are determined by the real forces noted above, none of these variables can adjust in the face of an excess demand and supply of money as they would in a closed economy.[9] Instead, the nominal money supply must adjust endogenously to changes in demand.

To see how this happens, suppose that the commercial banks in Canada create, through their domestic loan and discount policies, less money than Canadian residents want to hold. Canadians have an easy avenue to acquire more money – they sell nonmonetary assets. Since, by assumption, *all* Canadians want more money, the sale of assets is necessarily a sale to foreigners. The foreign currency acquired from this sale of assets is converted into Canadian dollars at the commercial banks. The Canadian banks thereby create additional Canadian money balances to meet the demand for them, and acquire U.S. dollar reserves in New York. Similarly, if Canadian residents find that they have too much money, perhaps because of generous loan and discount policies of the commercial banks, they spend the excess money abroad on nonmonetary assets. Canadians obtain the necessary foreign currency from the commercial banks which in turn are forced to reduce the Canadian money supply, losing U.S. dollar reserves in New York in the process.

Why do Canadian residents spend excess money holding on nonmonetary assets rather than on real goods and services? The reason is that excess

---

[9] Or in an open economy model where international capital movements cannot respond to market forces.

money holdings constitute a portfolio disequilibrium rather than excess spendable real income. It is useful to think of the portfolio decision as separate from the consumption–savings decision. Wealth-holders take care of portfolio imbalance by exchanging assets in the market. They adjust consumption flows when the fraction of their income saved is out of equilibrium. Virtually instantaneous gold flows and money-supply changes occur whenever and as long as domestic residents are out of portfolio equilibrium. Hence, excess or deficient money holdings never exist long enough to have wealth effects on consumption and saving.

As noted, the Canadian banks kept the bulk of their reserves in New York in either gold or U.S. dollar assets easily converted into gold. These primary and secondary reserves increase when the banks are stringent in their domestic loan and discount policies and decrease when they are lax. The commercial banks can thus control their reserve levels by appropriately adjusting their domestic credit policies. If reserves become too low, they tighten credit at home, forcing asset-holders into the international market to obtain desired money holdings. Assets are sold abroad and the U.S. dollar proceeds find their way into the reserves of the Canadian banks, which are forced to acquire them in exchange for Canadian deposits to maintain convertibility. If reserves get too high, the banks make additional loans and discounts. This excess money ends up in New York as domestic residents convert it into nonmonetary assets on the international market. International reserves are reduced as the banks supply the necessary foreign exchange, reacquiring the excess domestic money in return. It is important to realize that the commercial banks in Canada have *no* control over the domestic money supply. That is always equal to whatever Canadian residents want to hold. What the banks do control is the division of their asset portfolios between domestic loans and discounts and dollar assets in New York. They are driven to create the private sector's desired stock of money by their desire to profit as much as possible from domestic loans and discounts while maintaining adequate gold and U.S. dollar reserves in New York.

Thus the country's stock of international reserves is a function of the banking system's note and deposit liabilities and the various factors, such as interest rates, that affect the profit maximizing reserve ratios of the chartered banks. Gold holdings as a proportion of total reserves depend on these same factors. Changes in the gold stock and the stock of reserves have no causal effect on the Canadian price level. Indeed, the opposite is true. Changes in the price level due to real forces of demand and supply or monetary developments in the rest of the world cause the public to hold more money. This in turn causes the banks to create that money and hold larger reserves of U.S. dollar assets and gold to back it.

Modifications to incorporate Dominion notes

Dominion notes were issued after 1871 in both small and large denominations. Commercial banks were prohibited from issuing bank notes in denominations of less than five dollars, giving the government a monopoly over this part of the circulation. About 40 percent of the total stock of Dominion notes issued were held by the public in the form of small bills. The bulk of the remaining Dominion notes, the large denominations, were held by the commercial banks as reserves. The 1871 Bank Act also required that the banks hold generally one-half and no less than one-third of these primary reserves in Dominion notes. This was modified in 1881 to set the required ratio of Dominion notes to total primary reserves at no less than 40 percent. Both these provisions – the prohibition from issuing notes of lower denominations and the requirements relating to reserves – can be viewed as a tax on the chartered banks. The banks were forced to hold noninterest-bearing government created reserves instead of call loans and other U.S. dollar-denominated short-term earning assets. They were also forced to cede profitable note issue privileges to the government. After 1890, the banks were required to deposit a small fraction (5 percent) of their notes in the Circulation Redemption Fund, to be used to prevent the notes of failed banks from being quoted at a discount.

Dominion notes were backed in substantial part by government gold reserves and government offices were set up across the country to redeem them on demand. The likelihood of a public run on gold was small because Dominion notes were the only small bills available for circulation. The chartered banks could not make wholesale conversions of Dominion notes into gold without violating the law regulating the proportion of their reserves held in the form of these notes. The commercial banks had to hold reserves of gold and liquid U.S. dollar assets to back their notes and deposits as before 1871. Because the banks were forced to relinquish to the government that part of their note circulation consisting of small bills, their total note liabilities were smaller. On this score, less gold reserves were needed. To the extent that the government's gold reserve ratio against Dominion notes was the same as the banking system's gold reserve ratio against its notes, however, the total stock of gold in the country as a whole was not affected by the introduction of Dominion notes. The presence of Dominion notes does not fundamentally affect our analysis of how the system operated.

Comparison of the new view with Viner's theory

The above view of how the system functioned contrasts in important respects with Viner's modification of the traditional classical analysis. In his analysis, the Canadian price level was determined by the supply of money in Canada in accordance with local application of the quantity theory of money. If prices in Canada were too high, imports exceeded exports by more than the net capital inflow. Deposits in Canada were drawn down in exchange for foreign currency deposits, leading to a loss of secondary reserves by the chartered banks. This decline in the money supply caused the Canadian price level to fall, making domestic goods relatively cheaper and reducing the trade-balance deficit to equal the net capital inflow. Similarly, if prices in Canada were too low, Canadian bank deposits increased along with the banking system's outside reserves. This happened because imports exceeded exports by less than the net capital inflow. The rise in the money supply drove the price level in Canada up, making domestic goods less competitive in world markets and increasing imports relative to exports to match the net capital inflow. The essence of Viner's theory is that the balance-of-payments disequilibria cause monetary changes which cause price changes which, in turn, eliminate the balance-of-payments disequilibria.

The new view presented here differs on precisely this point. Because of international capital mobility, the domestic money supply adjusts automatically to the demand for money. Balance-of-payments disequilibria and gold flows are the process by which this adjustment occurs. Domestic prices are determined by world prices and the relative valuation world markets place on domestic as compared to foreign goods. Gold flows occur because price and income changes affect the demand for money and operate to bring the supply of money into line with the demand. They do not occur because price and income changes affect the balance of trade.

Purchasing-power parity and the monetary approach to the balance of payments

The theory developed here is obviously a close relative of the so-called monetary approach to balance-of-payments theory. The best statement of that approach within a gold standard context is by McCloskey and Zecher (1976, 1984). Balance-of-payments disequilibria are strictly monetary phenomena, processes that bring the demand for money into line with the supply. In the model presented above, perfect substitutability of domestic and foreign assets in portfolios implies a complete separation of monetary from real equilibrium. Balance-of-payments adjustments arise from monetary disequilibrium and have no impact on the real sector. In this respect our model accords well with the premises of McCloskey and Zecher and the other proponents of the monetary approach.

The analytical structure from which this result is derived, however, is fundamentally different from that of earlier writers on the monetary approach to the balance of payments. Except for those who viewed the balance of payments as a monetary phenomenon in the Humean sense that gold and money flows equilibrate relative prices, earlier proponents of the monetary approach used the purchasing-power parity theory as the cornerstone of their analysis.[10] In fact, McCloskey and Zecher (1984) deal almost exclusively with the relationship between purchasing power parity and the monetary approach.

The analysis in this present study does not support the purchasing-power theory as traditionally defined. Traded goods prices, net of transport costs and tariffs and measured in a single currency, must, of course, be the same everywhere. If the money stock in one country increases and everything else stays the same, moreover, a proportional devaluation of that country's currency is sufficient to prevent a balance-of-payments disequilibrium from occurring. There is no reason in general, however, for the ratio of domestic to foreign price levels to vary in proportion to the domestic currency price of foreign currency – that is, for the real exchange rate to be constant – as is required by the nontrivial definition of purchasing-power parity. For purchasing-power parity to hold in this sense, the ratio of nontraded to traded goods prices must be constant through time both at home and abroad. Where tastes and technology change and world investment is reallocated among countries from time to time in response to these changes, the relative price of nontraded to traded goods must change in different ways for different countries. The relative price of any country's output in terms of the rest of the world's output cannot be constant through time. There is no reason to regard the purchasing-power parity ratio of domestic to foreign prices as an equilibrium toward which the world economy is gravitating in some long run.

[10] See, for example, Johnson (1976, p. 153).

It is clear that the McCloskey and Zecher treatment of purchasing-power parity departs from the traditional definition in the direction of the view developed in the present study. They say, for example,

Our hypothesis says that prices are linked and therefore insensitive to internal forces such as monetary policy . . . , not that the prices are linked by some linear relationship having such and such a slope. (1984, p. 133)

[I]f Mars were connected to Earth by the market in chewing gum alone, the two price levels would nonetheless be fixed in relation to each other. (1984, p. 129)

Their view is perhaps best described as general equilibrium in more than one country at a time. The prices of traded goods are the same everywhere while the prices of nontraded goods vary from country to country according to local supply-and-demand conditions. Price levels are a combination of traded and nontraded goods' prices that move differently through time in different countries as tastes and technology change in different ways.

Movements of the real exchange rate over any period of time are just as likely to be up as down and may appear as a random walk. The drift or trend in the purchasing-power parity ratio over the long run does not represent long-run equilibrium. One cannot attach economic significance to what is, at the current state of knowledge, a purely statistical relationship. All observed values of the real exchange rate as it moves through time are fully consistent with equilibrium of the economy. To the extent that the observed equilibrium is not a long-run equilibrium, there is no presumption that long-run adjustments move the real exchange rate toward some single purchasing-power parity equilibrium value. The equilibrium at every point in time is a worldwide general equilibrium in which the prices of traded and nontraded goods and exchange rates observed are mutually consistent. This understanding, shared also by McCloskey and Zecher, is fully consistent with the law of one price, the unity of markets, and complete arbitrage subject to transport and other transactions costs that prohibit international exchange of nontraded goods.[11]

In the view presented here, the interdependence of the price levels in

---

[11] The linkage among price levels of different countries implied by the commonality of traded goods extends to nontraded goods only in a general equilibrium sense and is not well described by the concept of purchasing-power parity. McCloskey and Zecher attempt to extend the meaning of the term to incorporate the equilibrium of all prices. To most participants in the long debate over purchasing-power parity and to most present day economists, however, the term means more than a link between price levels. It means a rigid relationship between relative price levels and the exchange rate such that if one observed relative prices one could determine the equilibrium exchange rate.

all countries arises not because of the effects of specie flows on relative prices, as implied by the traditional classical theory. It occurs because of the simultaneous determination of all countries' relative prices within the framework of world real goods market equilibrium independent of gold and monetary movements.

McCloskey and Zecher argue that this simultaneous price level inter-dependence results from arbitrage in goods and capital markets; they devote enormous effort to examining relative price movements within and between countries. According to the new view outlined above, the interdependence arises strictly because capital can be freely bought and sold across inter-national boundaries – in other words, because of arbitrage in assets and the unity of capital markets. This unity of capital markets implies that when the residents of one country have an excess demand or supply of money they can reestablish portfolio equilibrium by a purchase or sale of assets abroad. No pressure on the domestic price level results. When capital markets are integrated, gold moves directly, without effects on relative domestic and foreign prices and the balance of trade. It is capital market integration, not purchasing-power parity, the unity of goods markets, or arbitrage in goods, that produces this result.

The situation is quite different without free trade in capital assets. An excess supply of money drives down domestic interest rates, no longer linked to interest rates in the rest of the world. This leads to a rise in the domestic price level and an expansion of domestic investment relative to savings and an equivalent increase in imports relative to exports. A gold outflow equal to the excess of imports over exports then occurs. Because capital markets are not integrated across countries, divergences between exports and imports represent the only avenue through which gold can move. This scenario, the standard one, occurs precisely because capital flows are assumed to be absent.

The clean separation of asset and goods market equilibrium in the formal analysis presented above results not only from capital market integration, but also from the assumption that domestic and foreign assets are perfect substitutes in portfolios and domestic and foreign interest rates are therefore equal. This latter assumption is formally relaxed in Chapter 9. The sharp dichotomy between the real and monetary sectors then disappears, but the fundamental results remain unchanged. Monetary factors can then have some effect on relative prices and the trade balance, but these effects are not of the sort implied by the traditional price-specie-flow mechanism.

4. An empirical overview

As Viner noted some sixty years ago, massive inflow of long-term capital into the Canadian economy in the early years of the twentieth century provides an excellent test case for theories about the response of the real and monetary sectors of an open economy to external shocks. Figure 4.1 plots the long-term, short-term, and total net capital inflows over the period 1871 to 1913.[1] There were periods before the turn of the century during which long-term capital inflow was relatively large, but nothing can compare with the magnitude of the inflows between 1904 and 1913, when the net inflow was well in excess of 10 percent of gross national product (GNP).

This phenomenon was related to other major happenings in the Canadian economy over the period. Capital inflow was accompanied by settlement on the Canadian prairies that began in the 1870s and accelerated noticeably after 1896, especially during the early years of the twentieth century when capital inflows were mammoth.[2] Canadian economic historians dispute the relationship of the prairie expansion to overall expansion of the economy, but recent research leaves little doubt that, although substantial economic growth occurred before 1896, there was an acceleration in the rate of growth around the turn of the century.[3] Whatever the role of settlement and staples in this expansion, the pace of growth is diffused through many activities. The average annual rate of growth of secondary manufacturing in Canada, for example, was about 5 percent between 1870 and 1890. It fell to 2 percent in the 1890s, but rose to 6 percent from 1900 to 1910.

---

[1] The data for this and succeeding figures are provided in Appendix B. The sources are given in Appendixes A and C.

[2] See Britnell (1939, chapter 4), Mackintosh (1939, chapters 3 and 4), and Buckley (1955, pp. 4–12).

[3] This dispute was initiated by Chambers and Gordon (1966) and is described in Pomfret (1981b, pp. 157–64). Urquhart (1986) is the most authoritative work on the pace of economic growth after 1870.

.l. 1890 Dollars

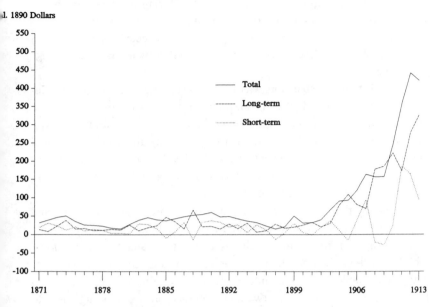

Figure 4.1. Long-term, short-term, and total real net capital inflows: short-term and total include errors and omissions, 1871–1913. Source: Appendix A.

Industries supplying agricultural equipment and railroad rolling stock grew rapidly. Real output of iron and steel products and transportation equipment grew at 12.4 percent per year, while wheat production rose at only 9.4 percent per year during the first decade of the twentieth century.[4] External capital flowed into nonagricultural activities as well as into farming to boost the overall rate of growth after 1896.

Two things are significant from the point of view of this study. Canada participated in an international economy throughout the period and her history provides episodes where the opportunity to invest in Canada exceeded the availability of domestic savings.[5] This is especially true in the years before 1900 when the domestic capital market was less well devel-

[4] See Bertram (1963). Urquhart's revised national income estimates tell a similar story and may even understate the relative growth of manufacturing because manufacturing and trading activities were often confounded in early census data.

[5] This has been observed even without the benefit of the latest national income estimates of Urquhart (1986). Edelstein (1982, chapter 12) provides a convenient summary of some of the early literature.

oped and capital inflows were more modest. During three periods of investment boom, the early 1870s, 1880–85, and 1900–14, the ratios of gross total fixed capital formation to GNP were respectively 20, 20, and 25–30 percent while the ratios of savings to GNP were only 12.8, 13.5, and 19 percent.[6]

Although prairie expansion was by no means the sole impetus to Canadian economic growth after 1896, it did absorb a good part of the capital inflow of those years. The settlement of the Canadian prairies began in earnest after 1896, made economically feasible by the conjunction of a number of factors – rising wheat prices, the development of red fife wheat and the chilled steel plow, and the lack of opportunities for further expansion on the northern subhumid plains.[7]

To develop major export production in the prairie region, the idle land was combined with quantities of labor and capital that were not available domestically. Given world conditions at the time and the international mobility of these factors, labor and capital flowed to Canada. In addition, many new staple-producing industries such as pulp and paper arose in Eastern Canada in the early twentieth century, also exploiting hitherto unused natural resources only after attracting external labor and capital.[8] It has been established that these factor movements actually preceded the surge in exports.[9] Investment and capital flows occurred as part of long swings in an Atlantic economy, trade and investment booming alternately in Europe and North America in response to shifting comparative advantages and investment opportunities.[10]

This study concerns the response of the real goods and asset markets to Canadian economic expansion, and the implications of this response for balance-of-payments adjustments and international gold movements. The theoretical analysis in the preceding chapter suggests a number of hypotheses with which to confront the data. Before formulating and testing these hypotheses, however, the data sources and the major movements in the time series are examined.

[6] See Urquhart (1986).
[7] See Dick (1980) for an analysis of the supply and demand factors influencing prairie wheat expansion.
[8] Aitken (1961, chapter 2) gives a good statistical account of the involvement of United States capital in Canadian nonagricultural industries.
[9] This precedence of investment has been noted by Ankli (1980) and Urquhart (1986).
[10] The sensitivity of investment to population movements and its long swing characteristics within the Atlantic economy have been noted by Buckley (1952, 1963), Cairncross (1953, pp. 37–64), and Thomas (1973, pp. 256–8).

The data

The data describing Canada's experience with the gold standard between 1871 and 1913 have evolved through successive reworkings of official trade, banking, price, and output statistics, aided at many points by unofficial sources and techniques of aggregation suggested by economic theory.

The sources, assembly, and characteristics of the data base are discussed in detail in Appendix A and the series themselves tabulated in Appendix B. Appendix C presents a detailed discussion of the sources and methods used in developing the Canadian price series.

The balance-of-payments data were developed by Professor Alasdair M. Sinclair for the national income estimates compiled by M. C. Urquhart and his associates.[11] Minor adjustments relating to the handling of nonmonetary gold flows are made following Rich (1988). Estimates of the nominal gross national product for Canada are also obtained from Urquhart's work. The real income series for the rest of the world is a weighted index of the available income series for six countries, the United States, the United Kingdom, Germany, Italy, Norway, and Sweden.[12]

Rich (1988), building on earlier estimates of Viner (1924), Hay (1968), and Macesich and Haulman (1971), provides the Canadian money and asset series used in our analysis. The index of the nominal money stock in the rest of the world is a weighted average of the nominal money supplies of seven countries, the above six plus France.

The price series are aggregations based on both earlier work and new constructions.[13] These consist of a price index for all Canadian goods, decomposed into series for traded and nontraded goods, and indexes of prices of all goods and nontraded goods in the rest of the world. The index of all prices in the rest of the world is a weighted average of the implicit GNP deflators for the six countries listed above. An index of nontraded goods prices in the rest of the world is obtained by combining the wholesale prices of selected items reported in the published data for Great Britain and the United States. Appendixes A and C discuss all procedures concerning the price data.

---

[11] See Urquhart (1986).
[12] France is excluded because her income data are thin and incomplete.
[13] See Appendix C and Dick (1986b) for the current status of this work.

The terms-of-trade data, in Urquhart and Buckley (1965), focus on subcomponents of traded goods and are from official trade statistics.

Exchange rates are fixed as a requirement of the gold standard. Before 1879, however, the United States was off gold. An estimate of the exchange rate for the years 1871–79 is obtained by taking a weighted average of the Canadian dollar prices of the U.S. dollar and the British pound. The weights are the proportions of Canadian trade accounted for by these two dominant trading partners.

Finally, the long-term interest rate series for Canada is from Neufeld (1972). Two alternative long-term rates are available for the United States, and one each for Great Britain, France, and Italy. The British and U.S. long-term series are from Friedman and Schwartz (1963). The long-term interest rates for France and Italy are from Fratianni and Spinelli (1984).[14] Two short-term interest rate series for the United States and one for Britain are also available from the same Friedman–Schwartz study.

An empirical overview of the 1871–1913 period

Figure 4.1 shows the composition of net capital inflow into Canada during the period 1871–1913. Errors and omissions, assumed to be primarily unmeasured short-term capital movements, are included in both the short-term and total net inflows. Although net inflows of capital occur throughout the period, it is not until after 1902 that the massive inflows begin. Long- and short-term capital flows show similar broad movements, although many of the year-to-year movements are in opposite directions. The major inflow of long-term capital in the twentieth century traces its beginnings to about 1896, while the upturn in the short-term capital inflow occurs somewhat later.

The pressure on domestic resources created by the net inflow of capital is measured in part by the increase in the trade balance required to finance it. Normally, a significant part of this required trade balance deficit is created by a rise in the prices of domestic nontraded goods in terms of traded goods. Figure 4.2 gives two measures of this pressure. One is a direct measure consisting of the sum of the total net capital inflow and the debt service balance and the other is an indirect measure equal to the negative of the trade balance. The two measures differ in that the direct measure does not include errors and omissions as a capital movement. If

---

[14] See Appendix A for further details.

Mil. Dollars

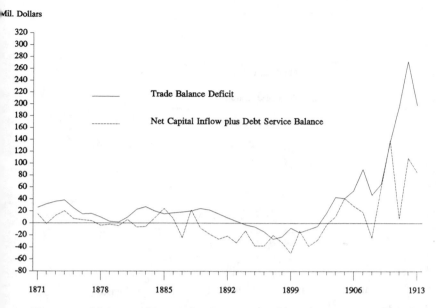

Figure 4.2. Measures of international pressure on domestic resource markets: Canada, 1871–1913. Source: Appendix A.

errors and omissions are largely unreported short-term capital flows, the negative of the trade balance is the more accurate of the two series.

Movements in the negative trade balance series correspond quite closely to the total net capital inflow in Figure 4.1, since the debt service balance, the difference between the two series, tends to grow rather smoothly over the 43-year period with an acceleration after 1908. There is no doubt that increasing pressure on domestic resources and on the relative price of nontraded goods occurred after the turn of the century.

The pressure on domestic resources associated with the net inflow of capital is only one factor affecting the general level of prices in Canada. World nominal price trends are also a major influence. Figure 4.3 gives the price indexes for all goods for Canada and nontraded goods for both Canada and the rest of the world. World prices show a generally downward trend from the early years of the period to 1896 and a sharp upward trend after that year.

Contrary to the belief of some economic historians, there is no evidence that the late nineteenth century was a period of stagnation. As indicated in Figure 4.4, Canadian real GNP grew rapidly after 1896 but experienced modest growth before that year. Real GNP grew more rapidly in Canada

1890 = 100

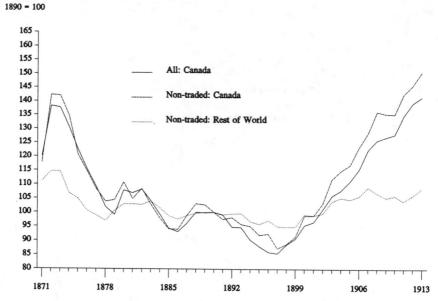

Figure 4.3. Price indexes: all goods and nontraded goods: Canada and the rest of the world, 1871–1913. Source: Appendixes A and C.

than in the rest of the world throughout the whole period. Real output growth in Canada was greater after 1904 than between 1896 and 1904 as might be expected, given that the major inflows of capital occur well after 1900. A substantial part of the real income growth after 1896 appears to be due to increases in human as well as physical capital, since per capita income in Canada grew only slightly faster after 1896 than before, as indicated in Figure 4.5.

The terms of trade, shown in Figure 4.6, increased steadily and very substantially from the beginning of the period to 1895. A fall of about 10 percent between 1895 and 1900 was followed by a slight increase between 1900 and 1908 and then a slight fall between 1908 and 1913. Over all, there was little trend after 1895.

As indicated in Figure 4.7, the real and nominal stocks of money in Canada grew steadily over the whole period except for slight decline associated with the recession of 1907 and a further slight decline in 1913. As in the case of real and nominal GNP, the rate of growth accelerated after 1896. The fraction of total currency holdings consisting of Dominion notes (Figure 4.8) increased dramatically from the early 1870s to 1886 and then flattened out. The ratio of deposits to total money holdings (Figure

890 = 100

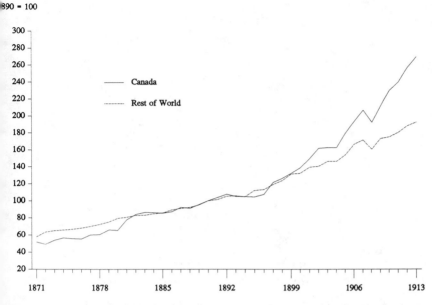

Figure 4.4. Real income: Canada and the rest of the world, 1871–1913. Source: Appendix A.

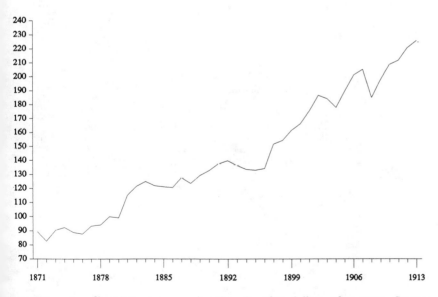

Figure 4.5. Real Income per capita: Canada, 1890 dollars, 1871–1913. Source: Appendix A.

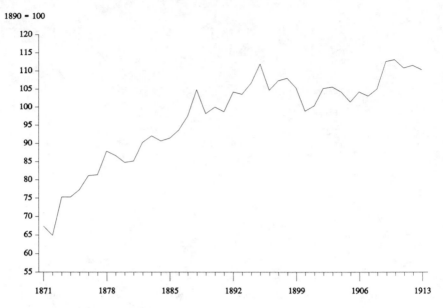

Figure 4.6. Terms of trade: Canada, 1871–1913. Source: Appendix A.

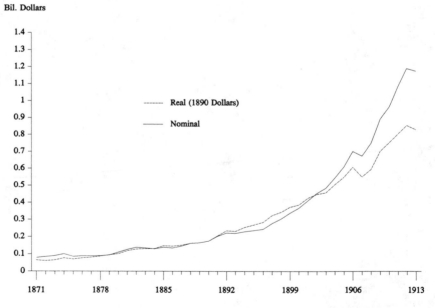

Figure 4.7. Real and nominal money holdings: Canada, 1871–1913. Source: Appendix A.

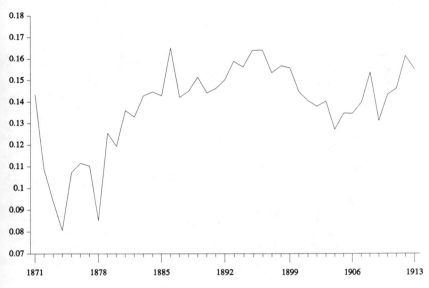

Figure 4.8. Ratio of Dominion notes to all currency: Canada, 1871–1913. Source: Appendix A.

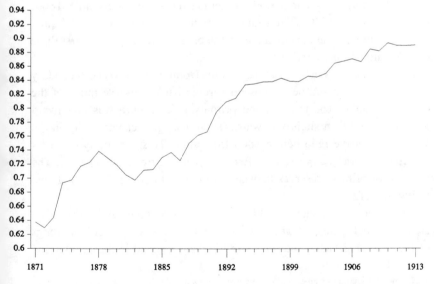

Figure 4.9. Ratio of bank deposits to the money supply: Canada 1871–1913. Source: Appendix A.

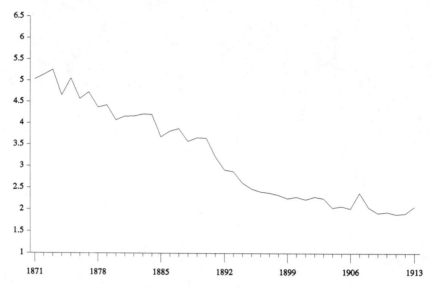

Figure 4.10. Income velocity of money: Canada, 1871–1913. Source: Appendix A.

4.9) increased sharply before 1894 and much more slowly thereafter. As Figure 4.10 indicates, the income velocity of money trended downward during the entire 43-year period, flattening out significantly after 1896. Evidently the public's desired ratio of money to income increased quite dramatically with the development of the banking system in the first three decades after Confederation.

Figure 4.11 gives the primary (gold plus Dominion notes) and secondary (call loans abroad and net claims on foreign banks) reserve ratios of the chartered banks. The trend of the primary reserve ratio was downward until 1900 and then slightly upward. There was greater variability in the secondary reserve ratio before 1890 than after. This variability obscures the trend in series before 1890. After that year, the trend was upward. The division of primary reserves between gold and Dominion notes is shown in Figure 4.12.

Total inflows of monetary gold, referred to as net monetary movements, are plotted in Figure 4.13 They consist of the increases in the gold holdings of the chartered banks and the Dominion government,[15] thus containing

[15] Net monetary gold movements plus the current account balance plus capital flows (defined to include errors and omissions) equal zero. Canada was a producer of gold during much of the period. Most of this gold was exported and is included in commodity exports.

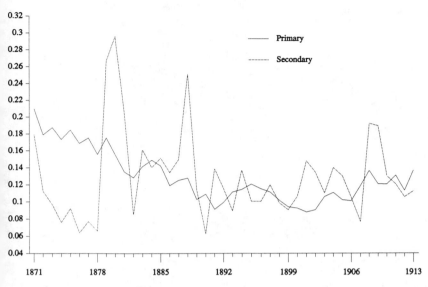

Figure 4.11. Chartered bank reserve ratios: Canada, 1871–1913. Source: Appendix A.

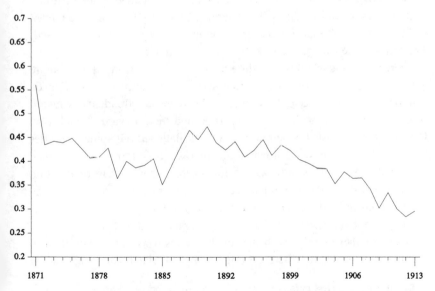

Figure 4.12. Chartered banks' ratio of gold to primary reserve holdings: Canada, 1871–1913. Source: Appendix A.

Mil. Dollars

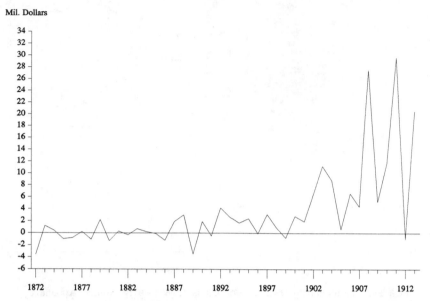

Figure 4.13. Net gold inflows: Dominion government plus chartered banks, Canada, 1871–1913. Source: Appendix A.

more information about gold movements than is contained in the series on chartered bank gold holdings. On average, monetary gold inflows tended to increase as nominal income and nominal money holdings increased. The trend in the rate of increase was upward after 1896.

Interest-rate movements are shown in Figures 4.14 and 4.15. Figure 4.14 plots the long-term interest rate series. Long-term rates in Canada and Britain, as well as U.S. corporate bond yields, trended downward from the beginning of the period to 1896 and then upward.[16] Yields on U.S. industrial bonds trended downward but flattened out somewhat after the late 1890s. The sharp down trend in U.S. long-term rates between 1871 and 1880 is consistent with a fall in the expected rate of inflation associated with the decline in the actual inflation rate occurring before the reestablishment of the gold standard in 1879. Otherwise, the movements in long-term interest rates in Canada, the United States, and Britain corresponded rather closely, with the level of rates lower in Britain than in Canada and the United States. Long-term industrial bond yields in the

[16] This pattern of interest rates is similar to the pattern of price movements indicated in Figure 4.3, a classic example of the so-called Gibson Paradox. Sargent (1973) and Barskey and Summers (1988) discuss alternative interpretations of this phenomenon.

cent Per Year

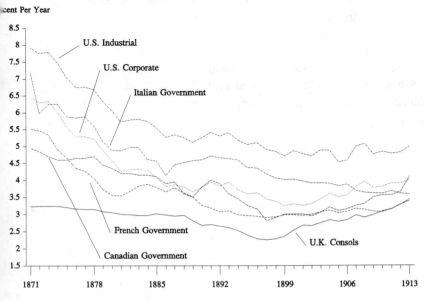

Figure 4.14. Interest rates on long-term bonds, 1871–1913: Canada, United Kingdom, United States, France, and Italy. Source: Appendix A.

cent Per Year

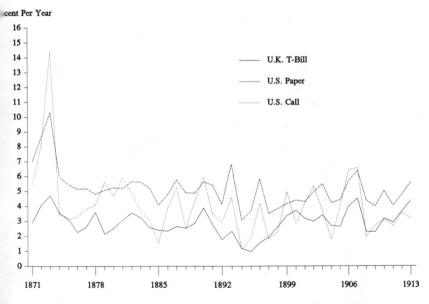

Figure 4.15. Short-term interest rates, 1871–1913: United States and United Kingdom. Source: Appendix A.

United States differed from the other series in that they did not trend upward after 1896. In this respect, they corresponded more closely with bond yields in France and Italy.

Short-term interest rates in the United States and United Kingdom, given in Figure 4.15, corresponded reasonably closely in the period after the 1879 Resumption. The fluctuations in the United States show greater amplitude than those in Britain, probably because the U.S. rates are for commercial paper and call loans while the U.K. rate is for treasury bills.

5. Statistical tests of goods and asset market adjustments

This chapter describes tests of some hypotheses about the adjustment of goods and asset markets, hypotheses that follow directly from the analysis of Chapter 3. They fall into two groups, hypotheses concerning the relationship between the inflows of long-term capital and the prices of goods produced and consumed in Canada, and hypotheses concerning the response of the Canadian monetary system to these capital inflows. The first deals with relative price and real adjustments, the second with adjustments in the asset markets. Additional hypotheses relating to timing and to the structure of our model versus the traditional classical one are formulated and tested in Chapters 6 and 7. The tests in this chapter show consistency of the evidence with the portfolio approach, but this evidence is also consistent with the traditional specie-flow model. The evidence in Chapter 7 favors the portfolio approach, though not decisively. In Chapter 6, the evidence on the process of balance-of-payments adjustment confirms the essential structure of the portfolio model we develop and decisively rejects the traditional classical approach.

Real adjustments

The real sector adjustments fall into two subgroups, those involving the adjustment of relative prices and the trade balance to the net capital inflow and those involving the effects of the capital inflow on the terms of trade. This section deals with these in turn.

Net long-term capital inflows, relative prices and the balance of trade

The inflow of long-term capital represents an injection of foreign savings into the domestic economy, augmenting the level of investment possible with domestic savings alone. This expansion of investment increases the aggregate demand for goods.

47

If the capital goods implanted in the investment process and the labor used to implant them are exclusively foreign goods and labor, a leakage to imports exactly equal to the net inflow of capital occurs. There is no increase in the aggregate demand for domestically produced goods. It is likely, however, that at least some of the labor and capital goods used in the investment process are nontraded goods. Domestic resources must therefore be found to produce them and aggregate demand for domestic output rises. At full employment, this increase in aggregate demand results in an increase in the price level.

For a small country like Canada, traded goods prices are determined abroad and are insensitive to domestic economic developments. They cannot rise in response to an increase in aggregate demand. The pressure of aggregate demand thus falls almost entirely on nontraded goods. Domestic nontraded goods prices rise, switching domestic expenditure toward traded goods and increasing imports. The rise in domestic costs in the face of unchanging export prices reduces the supply of exports.[1] The balance of trade thus deteriorates, reducing aggregate demand sufficiently to accommodate the pressure of investment expansion. Given the resulting equality of aggregate demand and supply, the balance-of-trade deficit created is just sufficient to finance the net capital inflow.

One consequence of the net inflow of capital should therefore be a rise in the relative price of domestic nontraded goods in terms of traded goods. Because there is an equivalent outflow of capital from the rest of the world, the prices of nontraded goods abroad should fall relative to traded goods prices. The Canadian economy, however, is very small in relation to the rest of the world. One would therefore not expect the shift of demand away from foreign nontraded goods to be very large in percentage terms. The rise in nontraded relative to traded goods prices in Canada, therefore, is not likely to be accompanied by a significant fall in the relative prices of nontraded goods abroad.

Causality should run from net long-term capital inflow to the trade balance. There is a direct effect of investment on imports at unchanged aggregate demand. There is also an indirect effect through changes in aggregate demand that stimulate nontraded goods output – the investment expansion increases the relative prices of domestic nontraded goods in terms of traded goods, increasing imports and reducing exports. Through-

---

[1] This is a historical equivalent of what has come to be known as the "Dutch disease." See Buiter and Purvis (1983).

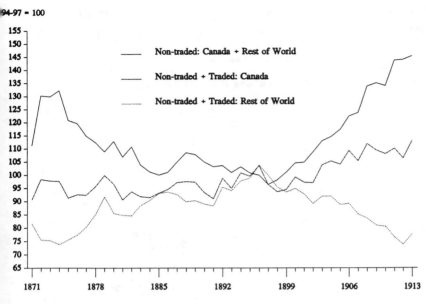

Figure 5.1. Relative traded and nontraded goods prices: Canada and the rest of the world, 1871–1913. Source: Appendixes A and C.

out these changes, regardless of causality, the equality of aggregate demand and aggregate supply implies that the trade balance deficit must equal the net capital inflow (plus the debt service balance) as a condition of equilibrium. Double entry bookkeeping, moreover, requires that the net capital inflow (plus debt service balance) be identically offset by a trade balance deficit, *ex post,* regardless of what determines the balance of trade.

Figure 5.1 plots the ratio of Canadian nontraded goods prices to those of the rest of the world, the ratio of Canadian nontraded to traded goods prices, and the ratio of nontraded to traded goods prices in the rest of the world. The index of the rest of the world's nontraded goods prices used here is a weighted average of selected U.K. and U.S. wholesale prices. The U.S. prices are converted into gold equivalents by dividing by the U.S. dollar price of the pound. This conversion is necessary to make Canadian and U.S. prices comparable in real terms, the United States being off gold in the years before 1879.

It is clear from the figure that after 1898 Canadian nontraded goods prices rose relative to both traded goods prices in Canada and nontraded goods prices abroad. The major part of the increase in nontraded relative

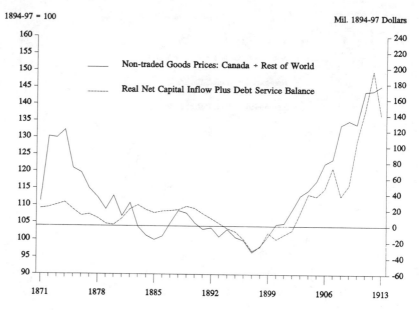

1894-97 = 100

Mil. 1894-97 Dollars

Figure 5.2. Relative nontraded goods prices and the real net capital inflow: Canada versus the rest of the world, 1871–1913. Source: Appendixes A and C.

to traded goods prices occurred before 1906, with a flattening out thereafter. The upward movement of the prices of Canadian nontraded goods relative to the prices of nontraded goods in the rest of the world was slightly different in timing but even more dramatic. The sharp downward movement of the ratio of nontraded to traded goods prices in the rest of the world seems unlikely because of Canada's size. It probably reflects the fact that other new lands like Australia and Argentina were also absorbing capital investment from the United States and United Kingdom at this time.

Figure 5.2 shows the relationship between the real net capital inflow (plus debt service balance) and nontraded relative to traded goods prices in Canada. The former variable measures the pressure on the domestic goods markets. Since errors and omissions are included as an unreported capital flow, this variable is the negative of the trade account balance. The turnaround in both series occurred in 1897, suggesting that the relative internal price adjustment and the net inflow of capital took place more or less simultaneously.

Table 5.1 presents a formal statistical test. The relative price variables

Table 5.1. *Real net capital inflows, relative prices, and the terms of trade*

	Relative prices					Real Net Capital Inflow plus Real Net Debt Service	Terms of Trade
	Nontraded: Canada ÷ Traded: Canada	Nontraded: Rest of World ÷ Traded: Canada	Nontraded: Canada ÷ Nontraded: Rest of World				
	(1)	(2)	(3)	(4)	(5)	(6)	(7)
Constant	96.44 (107.6)	90.30 (83.08)	107.14 (74.6)	108.05 (34.6)	106.72 (9.10)	−7.87 (−.204)	72.59 (27.64)
Real net capital inflow plus real net debt service	.085 (4.9)	−.105 (−5.03)	.248 (8.98)	.257 (6.65)	.265 (3.54)		−.142 (−4.36)
Canadian real income				−.011 (−.33)	−.047 (−.151)	2.81 (7.82)	.252 (9.56)
Rest of the world real income					.051 (.118)	−3.79 (−7.09)	
Non-traded goods prices:						.918	
Canada ÷ Nontraded goods prices: rest of world						(3.54)	
Number of observations	43	43	43	43	43	43	43
R-squared	.370	.381	.663	.664	.664	.891	.716
Standard errors	5.029	6.10	8.06	8.15	8.252	15.369	6.857
Durbin–Watson	.835	.277	.657	.676	.686	1.791	.439

Note: All prices are indexes with 1894–97 = 100, real incomes are in 1894–97 Canadian dollars, and all remaining real variables are in 1890 Canadian dollars. The figures in brackets are *t*-ratios.

are regressed on the real trade-balance deficit which, as noted, measures the pressure of the capital inflow and debt service requirements on Canadian productive resources. Variation in the real net capital inflow plus debt service requirement explains, in regression (1), about 37 percent of the variation in Canada's price of nontraded relative to traded goods. In regression (3), it explains over 65 percent of the variation in the price of nontraded goods in Canada relative to the price of nontraded goods in the rest of the world. Both regressions perform well. A negative relationship exists, as expected, between the net capital inflow and foreign nontraded goods prices relative to foreign (and Canadian) traded goods prices [regression (2)]. Nearly 39 percent of the variation in nontraded relative to traded goods prices in the rest of the world is explained by the net capital flow plus debt service balance. That the relationship is this strong is somewhat remarkable given the relative size of Canada in relation to the United States and Great Britain. As noted, it suggests that the development of the Canadian West was accompanied by simultaneous development of other new lands drawing capital from the United States and United Kingdom.

Variables other than the capital inflow undoubtedly helped determine relative domestic and foreign prices. The low Durbin–Watson statistics in all three regressions suggest this, indicating serial correlation in the residuals and excluded variables.[2]

Domestic and foreign real incomes are such variables. An expansion of real output and income either in Canada or abroad increases both the demand and supply of that part of the world's nontraded goods. It may lead to a rise or fall in their prices relative to the prices of traded goods and nontraded goods in the other part of the world. To the extent that the increase in output and income is permanent, the effect on relative nontraded goods prices will depend on two forces, relative bias toward or away from the nontraded good of the improvement of technology leading to the increase in output, and the relative bias toward or away from the nontraded good of the consumption effect of the resulting increase in permanent income. To the extent that the increase in output and income is transitory, it increases the production of nontraded goods but not the consumption, causing the prices of domestic relative to foreign nontraded goods to fall.

Regressions (4) and (5) in Table 5.1 indicate no relationship between Canadian and foreign real income and Canadian relative to foreign non-

---

[2] This will also bias our estimated coefficients if the excluded variables are correlated with the included ones.

traded goods prices. That one of the income variables alone is not significant suggests that the insignificance of the two variables when together is not due to multicollinearity.[3] A plot of the deviations of real GNP around trend in the same figure with the real net capital inflow plus debt service balance indicates that the major movements of the two series are broadly the same. Addition of the real income variables to the regression thus contributes nothing.

A frequently used procedure when low Durbin–Watson statistics are encountered in ordinary least squares (OLS) estimation is to reestimate the regression using a generalized least squares (GLS) estimator that transforms the data in such a way as to eliminate serial correlation in the estimated residuals.[4] The philosophy behind this approach is that serial correlation is a purely statistical problem – a violation of the assumption of independence of successive errors in the regression equation. The problem is not that the regression function is misspecified but that the error term chosen is inappropriate. According to this view, correct specification of the error term as a first-order autoregressive process leads to more efficient regression coefficient estimates. An alternative philosophy, adopted here, is to treat serial correlation of the estimated residuals as an indication of misspecification of the regression function component of the model.[5] As Carr has shown, standard procedures for purging the residuals of serial correlation when the problem is misspecification of the model may lead to a greater bias in the coefficients than would have occurred had no adjustment been made.[6]

Applying the AR1 model to the serially correlated residuals leaves the capital flow plus debt service variable insignificant in all regressions except (2). As in the case of simple first differencing, though somewhat less dramatically, information about trends in the series is lost by this transformation. The data appear to contain only one major piece of information about the relationship between the net capital inflow and domestic relative to foreign nontraded goods prices – the correspondence of the shifts in trend occurring around 1896 evident in Figure 5.2.

Consider now a completely different conception of the relation between relative prices and capital flows corresponding to popular wisdom and not

[3] The null hypothesis that the coefficients of both income variables together are zero is rejected at the 94 percent level.
[4] See, for example, Hildreth and Lu (1960) or Cochrane and Orcutt (1949).
[5] This interpretation is suggested by Griliches (1966, p. 44).
[6] See Carr (1972).

directly suggested by the new theory presented in Chapter 3. According to this view, the relationship takes the inverse form presented in regression (6) of Table 5.1. Making capital flows the dependent variable and relative prices the independent variable has a traditional interpretation. The balance of trade is determined by income and relative prices, with an increase in domestic income and a rise in domestic relative to foreign prices leading to a deterioration.

The results of regression (6) should not be interpreted in this way in the present context. The traditional interpretation allows for no distinction between a world of capital flows and a world of no capital flows. Viewing the trade balance as determined by relative prices masks the important causal influence of the net capital flow. According to our interpretation, the observed trade balance deficit and the rise in domestic relative to foreign prices are *both* a consequence of the net inflow of capital. The relative price adjustment is necessary to create a sufficiently negative trade balance to finance the capital inflow. A straightforward conventional interpretation of the equation with the trade balance as the dependent variable [regression (6) makes the negative of the trade balance the dependent variable] suggests that a fall in domestic relative to foreign prices generates an improvement of the trade balance. This is true only if the fall in the relative price of domestic in terms of foreign goods is brought about by a reduction in aggregate demand directly associated with a decline in the net inflow of capital.

This point deserves further attention. Consider the standard Keynesian income–expenditure equation:

$$Y - C - I = S - I = B_T \qquad (5.1)$$

where Y is income, C consumption, I investment, S savings, and B_T the balance of trade. A reduction in aggregate demand can occur from two sources, a shift in desired exports relative to imports or a shift in desired savings relative to investment. Shifts in planned savings relative to planned investment result in a change in the net capital flow. Given full employment, they lead to a change in relative domestic and foreign prices to bring the trade balance into line with this capital flow. Changes in desired exports or imports do not lead to a change in the capital flow at full employment, and thus cannot lead to a change in the trade balance. In this case, domestic prices must adjust relative to foreign prices to maintain the balance of trade at its original level. Variations in domestic relative to foreign prices that arise from shifts in desired exports and imports are thus uncorrelated with the trade balance deficit. On the other hand, variations in relative prices that arise from changes in desired savings and investment are positively correlated with it. If some part of the observed variation in relative prices over a particular period occurs because of variations in desired exports and imports, the regression coefficient relating relative prices to the trade balance deficit is biased toward zero. It is possible in some sample periods, moreover, that a decline in domestic relative to foreign prices due to an increase in desired imports relative to exports may be partly offset by the relative price effect of an independent increase in domestic investment. This could result in a negative correlation between the trade balance deficit and domestic relative to foreign prices.

The argument need be altered only slightly when there is less than full employment. Changes in the level of employment lead to changes in both the net capital flow (through the effect of income on savings) and desired imports. Some additional variation of domestic relative to foreign prices is then necessary to reestablish the equality between the net capital flow and the balance of trade.

The strong positive relationship between relative domestic and foreign prices and the net capital inflow (trade-balance deficit) observed in Table 5.1 occurs because the net capital inflow into Canada was so large that its effect on relative traded and nontraded goods prices completely dominated those other factors that independently affected desired exports relative to imports. If those other factors were significant, the estimated relationship between the trade balance and relative prices would be biased toward zero. The insignificant relationship between domestic and foreign incomes and the relative price variable occurs because rises in incomes are associated with increases in investment relative to savings and imports relative to exports of roughly the same magnitude, requiring little adjustment in relative prices to preserve equilibrium. Because of simultaneity, the magnitudes of the coefficients in the regressions above should be given little attention.[7]

---

[7] As Jerry Dwyer has pointed out to us, the least squares estimators of the two equations using alternatively the trade balance and relative prices as the dependent variable cannot both be consistent. If the ratio of relative price levels is endogenous and a function of the exogenous trade balance, then the trade balance cannot be endogenous and determined by exogenous relative price levels. In fact, of course, both variables are simultaneously determined by other forces.

The inflow of capital and the terms of trade

Another aspect of the effect of the net capital inflow on relative prices is the effect on the terms of trade. The standard neoclassical theory assumes that each country produces a single good and consumes its own good as well as the good produced in the rest of the world. An inflow of capital increases the price of the domestically produced good and hence export prices. The capital inflow thus improves the terms of trade.

As Viner recognized, this model is not directly applicable to the situation of a small country like Canada. Such countries produce an insignificant fraction of total world production of most of their export goods, and consume an insignificant fraction of world consumption of their import goods. The prices of exports and imports and the terms of trade are thus determined in the rest of the world.

The aggregate demand effect of the capital inflow should cause the prices of nontraded goods to rise, with export and import prices remaining unchanged. There is no reason for the terms of trade to change.[8]

Figure 4.6 indicates that the terms of trade increased by more than 70 percent between 1871 and 1896, declined somewhat to the turn of century, and then recovered moderately. The massive net capital inflow after 1896 was thus associated with a decline and/or more modest improvement in the terms of trade. Regression equation (7) in Table 5.1 bears this out. Once variations in real GNP are taken into account, the apparent effect of the net inflow of capital on the terms of trade is negative. The very low Durbin–Watson statistic, however, indicates serial correlation in the residuals and misspecification of the model. When the Cochrane–Orcutt technique is used, the effect of the capital inflow on the terms of trade becomes insignificant. A very weak positive relationship between the capital inflow and the terms of trade can be obtained by dropping real GNP from the equation and not correcting for serial correlation in the residuals. But the R^2 in that case is only 0.07 and the regression is significant at only the 10-percent level.

It is probable that the improvement in Canada's terms of trade before 1896 and after 1900 was the result of shifting world relative prices for her exports and imports unrelated to the growth of the domestic economy.[9]

---

[8] Viner (1924, pp. 231–7) argues that the terms of trade improved over the period 1900–13 as a result of the inflow of long-term capital. This is discussed in Chapter 8.

[9] The increasing world relative price of hard wheat, for example, favored Canada relative

The improvement in the terms of trade before 1896 may well have been a major factor stimulating the net inflow of capital that occurred after that year. The flattening of the trend in the terms of trade after 1896 could be interpreted as either an exogenous development or a result of the expansion of Canadian exports arising from the net inflow of capital. The latter explanation is not very plausible, however. Between 1900 and 1913, Canadian wheat production increased by about 125 million bushels, or about 7 percent of average world wheat output over the period. At an elasticity of world demand for wheat of -0.5, this would have produced a fall in the world price of wheat of around 15 percent. Since wheat made up no more than 25 percent of total Canadian exports,[10] the resulting fall in the terms of trade would have been about 4 percent. This magnitude is trivial compared to the shift in the trend of the terms-of-trade series after 1895.[11] It seems reasonable to conclude, therefore, that the terms-of-trade changes were exogenous.

Asset adjustments

Asset sector adjustments fall into several categories: (1) changes in the quantity of money demanded, (2) changes in the velocity of money, (3) changes in the composition of the public's money holdings, and (4) changes in the size and composition of the reserve holdings of the banking system.

According to the theory developed in Chapter 3, excess or deficient gold holdings of banks and/or private wealth-owners are eliminated by an exchange of gold and assets in the international capital market. No adjustment of domestic relative to foreign prices and the trade balance occurs. Indeed, the banking system has no control over the domestic money supply. If the public wants to hold more money, it sells assets (to foreigners) and presents the foreign exchange to the chartered banks for conversion into domestic currency. The banking system is forced to increase the domestic money supply, providing the level of money balances the public wishes to hold. In the process, secondary reserves in

---

to other sources of wheat in the world market. Technological changes in milling, transportation, and marketing were mainly responsible. See Harley (1980).

[10] See Taylor (1937). Canada was also a major producer of nickel, producing over 50 percent of the world supply, and nickel output and exports expanded very rapidly after 1900. Nickel, however, made up less than 1 percent of Canadian exports.

[11] See the interpretation provided by Ankli (1980).

New York or London increase. But the banking system does not have to hold these excess secondary reserves.

The banks can dispose of excess secondary reserves by buying bonds in the United States or Great Britain, or by expanding loans in Canada. An expansion of domestic loans creates excess money holdings that the private sector disposes of by purchasing assets abroad. The excess money is returned to the banks in exchange for the foreign currency required to purchase these assets, establishing the equilibrium level of secondary reserves.

The public's desired money holdings are explained by a standard demand function for money expressing the quantity of money demanded as a function of interest rates and wealth or income. Since the supply of money in the period under discussion was perfectly elastic to the country at a fixed price of gold, estimates of the demand for money should be free of the simultaneity bias often found in money-demand estimates for more recent time periods. This bias may arise from failure to incorporate reaction functions on the supply side.[12]

In the portfolio adjustment approach developed here, the money multiplier does not have an important role to play in determining the money supply. Base money (bank reserves and public Dominion note holdings) is chosen by the banks according to their desired ratios of reserves to deposit and note liabilities, and by the public according to its desired ratio of Dominion notes to deposit and bank note holdings. The banks also choose the division of reserve holdings among gold, Dominion notes, and secondary reserves in New York and London, subject to the legal provisions regarding the fraction of primary or cash reserves that must be held in Dominion notes. The banking system's stock of reserves and reserve components, therefore, is determined by short-term interest rates and the magnitude of note and deposit liabilities.

The public's holdings of Dominion notes as opposed to bank notes and deposits represents a transactions demand, since Dominion notes are the only notes available smaller than five dollars. The public's ratio of both Dominion and bank note holdings to bank deposits depends on the level of interest rates (since notes bear no interest), on some measure of transactions, and on wealth.

There is no presumption that an increase in the money supply precedes the rise in the price of nontraded relative to traded goods – money

---

[12] See, for example, Carr and Darby (1981).

holdings respond to the effects of price changes on desired holdings. Domestic price changes result from the effect on aggregate demand of the expansion of investment financed by the inflow of capital, and not from a prior change in the money supply. The causality runs from capital inflow to prices to money, not from capital inflow to money to prices.

The consistency of these adjustments with the maintained hypothesis can be established by demonstrating that the money stock, its components, the velocity of money, and the level and components of bank reserves are stable functions of the variables predicted by theory.

The demand function for money

International capital mobility combined with the relatively small size of the Canadian economy implies a strong similarity between portfolio equilibrium of Canadian residents in the aggregate and portfolio equilibrium of an individual in a large economy. Prices and interest rates adjusted for risk are fixed from the point of view of domestic residents, implying that estimates of the demand function for money should be free of simultaneity bias.[13]

Table 5.2 presents least squares estimates of the demand function for money for Canada in the 1871–1913 period. The log of the real quantity of money demanded is expressed as a function of the interest rate and the log of real income. Three alternative interest rates are used, the long-term rate on Canadian borrowings, the short-term rate on commercial paper in New York, and the British treasury bill rate.

These results present a satisfactory confirmation of the maintained hypotheses about the signs of the parameters in the demand function for money. The Durbin–Watson statistics, however, indicate serial correlation in the residuals, suggesting that some important explanatory variables are left out of the estimating equation. It is particularly interesting that both the long-term and short-term interest-rate coefficients are significant, with the U.K. treasury bill rate performing somewhat better than the U.S. commercial paper rate. The bulk of the capital inflow before 1914 was from the United Kingdom.[14]

In regressions (not shown) using the real money stock and real income

---

[13] Reactions on the supply side resulting from central bank policy were not present because there was no central bank or domestic short-term monetary policy – the chartered banks were forced to provide whatever stock of money the public wanted to hold.

[14] See Paterson (1976).

Table 5.2. Least squares estimates of the demand function for money: Canada, 1871–1913

	Log of the real money stock				
	(1)	(2)	(3)	(4)	(5)
Constant	-3.62 (-10.0)	-5.02 (-17.8)	-5.36 (-26.1)	-3.90 (-11.2)	-3.59 (-10.0)
Canadian long-term gov't bond rate	-.19 (-6.0)			-.15 (-4.8)	.17 (-5.1)
U.S. short-term commercial paper rate		-.04 (-2.8)			-.02 (-1.4)
U.K. treasury bill rate			-.076 (-4.2)	-.045 (-2.8)	
Log of real income	1.49 (36.9)	1.63 (43.8)	1.68 (54.3)	1.53 (38.1)	1.49 (37.3)
Number of observations	43	43	43	43	43
R-squared	.990	.984	.987	.992	.990
Standard error	.085	.106	.097	.078	.083
Durbin–Watson	.93	.51	.60	.89	.81

Note: The figures in brackets are t-ratios.

without taking logs of the variables, the long-term Canadian and short-term U.S. interest-rate coefficients are insignificant but correctly signed. The U.K. interest-rate variable is correctly signed and significant at only the 10-percent level. First-order serial correlation is again present in the residuals.

A visual examination of movements in interest rates in Canada, the United States, and Great Britain in Figures 4.14 and 4.15 reveals a number of features of the data that must be considered when interpreting the above results. First, note that before 1890 long-term rates in Canada and the United States fell very substantially relative to rates in the United Kingdom. This probably reflects the growth and development of the capital market in North America that brought a reduction in and more efficient measurement of risk. Moreover, it is apparent from Figure 4.9 that there was substantially greater growth of deposit banking before 1894 than after that year. Figure 4.10 indicates that the velocity of money also fell much more steeply before 1895 than after. Significant differences in the behavior of the reserve ratios of the chartered banks before and after 1890 are also apparent from Figure 4.11. All these factors suggest that the money and asset markets were developing more rapidly before 1890 than after.

Before 1880, long-term U.S. interest rates fell relative to U.K. and Canadian rates. Short-term U.S. interest rates fell relative to short-term U.K. rates in the early seventies. These higher and declining U.S. rates are likely the result of a reduction in the U.S. inflation rate as the Americans prepared to resume convertibility of the U.S. dollar into gold in 1879.

To examine the impact of these considerations the sample is split and the regressions rerun for the 1871–89 and 1890–1913 subperiods separately. In the earlier period, the long-term interest rate turns out to be significant only at the 7.5 percent level when the U.K. treasury bill rate is used as the short rate. Otherwise, the long- and the short-term rates are significant at the 5 percent level. The Durbin–Watson statistics are now too high.[15] In the later period, both short-term and long-term interest rates are significant. The Durbin–Watson statistics are too low except where both short-term and long-term interest rates are included in the regressions. Table 5.3 gives the flavor of these results.

For the 1890–1913 period, with both long-term and short-term interest rates included, the Durbin–Watson statistics indicate no serial correlation in the residuals. The model is properly specified, consistent, and without

---

[15] The Ljung-Box Q-statistic indicates no serial correlation in the residuals.

Table 5.3. *Least squares estimates of the demand function for money: Canada, 1871–89 and 1890–1913*

	Log of the real money stock					
	1871–89		1890–1913		1871–1913	
Constant	−1.95 (−1.8)	−1.47 (−1.5)	−3.87 (−15.2)	−3.26 (−11.0)	−3.80 (−16.2)	−3.27 (−13.0)
Canadian long-term gov't bond rate	−.138 (−1.9)	−.155 (−2.4)	−.176 (−6.2)	−.156 (−4.1)	−.172 (−6.8)	.163 (−5.5)
U.S. short-term commercial Paper rate		−.024 (−3.1)		−.040 (−2.7)		−.30 (−3.8)
U.K. treasury bill rate	−.038 (−2.2)		−.067 (−5.1)		−.058 (−5.6)	
Log of real income	1.20 (9.2)	1.13 (9.4)	1.55 (40.9)	1.45 (35.3)	1.54 (44.6)	1.45 (41.7)
Dummy					2.56 (5.1)	2.11 (3.8)
Dummy × log of real income					−.423 (−5.5)	−.36 (−4.1)
Number of observations	19	19	24	24	43	43
R-squared	.986	.989	.991	.984	.997	.996
Standard error	.044	.040	.049	.064	.047	.054
Durbin–Watson	2.88	2.36	1.90	1.71	2.30	1.85

Note: The figures in brackets are *t*-ratios.

simultaneity bias. In fact, these estimates are among the very few money-demand function estimates that are not burdened with serial correlation in the residuals, an endemic problem.[16] For a small country in a world of capital mobility, the portfolio theory predicts no serial correlation in the residuals even when it is present in the residuals of the estimating equations for the world as a whole.

Regressions for the entire period with dummy variables for the constant term and real income in the earlier subperiod yield much lower standard errors. The Durbin–Watson statistics are in the acceptable range. In these regressions, a one-percentage-point increase in both long-term and short-term rates is associated with little more than a 0.2 percent reduction in the level of real money holdings. This implies an interest elasticity of demand for money balances, computed at the mean, of about 0.75, somewhat larger than the long-run interest elasticities of demand for money estimated by Clinton (1973) for the period 1955–70. The estimates also reflect the pattern, noted by Clinton, that the elasticity is lower for the short-term rate than for the long-term rate. The income elasticity of demand for money for the period after 1890 is in the neighborhood of 1.5, somewhat higher than Clinton's estimates. This is also considerably higher than estimates obtained by Carr and Darby (1981) using quarterly data for the period 1951 to 1976.

The rapid growth of population during 1871–1913 makes it worthwhile to rerun the regressions with both real GNP and the real money stock in per capita terms. These results are shown in Tables 5.4 and 5.5.

For both the whole period and the two subperiods the results are essentially the same as when the real money stock and real income were not in per capita terms. The long-term interest elasticity is now significant at the 5-percent level for the earlier subperiod. The income elasticities of demand for money are somewhat higher than when the real money stock and real GNP variables were not in per capita terms. Again, the Durbin–Watson statistics are unacceptable in the regressions for the whole period and the early subperiod, but become acceptable in the 1890–1913 regressions and the 1871–1913 regressions that include the dummy variables.[17]

The determinants of velocity

The income velocity of money is, of course, closely related to the demand function for money. Estimating equations for velocity consistent with those

---

[16] For a wide-ranging discussion of the problem, see Carr (1983).
[17] The Ljung-Box Q-statistics again indicate no serial correlation in either period.

Table 5.4. *Least squares estimates of the demand function for per capita real money holdings: Canada, 1871–1913*

	Log of the real money stock				
	(1)	(2)	(3)	(4)	(5)
Constant	−4.58 (−8.7)	−6.00 (−17.6)	−6.43 (−25.8)	−5.14 (−9.9)	−4.56 (−8.8)
Canadian long-term gov't bond rate	−.16 (−4.2)			−.11 (−2.8)	.14 (−3.4)
U.S. short-term commercial paper rate		−.039 (−2.8)			−.022 (−1.6)
U.K. treasury bill rate			−.079 (−4.4)	−.055 (−3.0)	
Log of real income	1.83 (22.3)	2.03 (32.9)	2.12 (42.1)	1.93 (23.4)	1.83 (22.8)
Number of observations	43	43	43	43	43
R-squared	.978	.973	.978	.982	.979
Standard error	.097	.107	.096	.089	.095
Durbin–Watson	.86	.64	.78	.85	.75

Note: The figures in brackets are *t*-ratios.

Table 5.5. *Least squares estimates of the demand function for per capita real money holdings: Canada, 1871–89 and 1890–1913*

	Log of the real money stock					
	1871–89		1890–1913		1871–1913	
Constant	−1.58 (−1.5)	−1.28 (−1.4)	−5.52 (−13.3)	−4.27 (−9.1)	−5.27 (−14.3)	−4.23 (−11.0)
Canadian long-term gov't bond rate	−.167 (−2.6)	−.170 (−3.0)	−.122 (−3.8)	−.111 (−2.4)	−.129 (−4.6)	.127 (−3.7)
U.S. short-term commercial paper rate		−.025 (−3.4)		−.047 (−2.7)		−.034 (−3.7)
U.K. treasury bill rate	−.042 (−2.4)		−.088 (−5.5)		−.072 (−6.0)	
Log of real income	1.21 (7.4)	1.15 (7.9)	2.03 (24.9)	1.78 (20.3)	1.99 (27.8)	1.77 (24.6)
Dummy					3.42 (5.4)	2.54 (3.5)
Dummy × log of real income					−.737 (−5.8)	−.565 (−3.9)
Number of observations	19	19	24	24	43	43
R-squared	.977	.982	.976	.955	.994	.991
Standard error	.045	.040	.056	.076	.052	.063
Durbin–Watson	2.81	2.31	1.77	1.48	2.13	1.60

Note: The figures in brackets are *t*-ratios.

Table 5.6. *Least squares estimates of the income velocity of money: Canada, 1871–1913*

	Log of the income velocity of money							
	1871–1913		1871–89		1890–1913		1871–1913	
Constant	3.90 (11.2)	2.04 (2.4)	1.95 (1.8)	2.31 (2.0)	3.87 (15.2)	3.52 (3.81)	3.80 (16.2)	3.26 (4.4)
Canadian long-term gov't bond rate	.152 (4.8)	.223 (5.3)	.138 (1.9)	.095 (1.1)	.176 (6.2)	.187 (4.7)	.173 (6.8)	.189 (5.7)
U.K. treasury bill rate	.045 (2.8)	.026 (1.5)	.038 (2.2)	.028 (1.4)	.067 (5.1)	.062 (3.5)	.058 (5.6)	.053 (4.1)
Log of real income	−.534 (−13.2)		−.20 (−1.5)		−.554 (−14.6)		−.538 (−15.6)	
Log of per capita real income		.018 (.08)		−.045 (−.22)		−.453 (−1.8)		−.378 (−1.8)
Log of population		−1.20 (−4.3)		−.788 (−1.2)		−.663 (−2.4)		−.720 (−3.0)

Dummy							−2.56 (−5.1)	−2.17 (−3.0)
Dummy × log of real income							.423 (5.5)	
Dummy × log of per capita real income								.274 (1.0)
Dummy × log of population								.646 (1.2)
Number of observations	43	43	19	19	24	24	43	43
R-squared	.952	.958	.888	.895	.926	.927	.983	.984
Standard error	.078	.073	.044	.044	.049	.050	.047	.048
Durbin–Watson	.894	.995	2.876	2.949	1.896	1.883	2.304	2.285

Note: The figures in brackets are *t*-ratios.

for the demand function for money are given in Table 5.6. Only the estimates that include both Canadian long-term and U.K. short-term interest rates as independent variables are shown. All variables except interest rates are in logs.

As in the case of the demand for money estimates, the equations perform well. The Durbin–Watson statistics indicate the presence of serial correlation in the residuals in the 1871–1913 regressions not containing dummy variables and in the 1871–89 regressions. They indicate no serial correlation in either the 1871–1913 regressions with dummy variables or the 1890–1913 regressions.[18] When velocity and the income and population variables are not in logs the results (not shown) are essentially the same except that the Durbin–Watson statistics indicate no evidence of serial correlation in the residuals for the whole period. When the sample is split, positive serial correlation is present in the residuals for the early subperiod but no serial correlation is present for the later one.[19]

When the income variable is split into its per capita income and population components, population is significant and per capita income insignificant in the regressions for the whole period without dummy variables. When dummies are included for the constant term and the income and population variables, the per capita income variable becomes significant at the 10 percent level. The results are the same for the 1890–1913 subperiod alone – population is significant at the 5 percent level and per capita income at the 10 percent level. Both variables are insignificant in the regressions for the 1871–89 period. When the population variable is dropped the per capita income variable becomes significant in all regressions except the one for the subperiod 1871–89.

The relationship between real income and velocity is negative in all regressions. This is consistent with the well-known downward trend of velocity in the period extending from the beginning of World War II back well into the nineteenth century.[20] The effect of interest rates on velocity is positive, reflecting the negative relationship between the demand for money and interest rates.

[18] The Ljung-Box Q-statistics indicate serial correlation in the residuals over the whole period but not in either subperiod.

[19] In this case the Ljung-Box Q-statistic indicates rejection of the hypothesis of serial correlation for the whole period and for both subperiods.

[20] The long-run behavior of velocity is analyzed in detail by Bordo and Jonung (1981, 1987). They ascribe this decline in velocity to the monetization of the economy associated with the shift of the population from subsistence farming to commercial farming and urban manufacturing.

Table 5.7. *Least squares estimates of the public's ratio of currency to deposits: Canada, 1871–1913*

	Log of the ratio of currency to deposits			
	1871–1913	1871–89	1890–1913	1871–1913
Constant	3.92	−2.90	3.73	3.71
	(6.7)	(−1.1)	(13.5)	(9.2)
Canadian long-term gov't bond rate	.074	.275	.080	.101
	(1.4)	(1.6)	(2.6)	(2.3)
U.K. treasury bill rate	.079	.107	.094	.099
	(2.9)	(2.6)	(6.7)	(5.6)
Log of real income	−.888	.082	−.875	−.885
	(−13.2)	(.26)	(−21.3)	(−14.9)
Dummy				−4.01
				(−4.6)
Dummy × log of real income				.666
				(5.0)
Number of observations	43	19	24	43
R-squared	.932	.673	.960	.975
Standard error	.130	.107	.053	.081
Durbin–Watson	.439	.896	2.012	1.175

Note: The figures in brackets are *t*-ratios.

The composition of money holdings

One would expect a negative relationship between the ratio of currency to deposits held by the public and the rate of interest. Rising interest rates increase the opportunity cost of holding noninterest bearing currency. In a growing economy with a developing banking system and increasing proportion of large scale transactions, the public is expected to increase its holdings of deposits relative to currency as real income increases.

Regressions of real GNP and short-term and long-term interest rates on the currency/deposit ratio are shown in Table 5.7. The estimated coefficients are significant for the period as a whole and for the 1890–1913 subperiod, but not for the subperiod 1871–89. The Durbin–Watson statistics for the 1890–1913 regressions indicate no serial correlation in the residuals. The interest-rate coefficients, however, have the wrong signs.

The positive relationship between the level of interest rates and the currency/deposit ratio arises from two facts. First, the quantity of money is negatively related to interest rates. Second, the deposit component of this money stock is much more sensitive to interest rates than the currency component. Given the technology of transactions making at the time, it was easier for holders of cash to economize on lower (and often zero) interest-bearing deposits than on noninterest bearing currency. To ferret out these effects, separate demand functions are estimated for currency and deposits using interest rates and real GNP as independent variables. These are shown in Table 5.8.

The demand for currency, measured in real terms, is negatively related to the long-term Canadian interest rate and positively related to real GNP during the period as a whole and the 1890–1913 subperiod. But it does not respond negatively, or significantly, to short-term interest rates. Indeed, neither the U.S. corporate paper rate nor U.K. treasury bill rate as proxies for the short-term interest rate turn out to be significant in regressions that exclude the Canadian long-term rate.

The real deposit estimating equations yield results very similar to the demand for money estimates – the coefficients of the log linear estimates are almost the same.

These results confirm that both deposit and currency components of the desired money stock are negatively related to interest rates. Long-term interest rates alone, however, appear to be relevant in the case of currency, with the interest elasticities being greater (in absolute value) in the case of deposits. This accounts for the fact that the currency/deposit ratio is positively related to interest rates. The income elasticity of demand for deposits is also much greater than the income elasticity of demand for currency, accounting for the negative relationship of the currency/deposit ratio to GNP. A Cochrane–Orcutt correction for serial correlation in the residuals yields no substantive change in these results.

The composition of chartered bank reserves

One might expect the reserve ratio of the banking system to be negatively related to interest rates because higher interest rates raise the opportunity cost of holding low and zero interest bearing reserves. This might particularly be the case for primary reserves (gold and Dominion notes) that bore no interest. In the case of secondary reserves (call loans in New York and London and deposits in foreign banks), the situation is more complicated.

Since call loans and deposits in foreign banks bear interest, the oppor-

Table 5.8. *Least squares estimates of the demand for currency and deposits: Canada, 1871–1913*

	Log of real currency				Log of real deposits			
	1871–1913	1871–89	1890–1913	1871–1913	1871–1913	1871–89	1890–1913	1871–1913
Constant	−1.10 (−4.0)	−4.76 (−2.8)	−1.11 (−5.0)	−1.09 (−3.8)	−5.02 (−11.5)	−1.86 (−1.2)	−4.84 (−16.8)	−4.81 (−16.6)
Canadian long-term gov't bond rate	−.113 (−4.5)	.066 (.58)	−.119 (−4.8)	−.099 (−3.2)	−.187 (−4.7)	−.209 (−2.0)	−.198 (−6.2)	−.189 (−6.3)
U.K. treasury bill rate	.013 (1.0)	.035 (1.3)	.012 (1.0)	.019 (1.5)	−.066 (−3.3)	−.072 (−2.9)	−.083 (−5.6)	−.079 (−6.2)
Log of real income	.809 (25.7)	1.27 (6.2)	.813 (24.6)	.798 (18.9)	1.70 (33.6)	1.19 (6.3)	1.69 (39.3)	1.68 (39.6)
Dummy				−1.11 (−1.8)				2.89 (4.6)
Dummy × log of real income				.182 (1.9)				−.484 (−5.1)
Number of observations	43	19	24	43	43	19	24	43
R-squared	.983	.943	.978	.986	.989	.976	.990	.996
Standard error	.061	.069	.043	.058	.098	.064	.056	.058
Durbin–Watson	.833	.947	1.710	1.055	.813	2.201	1.899	2.151

Note: The figures in brackets are *t*-ratios.

tunity cost to banks of holding them depends on the differential in interest rates between these and other assets. These rates, in turn, depend on the willingness of the banking system in the world as a whole to hold these assets. If capital markets function well and different assets are good substitutes for each other in portfolios, not much difference in interest rates would be observed between secondary reserves and other short-term assets. The interpretation of an observed partial correlation of short-term interest-rate changes with secondary reserve holdings must take into account the covariance between interest rates on secondary reserves and on other competing assets in bank portfolios.

A decrease in secondary reserve holdings might result from a general increase in short-term rates because the rates on call loans and net claims on foreign banks do not rise as much as interest rates in general. The cost of holding secondary reserves increases. Alternatively, in boom periods when short-term interest rates are high, banks might hold lower ratios of reserves to liabilities because of risk considerations. To unravel the effects of interest rates on bank reserves we would need interest-rate data on all major assets in the banks' portfolios.

Regression analyses of the determinants of the chartered banks' primary, secondary, and total reserve holdings are presented in Tables 5.9 and 5.10. The ratios of reserve holdings to note and deposit liabilities are regressed on the short-term interest rate and real note and deposit liabilities. The latter variable takes into account the possibility that reserve ratios may increase or decrease with the scale of the banking system. In all regressions, the British treasury bill rate is used as the relevant short-term rate. When the U.S. commercial paper rate or the U.S. call loan rate is used, the results are essentially the same but the fit is not quite so good.[21]

Table 5.9 gives the regressions for the ratio of total reserves to note and deposit liabilities. In the analysis of the demand for money earlier in this chapter, it is found that the financial system before 1890 was affected by factors that were not present after that year. These factors include the growth and development of the domestic capital market and the associated reduction in the costs of holding money and other financial assets in the years following Confederation. There was a sharp increase in money holdings, a shift toward deposit banking, and a general decline in interest rates in Canada relative to Great Britain.

---

[21] Most capital entering Canada during the period under study came from the United Kingdom rather than the United States, suggesting that the Canadian and U.K. financial markets may have been more highly integrated than the Canadian and U.S. markets.

Table 5.9. *Least squares estimates of the reserve ratios of the chartered banks: Canada, 1871–1913*

	Ratio of total reserves to currency and deposit liabilities			
	1871–1913	1871–89	1890–1913	1871–1913
Constant	.315	.508	.025	.261
	(9.27)	(4.49)	(15.6)	(8.76)
U.K. treasury bill rate	−.012	−.046	−.028	−.034
	(−1.12)	(−1.8)	(−4.9)	(−3.4)
Log of real chartered bank	−.068	−.71	.131	.141
liabilities	(−1.71)	(−1.4)	(4.9)	(2.76)
Dummy				.196
				(4.21)
Dummy × log of real				−.748
chartered bank liabilities				(−2.19)
Number of observations	43	19	24	43
R-squared	.109	.186	.608	.478
Standard error	.059	.066	.023	.047
Durbin–Watson	.894	1.115	1.438	1.249

Note: The figures in brackets are *t*-ratios.

Accordingly, the sample is again split at 1890. As can be seen from the table, this split is important. The scale variable is negative before 1890 and for the period as a whole when no dummy variables are included, but positive for the 1890–1913 subperiod. This strongly suggests that the banks responded to a different environment and forces before and after 1890. The regression coefficients are much more significant in the later subperiod, the explanatory power of the equation is higher, and the Durbin–Watson statistic is close to rejecting serial correlation. In the earlier subperiod, the interest-rate variable is significant at only the 10 to 15 percent level and the Durbin–Watson statistics indicate serial correlation in the residuals and misspecification of the equation.

When the reserve ratio is split into its primary and secondary components, as in Table 5.10, the conclusion that there is an underlying structural shift around 1890 is confirmed. In addition, there is no evidence that primary reserve holdings respond more strongly than secondary reserves to short-term interest-rate changes.

Table 5.10. *Least squares estimates of the primary and secondary reserve ratios of the chartered banks: Canada, 1871–1913*

	Primary reserve ratio (gold and Dominion notes)				Secondary reserve ratio (call loans and net claims on foreign banks)			
	1871–1913	1871–89	1890–1913	1871–1913	1871–1913	1871–89	1890–1913	1871–1913
Constant	.13	.26	.10	.105	.18	.24	.13	.146
	(8.3)	(14.1)	(13.5)	(15.18)	(6.4)	(2.1)	(7.8)	(4.86)
U.K. treasury bill rate	.01	−.01	−.01	−.01	−.02	−.04	−.02	−.02
	(1.7)	(−1.5)	(−2.1)	(−2.59)	(−2.0)	(−1.6)	(−3.0)	(−2.54)
Log of real chartered bank liabilities	−.07	−.80	.05	.05	−.003	.24	.08	.097
	(−3.9)	(−9.9)	(3.6)	(3.87)	(−.10)	(.48)	(3.0)	(1.89)
Dummy				.15				.033
				(13.8)				(.704)
Dummy × log of real chartered bank liabilities				−.849				.276
				(−10.7)				(.806)
Number of observations	43	19	24	43	43	19	24	43
R-squared	.290	.872	.384	.886	.092	.208	.372	.263
Standard error	.027	.011	.011	.011	.051	.066	.025	.047
Durbin–Watson	.389	1.972	1.340	1.757	1.065	1.166	1.399	1.26

Note: The figures in brackets are *t*-ratios.

6. Evidence on the process of balance-of-payments adjustment

The evidence in the previous chapter is fully consistent with the portfolio approach to balance-of-payments adjustment, but it is also consistent with the traditional theory, thus providing little basis for discriminating between the two. In this chapter we present evidence on the balance-of-payments adjustment process that strongly supports the portfolio theory and is strongly inconsistent with the workings of the standard price-specie-flow mechanism.

According to both the portfolio and traditional theories, the balance-of-payments surplus equals the increase in the stock of gold and secondary reserve holdings of the chartered banks plus the increase in the government's gold holdings. These two components together are referred to below as reserve money. The first is by far the dominant component.

The portfolio theory explains the inflow of reserve money during our period as the result primarily of increases in the quantity of money demanded by the public. The banking system created money to satisfy Canadian demands for additional note and deposit holdings, acquiring in the process the necessary gold and secondary reserve holdings to back these additional liquid liabilities. The demand for money rose due to the desire of domestic residents to transact the increased volume of nominal income resulting from the development of the Canadian economy. In addition, desired money holdings changed because of changes in world prices that resulted from expansions of the gold stock and changes in the demand for money in the world as a whole.

The portfolio theory predicts that the rate of change through time in chartered bank reserves and government gold holdings is explained by the rates of change of two sets of factors, those that cause changes in the nominal quantity of money demanded – prices, real income, and world interest rates – and those that determine the ratio of reserve money to the nominal money supply.

75

The stock of reserve money can be expressed

$$R = \delta(r^*, H, Z) \cdot M \tag{6.1}$$

where δ (r^*, H, Z) is the equilibrium ratio of reserve money to the total money stock, r^* is the world interest rate, H is a scale variable denoting the size of the banking system, and Z ($= DSB/P$) is the real debt service balance. The evidence below suggests that a rise in the real debt service deficit increases the banking system's desired ratio of reserves to monetary liabilities. When there is a large outstanding stock of domestic assets owned by foreigners, higher international reserves are held against potential future international transactions.[1] Substitution of the domestic demand for money function (3.20) into equation (6.1) yields

$$R = \delta(r^*, H, Z) \cdot P \cdot L(r^*, Y) \tag{6.2}$$

The balance-of-payments surplus is the rate of growth of reserve money:

$$dR/dt = [\delta\ (r^*, H, Z) \cdot L\ (r^*, Y)\ ]\ dP/dt + [\delta\ (r^*, H, Z) \cdot P \cdot L_{r_*}$$
$$+\ M \cdot \delta_{r_*}]\ dr^*/dt + [\delta\ (r^*, H, Z) \cdot P \cdot L_y]\ dY/dt$$
$$+\ [M \cdot \delta_h]\ dH/dt + [M \cdot \delta_z]\ dZ/dt \tag{6.3}$$

δ_j and L_j ($j = r^*, y, h, z$) are the partial derivatives in the functions δ (r^*, H, Z) and $L(r^*, Y)$; dP/dt and dY/dt are the equilibrium rates of growth of Canadian income and prices; dH/dt, the growth of the banking system, is exogenous and could possibly be represented by some function of dY/dt or dM/dt; dZ/dt, the rate of growth of the real debt service balance, is determined by the capital inflows of previous periods. Finally, dr^*/dt is determined abroad.

Equation (6.3) can be converted into a useful estimating equation by putting it in first-difference form and dividing both sides by the price level at time $t - 1$ to put the change in reserves in real terms. The resulting estimating equation for the real balance-of-payments surplus is:

---

[1] In Dick and Floyd (1991) we did not include the real debt service balance as a determinant of the ratio of reserve money to the total money stock. A weak association was found between domestic and foreign real incomes and real long-term capital flows and the real international reserve flows, a finding contrary to the portfolio theory. The evidence to follow shows that modifying the specification to incorporate the real debt service balance as a determinant of the banking system's international reserve holdings removes that minor inconsistency with portfolio theory.

$$(R_t - R_{t-1}) / P_{t-1} = \beta_0 + \beta_r (R_{t-1}/P_{t-1}) (r_t^* - r_{t-1}^*)$$
$$+ \beta_y (R_{t-1}/P_{t-1}) [(Y_t - Y_{t-1}) /Y_{t-1}]$$
$$+ \beta_h (R_{t-1}/P_{t-1}) [(H_t - H_{t-1})/H_{t-1}]$$
$$+ \beta_z (M_{t-1}/P_{t-1}) [Z_t - Z_{t-1}]$$
$$+ \beta_p (R_{t-1}/P_{t-1}) [(P_t - P_{t-1})/P_{t-1}] + u_t \quad (6.4)$$

where

$$\beta_r = \frac{1}{L}\frac{\partial L}{\partial r^*} + \frac{1}{\delta}\frac{\partial \delta}{\partial r^*} < 0$$

$$\beta_y = \frac{Y}{L}\frac{\partial L}{\partial Y} > 0$$

$$\beta_h = \frac{H}{\delta}\frac{\partial \delta}{\partial H}$$

$$\beta_z = \delta_z < 0$$

$$\beta_p = 1.0$$

$$u_t = \text{random error term}$$

A priori, β_h can be positive or negative. Notice that division of the entire equation by R_{t-1}/P_{t-1}, would reduce the left side to the relative change in R/P and the right side to the sum of the β_j's, each multiplied by the relative changes in the relevant exogenous variable (absolute change in the case of the interest rate and $1/\delta$ times the absolute change in the case of the real debt service variable).

The traditional classical approach to the balance of payments is radically different. The standard specie-flow mechanism treats the balance of payments as the sum of three independent components: (1) the balance of trade, determined by domestic and foreign real incomes and domestic relative to foreign prices; (2) the inflow of long-term capital, exogenously determined; and (3) the inflow of short-term capital, which is positively related to the differential of domestic over foreign interest rates. Although the capital components are usually not formulated rigorously, the implied expression for the determinants of the real reserve flow is

$$dR/P = B_T(P/P^*, Y, Y^*) + Z + LC + C(r - r^*) \quad (6.5)$$

where $B_T(P/P^*, Y, Y^*)$ is the balance of trade, LC is the real net inflow of long-term capital, and $C(r - r^*)$ is the real short-term net capital inflow expressed as a function of the differential of domestic over foreign real interest rates. According to the standard view, the partial derivatives of the relative price and domestic income variables in the balance-of-trade function are negative, while the partial derivative of foreign income in that function is positive. The net capital inflow is positively related to the differential of the domestic over the foreign interest rate.

Although many models do not do so, there is reason to include the net capital flow as a determinant of the balance of trade. The traditional literature on the transfer problem argues that a flow of capital into the domestic economy is associated with an equivalent reduction in foreign spending and increase in domestic spending.[2] These spending changes have direct effects on domestic and foreign imports, leading to a negative relationship between the long-term capital inflow and the trade balance. In the portfolio approach, increases in the capital inflow involve a reallocation of world investment toward the domestic economy or a decline in domestic relative to world saving. To the extent that an increase in domestic investment leads to an increase in imports of capital goods or a change in savings behavior leads to an increase in consumption of import goods, the capital inflow will deteriorate the trade balance at each level of the exchange rate.[3]

On the basis of the above discussion, equation (6.5) yields two estimating equations of interest:

$$B_T = \alpha_0 + \alpha_p P_t/P_t^* + \alpha_y Y_t + \alpha_y^* Y_t^* + \alpha_{lc} LC_t + v_t \quad (6.6)$$

$$(R_t - R_{t-1}) / P_{t-1} = \gamma_0 + \gamma_p P_t / P_t^* + \gamma_y Y_t + \gamma_y^* Y_t^*$$
$$+ \gamma_z Z_t + \gamma_{lc} LC_t + \gamma_c [r_t - r_t^*] + w_t^* \quad (6.7)$$

where

$$\alpha_p = \gamma_p < 0$$
$$\alpha_y = \gamma_y < 0$$
$$\alpha_y^* = \gamma_y^* > 0$$
$$\alpha_{lc} < 0$$
$$0 < \gamma_{lc} < 1.0$$
$$\gamma_z = 1.0$$
$$\gamma_c > 0$$

v_t and w_t = random error terms

If the income variables as measured do not fully reflect the influence of repatriated earnings, the real debt service balance should be included in

---

[2] See Johnson (1958b).
[3] Whatever these effects on the trade balance, however, its ultimate level must be driven equal to the net inflow of capital by international relative price (that is, real exchange rate) adjustments. Note that unless savings change, these shifts do not involve changes in the levels of income and wealth in either country. Capital owned by the capital exporting country's residents is simply employed abroad.

the balance-of-trade equation with a negative sign and the coefficient γ_z will be less than unity in (6.7). Furthermore, it could be argued that the real balance of trade might also be a function of the differential between domestic and foreign interest rates. Higher domestic relative to foreign interest rates would reduce domestic relative to foreign investment, lowering imports and increasing exports and thereby improving the balance of trade.

Tests of restrictions implied by the two theories

Our first empirical tests take advantage of the fact that the balance of trade is identically determined by relative prices and incomes and perhaps the real long-term capital inflow under the two alternative hypotheses, while the portfolio-adjustment and price-specie-flow mechanisms have radically different implications with respect to the determinants of the balance-of-payments surplus. Under the portfolio approach, the real international reserve inflow is determined by the rate of change in the desired reserve holdings of the banking system, given by equation (6.4), and is independent of the balance of trade. This implies that $\gamma_p = \gamma_y = \gamma_y^* = \gamma_{lc} = \gamma_c = \gamma_z = 0$ in equation (6.7). Under the classical approach, the balance of trade, real debt service balance, and long-term real net capital inflow are additive components of the real international reserve flow, implying, as noted above, that $\alpha_p = \gamma_p$, $\alpha_y = \gamma_y$, $\alpha_y^* = \gamma_y^*$, and $\gamma_z = 1.0$ in equations (6.6) and (6.7).

Table 6.1 presents the estimates of (6.6) and (6.7). In testing these restrictions, allowance must be made for the fact that the error terms v_t and w_t are jointly distributed. Accordingly, estimation proceeds using the seemingly unrelated regression (SUR) technique. To allow for the fact that our measures of domestic and foreign incomes may not be wholly adequate, and for the possibility that domestic and foreign interest differentials may affect the balance of trade, we add the real debt service balance and interest-rate differential variables to the balance-of-trade estimating equation. To the extent that these variables do not belong, the conclusions are biased in favor of the traditional price-specie-flow theory and against the portfolio approach.[4]

---

[4] The inclusion of independent variables that are unrelated to the dependent variable (and to the other independent variables) should not reduce the unrestricted residual sum of squares, nor should it affect the restricted residual sum of squares when the coefficients of these variables are restricted to equal zero. So the sample X^2 should not be affected. But the number of restrictions increases equally with the number of these variables included, raising

Table 6.1. *Estimates of the balance of trade and balance of payments with cross equation restrictions: Canada, 1872–1913*

	OLS	SUR		
	Real trade account surplus (1)	Real trade account surplus (2)	Real balance-of-payments surplus (3)	Real trade account surplus (4)[a]
Constant	27.21 (.509)	75.27 (1.33)	−71.48 (−1.15)	72.34 (1.48)
Canadian price level ÷ rest of world price level	−1.25 (−3.03)	−1.74 (−3.56)	.506 (.951)	−1.38 (−4.01)
Canadian real income	−3.25 (−6.31)	−2.81 (−5.44)	−1.31 (−2.33)	−2.66 (−6.22)
Rest of world real income	4.36 (6.27)	4.21 (5.94)	1.52 (1.96)	3.51 (5.50)
Long-term real net capital inflow	.020 (.159)	.111 (.880)	.263 (1.92)	−.078 (−.744)
Canadian long-term interest rate ÷ U.K. long-term rate		−.518 (−.036)	−10.24 (−.647)	
Real debt service balance		.990 (1.764)	−.339 (−.554)	
Number of observations	42	42	42	42
R-squared	.897	.906	.229	.876
Standard error	16.406	16.171	17.654	17.721
Durbin–Watson	1.76	1.945	2.385	1.41

[a] In calculating this regression, the coefficients of all variables except the constant term and the real debt service balance in the balance-of-payments equation are constrained to equal zero, as is the coefficient of the real debt service balance in the balance-of-trade equation. The interest-rate differential coefficient is not reported.

Note: The figures in brackets are *t*-ratios.

Regression (1), estimated by ordinary least squares, shows the trade balance result consistent with both theories. The real long-term net capital inflow variable is insignificant with the wrong sign. The income and relative price variables are highly significant with the correct signs.[5] Regressions

the critical value of χ^2 and making it less likely that the restrictions will be rejected by the data at usual significance levels. We would like to thank Dwayne Benjamin and Angelo Melino for helpful discussions on the application of this technique.

[5] In reporting the results in this and all succeeding tables, it is sufficient for our purposes to interpret the statistical significance of the estimated coefficients without commenting on their magnitudes. Our purpose is to discriminate between the two major hypotheses using reduced forms rather than to estimate the structural models underlying these hypotheses.

(2) and (3) report the results of (SUR) estimation with no restrictions imposed. The classical specie-flow restrictions that the coefficients of relative prices and incomes are the same as in the balance-of-trade equation are rejected by the data with a $\chi^2(3)$ value of 39.3 and an infinitesimal P-value. If we add the restrictions that the coefficients of the real debt service balance be unity in the balance-of-payments equation and zero in the balance-of-trade equation, the null hypothesis is rejected with a $\chi^2(5)$ value of 60.4 and an infinitesimal P-value.[6]

The portfolio hypothesis that the coefficients of all variables in the balance-of-payments equation except the debt service balance are zero can only be rejected at the 15 percent level with a $\chi^2(5)$ value of 8.1. Adding the further restriction that the debt service variable have a zero coefficient in the trade balance equation reduces the rejection level to 6 percent with a $\chi^2(6)$ value of 12.13.[7] That no restriction is imposed in these tests on the coefficient of the real debt service balance in the balance-of-payments equation is important. If the coefficient of the real debt service variable is restricted to zero in the balance-of-payments equation, with no corresponding restriction imposed on the balance-of-trade equation, the rejection level is reduced from 15 percent to nearly 5 percent with a $\chi^2(6)$ value of 12.4. If, in addition, the coefficient of this variable in the balance-of-trade equation is also restricted to zero, the portfolio hypothesis must be rejected at the 1 to 2 percent level with a $\chi^2(7)$ value of 17.4.[8] These χ^2 values are still much lower, it should be noted, than those obtained in the case of the classical specie-flow restrictions. One might restrict the real debt service balance to zero in the balance-of-payments equation on the grounds that it is the rate of change of this variable, not the level, that is a determinant of the real reserve flow under the portfolio theory. Since the correlation between the two debt service balance variables in equations (6.4) and (6.7) is

The sizes of the reduced form coefficients are of little interest since they do not typically serve to reveal structural magnitudes.

[6] Adding a further restriction that the coefficient of the interest-rate differential be zero in the balance-of-trade equation changes nothing.

[7] Imposing as well the restriction that the interest-rate differential variable have a zero coefficient in the trade balance equation raises the rejection level back to 8 percent.

[8] The fall in the P-value when the coefficient of the real debt service variable is constrained to zero in the balance-of-trade equation arises because, as can be seen from column (2) in Table 6.1, that variable is quite significant in the unconstrained regression. Since the variable also has the wrong sign, it is measuring in that regression something other than what we want to measure. Constraining the coefficient of the interest-rate differential variable in the balance-of-trade equation to zero does not change the P-value materially.

0.9, however, it would seem inappropriate to impose this restriction.[9] The constrained balance-of-trade regression is shown in column (4) of Table 6.1.

As is evident from the real reserve flow regression (3) in Table 6.1, the real long-term capital inflow and real output variables show some strength, with the expected signs, in determining the real reserve inflow. The crucial relative price and interest rate variables, however, are insignificant with the wrong signs.[10] The portfolio theory clearly outperforms the traditional specie-flow theory.

Estimation of the portfolio theory balance-of-payments equation

Table 6.2 presents the regression results for equation (6.4). The price level variable, which is insignificantly different from the value of unity suggested by our theory, is constrained to equal unity in regression (2). The debt service variable is significant and negative, indicating that the bigger the increase in the real deficit on debt service, the greater the real reserve inflow.[11] Because of shifts in the structure of the banking system before 1890, a dummy variable equal to unity for the years 1871–89 and zero otherwise was included. It is barely significant at the 5 percent level in a two-tailed test. Dummy variables allowing the coefficients to take different values in the two subperiods were insignificant. Finally, the standard error of estimate of regression (1) is under 10. This is substantially below the standard error of 17.7 in the price-specie-flow regression reported in column (3) of Table 6.1.

---

[9] This restriction was imposed in Dick and Floyd (1991), along with the restrictions that the coefficients of the real long-term net capital inflow and interest-rate differential variables are zero in the balance-of-trade equation. These restrictions, which were applied to SUR regressions that omitted the real debt service balance variable from both the balance-of-payments and balance-of-trade equations, could not quite be rejected at the 5 percent level.

[10] Also, the regression is not significant at the 5 percent level.

[11] One might be tempted here to venture an alternative explanation of this debt service effect on real reserve holdings, attributing it simply to the expansion of the volume of trade rather than to the debt service deficit per se. While the real value of exports plus imports does behave in a manner similar to the debt service deficit, exports plus imports taken as a fraction of real income does not.

Table 6.2. *Estimation of the real reserve flow under the portfolio theory: Canada, 1872–1913*

	Real balance-of-payments surplus	
	(1)	(2)[a]
Constant	6.38	6.43
	(2.87)	(2.38)
Price level variable	1.03	1.0
	(1.62)	
Foreign real interest-rate variable	−.17	−.17
	(−5.78)	(−5.89)
Canadian real income variable	−1.18	−1.18
	(−2.32)	(−2.41)
Scale of banking system variable	.734	.731
	(2.39)	(2.44)
Debt service variable	−.003	−.003
	(−4.51)	(−4.78)
Dummy variable	−6.03	−6.08
	(−1.73)	(−1.84)
Number of observations	42	42
R-squared	.780	.774
Standard error	9.423	9.292
Durbin–Watson	1.979	1.971

[a]In calculating this regression, the coefficients of the price-level variable is constrained to equal unity.
Note: The figures in brackets are t-ratios.

Nonnested hypotheses tests

The above results are corroborated by nonnested hypotheses tests concerning the determinants of the reserve flow.[12] We regressed the real balance-of-payments surplus on all variables suggested by both the traditional and portfolio theories, that is, on all the independent variables in equations (6.4) and (6.7). First, the hypothesis that the coefficients of the relative price, income, interest rate differential, long-term capital flow, and level of real debt service variables are zero – the price-specie-flow variables contribute nothing to the explanation of the real reserve flow – can only be rejected at about the 12 percent level with a value of $F(6,29)$

[12] We would like to thank Rick Simes, Greg Jump, Angelo Melino, and Allan Hynes for helpful discussions relating to this approach.

$= 1.84$. Second, the hypothesis that the coefficients of all variables from the portfolio theory are zero is rejected with a value of $F(6,29) = 18.62$ and an infinitesimal P-value. The portfolio variables dominate in determining the real reserve flow. Finally, the hypothesis of the portfolio theory that the coefficient of the price variable in the portfolio equation is unity and that the relative price, income, long-term capital inflow, interest differential, and real debt service balance coefficients are all zero cannot be rejected – the P-value is 0.179 with a value of $F(7,29) = 1.57$.[13]

These results are further corroborated using Davidson–MacKinnon J-tests.[14] The specie-flow equation and portfolio balance-of-payments equations (6.7) and (6.4) were estimated separately. The predicted values from each equation were then included in the other equation and the regressions rerun. The hypothesis that the predicted value from the portfolio balance-of-payments equation has a zero coefficient in the specie-flow equation is overwhelmingly rejected with a value of $F(1,34) = 114.4$ and an infinitesimal P-value. The hypothesis that the predicted value from the specie-flow equation has a zero coefficient in the portfolio equation is also rejected, but with a much smaller value of $F(1,34)$ of 4.87 and a larger P-value of 0.036. The J-test gives ambivalent results for two reasons. First, the real debt service balance, which is important in determining the balance-of-payments surplus in the portfolio approach, is included in calculating the predicted values of the specie-flow equation, providing strength for the wrong reason when these predicted values are included in the portfolio regression. Second, as Godfrey (1985) has shown, the experimental evidence for small samples indicates that the J-test tends to reject both the true and the false models more frequently than does the standard F-test.

The F- and J-tests are special cases of a complete parameter encompassing test.[15] The F-test tests whether the means of the explanatory variables in one model are consistent with the predictions of the other; the J-test tests whether the variance of the error term in one model is consistent with the predictions of the other. The complete parameter encompassing test is a joint test of the consistency of the means and conditional variance of one model with the predictions of the other. The data reject the classical model's predictions of the parameters in the portfolio model with an $F(6,$

[13] The real debt service variable whose coefficient is constrained to zero here is the one from the classical equation (7.7). The coefficient of the real debt service variable in the portfolio equation (7.4) is left unconstrained.
[14] See Davidson and MacKinnon (1981).
[15] See Mizon and Richard (1986).

36) statistic of 4.63 and a *P*-value of 0.0014. At the same time, the portfolio model's predictions of the parameters in the classical model cannot be rejected, the $F(6, 36)$ statistic being 1.61 and the *P*-value 0.171.[16]

Capital flows and interest-rate differentials

We conclude this chapter by investigating whether there is any empirical relationship of capital flows to the differential between domestic and foreign interest rates. The traditional specie-flow mechanism postulates that short-term capital tends to move into a country whose interest rates increase relative to interest rates abroad. In the regression results that follow, short-term and total capital flows are defined to include errors and omissions. The ratio of domestic to foreign interest rates gives a slightly better fit than the difference between them.[17] Neufeld's long-term borrowing rate was used for Canada and the U.K. consol rate for the rest of the world.[18] The results for short-term real net capital inflows are given in Table 6.3 and those for total real net capital inflows are presented in Table 6.4. The results for long-term real net capital inflows were similar to those for the total and are not shown.

As indicated in the three columns on the left in Table 6.3, the interest-rate differential has the correct sign but is insignificant by the usual criteria. When the two income variables are replaced by the ratio of Canadian to rest of the world income, imposing the assumption that the income coefficients are equal but opposite in sign, the interest differential variable becomes significant at about the 5 percent level in the regression for the whole period but the standard error of the regression increases. The relationship between short-term real capital inflows and Canadian/foreign interest-rate differentials is not highly significant, but it is in the direction predicted by the traditional theory.

---

[16] Letting **Y** be the vector of observations on the dependent variable, **X** be the $n \times k$ matrix of observations on the independent variables in the equation of the null hypothesis, and **Z** be the $n \times q$ matrix of observations on those independent variables in the alternative equation that are not also specified in the null, it follows from Mizon and Richard (1986, p. 669, equation 3.11) that a complete parameter encompassing test can be based on the statistic

$$S = \mathbf{Y'M_xZ(Z'M_xZ)^{-1}Z'M_xY}/s^2q$$

where $\mathbf{M_x = I - X(X'X)^{-1}X'}$ and $s^2 = \mathbf{Y'M_xY}/(n - k)$

and S is distributed as $F(n - k, q)$. We would like to thank G.S. Maddala for helpful discussions regarding this test.

[17] Long-term interest rates had to be used because short-term rates were unavailable.

[18] When U.S. long-term rates were used, the results were less favorable to the traditional view.

Table 6.3. *Regressions of short-term real net capital inflows on domestic/foreign interest-rate differentials: Canada, 1871–1913*

	Short-term real net capital inflows					
	1871–1913	1871–89	1890–1913	1871–1913	1871–89	1890–1913
Constant	−83.22 (−.7)	−94.10 (−.6)	23.42 (.1)	−283.87 (−2.7)	−126.30 (−1.2)	−339.48 (−2.2)
Canadian long-term gov't bond rate ÷ U.K. consol rate	77.90 (1.3)	73.84 (.9)	42.50 (.3)	99.74 (2.0)	60.88 (1.2)	105.57 (1.4)
Canadian real income	1.34 (2.9)	.98 (1.1)	1.82 (1.6)			
Rest of world real income	−1.46 (−1.8)	−.88 (−.6)	−2.52 (−1.0)			
Canadian real income ÷ rest of world real income				165.55 (3.7)	57.01 (1.2)	207.03 (3.0)
Number of observations	43	19	24	43	19	24
R-squared	.375	.133	.363	.294	.098	.316
Standard error	25.6	13.1	33.7	26.8	12.9	34.0
Durbin–Watson	1.79	2.25	1.84	1.66	2.29	1.72

Note: The figures in brackets are *t*-ratios.

Table 6.4. *Regressions of total real net capital inflows on domestic/foreign interest-rate differentials: Canada, 1871–1913*

	Total real net capital inflows					
	1871–1913	1871–89	1890–1913	1871–1913	1871–89	1890–1913
Constant	−36.24 (−.4)	305.22 (4.8)	−212.01 (−1.1)	−723.28 (−5.1)	107.88 (2.0)	−1014.79 (−8.0)
Canadian long-term gov't bond rate ÷ *U.K. consol rate*	91.63 (2.0)	−146.22 (−4.6)	176.77 (2.1)	183.59 (2.8)	−83.20 (−3.2)	225.60 (3.7)
Canadian real income	4.53 (12.6)	1.36 (3.9)	4.29 (5.5)			
Rest of world real income	−5.56 (−8.2)	−2.25 (−3.9)	−4.31 (−2.6)			
Canadian real income ÷ *rest of world real income*				523.14 (8.8)	45.91 (1.9)	726.59 (12.9)
Number of observations	43	19	24	43	19	24
F-squared	.930	.837	.944	.763	.722	.907
Standard error	19.8	5.3	22.3	36.1	6.7	28.0
Durbin–Watson	1.50	1.83	1.84	.666	.613	1.61

Note: The figures in brackets are *t*-ratios.

In the total capital flow regressions in Table 6.4 the interest differential is significant but does not uniformly have the correct sign. A significant and negative relationship between the interest differential and the long-term net capital inflow is obtained for the subperiod 1871–89. A decline in Canadian (and U.S.) interest rates relative to U.K. rates in the face of the inflow of long-term capital was evidently associated with the structural changes in the financial system in North America in the period before 1890 noted in Chapter 4. After 1890, the relationship between total real net capital inflows and the ratio of Canadian to rest of the world long-term interest rates was positive as the traditional theory would predict. But these results are not inconsistent with a portfolio interpretation. After 1890, the expansion of the Canadian economy entailed increasing commitments of capital by foreign investors. It was not unreasonable of those investors to demand a higher interest rate as their risk exposure became greater.

7. Some further evidence on structure and timing

There are two principal important implications for the temporal relationships among money, real income, and prices in Canada and the rest of the world that some researchers might wish to draw from the portfolio theory. Although timing and causation are not the same thing, evidence on timing does offer a complementary source of information about the underlying structure of these relationships and the reasonableness of the portfolio theory vis-à-vis the price-specie-flow theory.

The first implication of the portfolio theory developed in this study is that Canadian prices cause Canadian money and not vice versa as in the price-specie-flow mechanism. One might expect, therefore, to observe changes in Canadian prices preceding changes in Canadian money. The second implication is that foreign real and monetary factors cause Canadian prices and money. Although this is also an implication of price-specie-flow theory, one would not expect to observe much, if any, lag between changes in these factors and changes in Canadian prices and money if the portfolio theory were true. Under the price/income-specie-flow theory, there would be long lags because that mechanism operates through goods rather than through asset markets.

Before proceeding it is useful to develop more formally some of the implications of alternative theories with respect to the statistical relationship between money and prices. This formal analysis is motivated by the theoretical model developed in Chapter 3, but is designed somewhat differently to accommodate the statistical problems that arise in the tests that follow.

Formal specification of the alternative theories

The portfolio theory

Consider a small country embedded in a world in which capital markets are fully integrated. Assume that the income and interest elasticities of demand for real money balances and the response elasticities of output to interest rates are the same in the small country as in the rest of the world. Let domestic and foreign assets be perfect substitutes in portfolios and suppose that neither the real nor the nominal exchange rates of the small country are expected to change. Domestic and foreign interest rates are thus equal.

The portfolio theory postulates that under these circumstances the levels of output, interest rates, and prices in the world as a whole are independent of real and monetary forces in the domestic economy. The levels of prices, real income, and the interest rate in the rest of the world can be expressed formally:

$$P_t^* = P^*(\{M^*\}_t, \{X^*_t\}) \qquad (7.1)$$

$$Y_t^* = Y^*(\{M^*\}_t, \{X^*\}_t) \qquad (7.2)$$

$$r_t^* = r^*(\{M^*\}_t, \{X^*\}_t) \qquad (7.3)$$

where P_t^*, Y_t^*, and r_t^* are the levels of prices, real income, and interest rates, and $\{M^*\}_t$ and $\{X^*\}_t$ are the vectors of current and past monetary and real factors in the rest of the world at time t. Given that domestic and foreign interest rates are equal and the relevant response elasticities in the home and foreign economies are the same, domestic income and prices are determined by the same forces that determine income and prices abroad, together with any additional exogenous real factors affecting the domestic economy. The reduced form determinants of domestic prices, income, and interest rates can thus be formally expressed:

$$P_t = P_t^* + F(\{Z\}_t) \qquad (7.4)$$

$$Y_t = Y_t^* + \theta + G(\{Z\}_t) \qquad (7.5)$$

$$r_t = r_t^* \qquad (7.6)$$

where unstarred variables are domestic ones, θ is a scale factor by which domestic and foreign income differ, and $\{Z\}_t$ is a vector of current and past exogenous real factors affecting the domestic economy at time t.

The domestic and foreign demand functions for money can be written:

$$M_t = P_t L(\{r^*\}_t, \{Y\}_t) \qquad (7.7)$$

$$M_t^* = P_t^* L^*(\{r^*\}_t, \{Y^*\}_t) \qquad (7.8)$$

The foreign demand function for money is already embedded in the reduced form equations (7.1) through (7.3). The domestic one, on the other hand, is not embedded in the Canadian reduced form equations (7.4) through (7.6).[1] The factors that cause domestic output and prices to differ from foreign output and prices are the scale factor θ and the independent exogenous real domestic influences $\{Z\}$. Neither of these is affected by either the quantity of money or desired money holdings. The domestic nominal money stock M_t is thus determined endogenously by real and monetary influences in the outside world combined with those exogenous real influences $\{Z\}$ which are present in the domestic economy but not abroad.

In the portfolio theory, balance-of-payments disequilibria are the process by which the domestic supply of nominal money balances is brought into line with the demand. When domestic residents hold too much money, they reestablish portfolio equilibrium by buying assets abroad. The conversion of domestic currency into foreign currency at the commercial banks directly reduces the domestic money supply and the banks' liquid foreign assets by the same amount. To prevent their reserves from becoming inadequate, the banks contract their domestic loan portfolios. This directly reduces the money holdings of domestic residents without forcing them to resort to the international capital market to achieve portfolio equilibrium. The process continues until nominal money holdings are reduced to the desired level and the banks have decumulated sufficient liquid foreign assets to reestablish appropriate reserve levels. Where all bank notes held as money are demand liabilities of the commercial banks and holdings of subsidiary coins do not change, this reduction of reserves represents a balance-of-payments deficit.

Similarly, if the public finds itself with too little money, it sells assets abroad, increasing the banking system's liquid reserves. To prevent excess accumulation of reserves, the banks expand domestic loans, thereby directly creating additional domestic money without forcing the public into the international capital market. The net increase in reserves that backs the public's increased money holdings represents a balance-of-payments surplus.

The balance-of-payments surplus is usually defined as the excess of autonomous receipts from abroad over autonomous payments abroad. Normally, this equals the net induced accumulation of gold and foreign exchange reserves by the government. This definition, however, has no meaning in the present context.

Although the government was, in our period, committed to buying and

[1] The argument here is developed formally in Chapter 3.

selling gold to maintain convertibility of Dominion notes, it had no com-
mitment to maintain the external value of bank notes and deposits, the
main components of the money stock. The chartered banks, acting on their
own, maintained convertibility of their notes and deposits into gold –
otherwise the public would not have held them. It is appropriate, therefore,
to include the net accumulation of gold and secondary reserves of the
chartered banks as part of the balance-of-payments surplus. The other part
is the additions to government gold holdings. Changes in the chartered
banks' reserves of Dominion notes are not included in the balance of
payments since they involve no transactions with the rest of the world.

Let R_t be the stock of reserve money, defined as the gold and secondary
reserve holdings of the chartered banks plus the gold holdings of the
government. And let δ be the ratio of the stock of reserve money to the
domestic money stock. When δ is constant, the balance-of-payments surplus can then be expressed:

$$B_t = R_t - R_{t-1} = \delta\,(M_t - M_{t-1})$$
$$= \delta\,[P_t\,L(\{r^*\}_t, \{Y\}_t) - P_{t-1}\,L(\{r^*\}_{t-1}, \{Y\}_{t-1})]$$
$$(7.9)$$

The traditional classical theory

In the traditional classical specie-flow mechanism, domestic and foreign
interest rates are not jointly determined by conditions of world portfolio
equilibrium. Instead, each country's interest rate is determined strictly by
the interaction of real and monetary conditions at home. Where international capital movements are incorporated, they are treated as a function
of the differential between domestic and foreign interest rates. The domestic
and foreign economies are formally linked in the traditional model through
their common trade balance. They may also be linked through the effects
of their independently determined interest rates on capital flows and the
balance of payments. The rates of change of the domestic and foreign
money supplies are directly determined by the disequilibrium in the balance
of payments.[2]

---

[2] This statement assumes that the world gold stock is constant. When it is not, the world
money supply is increasing by some multiple of the rate of increase of the world stock of
gold. Relative prices operate through the balance of payments to shift gold (or secondary
claims on it) from the country that mines it to the rest of the world at an equilibrium rate.
In the present context, gold mined in Canada is treated as a commodity export and, since

Because of the above linkages, the levels of prices, income, and interest rates in each country depend on the vectors of past real and monetary disturbances in both countries. Real or monetary changes in a country affect its output and prices and lead to a change in the trade balance. This in turn leads to changes in output and prices in the other country. Canada is extremely small, however, in relation to the rest of the world. While domestic exports and imports are of significant size in relation to the domestic income, they are tiny in relation to income abroad. Real and monetary forces in Canada therefore have little effect on foreign income, prices, and interest rates.

Foreign and domestic interest rates, prices, and incomes are thus determined according to the following reduced form equations:

$$P_t^* = P^*(\{M^*\}_t, \{X^*\}_t) \tag{7.10}$$

$$Y_t^* = Y^*(\{M^*\}_t, \{X^*\}_t) \tag{7.11}$$

$$r_t^* = r^*(\{M^*\}_t, \{X^*\}_t) \tag{7.12}$$

$$P_t = P(\{M\}_t, \{X\}_t, \{M^*\}_t, \{X^*\}_t) \tag{7.13}$$

$$Y_t = Y(\{M\}_t, \{X\}_t, \{M^*\}_t, \{X^*\}_t) \tag{7.14}$$

$$r_t = r(\{M\}_t, \{X\}_t, \{M^*\}_t, \{X^*\}_t) \tag{7.15}$$

where $\{X\}_t$ is the vector of current and past real forces of demand, technology, and such affecting the domestic economy, and the other variables are as previously defined. The real domestic forces defined by the vector $\{Z\}$ in the formal description of the portfolio model are contained in the vector $\{X\}$. Equations (7.10), (7.11), and (7.12) reproduce (7.1), (7.2), and (7.3). Equations (7.13), (7.14), and (7.15) are the domestic economy equivalents of (7.10), (7.11), and (7.12) except that $\{M^*\}_t$ and $\{X^*\}_t$ do not drop out – the foreign economy is large in relation to the domestic one. Were the domestic economy of significant size in relation to the foreign one, $\{M\}_t$ and $\{X\}_t$ would also appear in (7.10), (7.11), and (7.12).

At each point in time, the nominal money supplies at home and abroad are exogenously determined by the vector of past balance-of-payments deficits and surpluses. The domestic and foreign demand functions for money, given by equations (7.7) and (7.8) above, are embedded in the

gold coins were not minted at all in Canada before 1908, all inflows of monetary gold are treated as a surplus item in the balance of payments. The overall balance-of-payments surplus also includes inflows of secondary reserves.

reduced form equations (7.13) through (7.15) and (7.10) through (7.12) respectively.

The balance of payments in the traditional price-specie-flow mechanism is presented as the sum of three factors: (1) the balance of trade in goods and services plus net repatriated earnings on capital; (2) exogenous net capital movements of the sort associated with the development of the Canadian West; and (3) endogenous net short-term capital movements that are a response to the differential between domestic and foreign interest rates. The trade balance is expressed as a function of domestic and foreign incomes and the relative price of domestic in terms of foreign goods. Setting the exchange rate equal to unity, the balance of payments becomes:

$$B_t = R_t - R_{t-1} = B_T(\{P/P^*\}_t, \{Y^*\}_t, \{Y^*\}_t) \qquad (7.16)$$
$$+ DSB_t + CE_t + C(\{r/r^*\}_t)$$

where the function B_T is the balance of trade, $\{P/P^*\}_t$ and $\{r/r^*\}_t$ are the vectors of current and past relative domestic and foreign prices and interest rates at time t, DSB_t is the debt service balance, CE_t is the exogenous component of the net capital inflow, and $C(\{r/r^*\}_t)$ is the capital flow component that depends on interest-rate differentials. All other variables are as previously defined. The rate of growth of the domestic money stock can be expressed:

$$(M_t - M_{t-1}) = (1/\delta)(R_t - R_{t-1}) \qquad (7.17)$$

Causal versus statistical relationships between money and prices

The portfolio theory

In this model, an unanticipated increase in the level of foreign money causes world interest rates to fall, stimulating increases in output not only in the rest of the world but in Canada as well. In the longer term, such monetary changes are reflected in the level of prices both in Canada and abroad.[3]

[3] We adopt the working assumption that fully anticipated exogenous changes in the money supply lead to immediate price level changes with no effect on real interest rates, but we recognize that there is substantial evidence that anticipated changes in the nominal money supply also have had effects on real output and interest rates (Gordon, 1990). It turns out that our analysis here is fundamentally unaffected by whether price changes are or are not anticipated and whether anticipated price changes do or do not have effects on real output.

Consider, for example, a situation in which all exogenous real factors both at home and abroad, $\{X^*\}$ and $\{Z\}$, have been constant in the relevant past and remain so. Since the response elasticities of output to interest rates and the interest rate and income elasticities of demand for money are the same at home and abroad, the endogenous variations in the domestic money supply through time will be synchronized exactly with the exogenous variations in the money supply abroad.

An important implication is that, even though domestic money is caused by domestic income and prices (and changes in world interest rates in the short run when prices are inflexible), changes in the domestic money supply precede changes in domestic income and prices when changes in the money supply abroad precede the resulting changes in foreign income and prices. When the foreign money supply unexpectedly expands, the world interest rate is driven down and foreign output is driven up until foreign residents are willing to hold their new higher stock of money. Since domestic interest rates equal foreign rates, and domestic output is driven up in proportion to the increase in foreign output, the demand of domestic residents for money balances increases in exactly the same proportion as the quantity of money increases abroad. Domestic residents satisfy this increased demand for money by selling assets in the international capital market.

Under the circumstances postulated, regressing domestic income or prices on current and past levels of the domestic money stock yields exactly the same fit obtained by regressing domestic income or prices on current and past levels of the foreign money stock. This occurs even though the causation runs from income and prices to money in the domestic economy and from money to income and prices in the world at large.

Consider now the case of random shifts in the domestic demand function for money, with the foreign demand function remaining stationary. Domestic residents adjust their money holdings to meet the demand by buying or selling nonmonetary assets in return for money in the international market. Output in the domestic economy is unaffected and money supply changes appear that do not correlate with observed real income changes. Foreign money should predict domestic output and prices better than domestic money does.

Random shifts in the foreign demand function for money, unmatched by corresponding variations in the demand for money at home, have the opposite effect. Both domestic and foreign output and prices vary in response to the shifts in the foreign demand function for money. These output and price level changes lead to corresponding variations in the quantity of money demanded by domestic residents which, in turn, bring about equivalent changes in the domestic money supply. Since by construction the world output and price changes result from shifts in the foreign demand for money, not the supply, domestic money predicts both domestic and foreign output and prices better than foreign money does, even though there is no causal relationship between the domestic money supply and output and prices in the rest of the world.

Assume now that the money supplies and demand functions for money do not shift and consider the effect of independent variations in domestic and foreign real factors, $\{Z\}$ and $\{X^*\}$. Suppose first that there are exogenous variations in domestic real factors unmatched by corresponding variations in the same forces abroad. Domestic output and prices change relative to output and prices abroad, leading to changes in the domestic quantity of money demanded in the same direction. As domestic residents satisfy this change in their demand for money holdings by adjusting their asset portfolios, domestic money adjusts in step with the variations in income and prices in the home economy. Variations in the domestic money supply are better correlated with the variations in domestic income and prices than are variations in the foreign money supply. Foreign money explains foreign output and prices better than domestic money does.

Now take the opposite case where the domestic and foreign nominal money supplies and demand functions for money are unchanged and variations in real factors abroad occur unmatched by corresponding variations in domestic real factors. The quantity of money demanded abroad changes, resulting in foreign output and price changes that spill over into the domestic economy through interest-rate and trade balance adjustments. A real expansion abroad ultimately causes prices to fall in both economies. Foreign and domestic output both rise. The desired money holdings of domestic residents increase and the nominal quantity of money rises as they readjust their portfolios. This increase in the domestic nominal quantity of money is correlated with the rise in foreign output and the decline in foreign prices in the face of no change in the foreign money supply. Domestic money therefore explains variations in foreign output and prices better than foreign money does. Domestic money also predicts domestic income and prices better than does foreign money. Canadian money is positively related to output levels and negatively related to price levels in both parts of the world. Foreign money remains unchanged by assumption.

Clearly, regressions of domestic income or prices on the current and lagged nominal money stocks at home and in the rest of the world are not likely to establish that foreign money causes domestic output and prices while domestic money does not. Depending on the sources of the variations in the data, it is quite possible that domestic money may explain both domestic and foreign output and prices better than foreign money does, even though the domestic economy happens to be trivial in size. The correlation between domestic money and domestic and foreign prices, moreover, may be negative if the variations in domestic money result from real forces affecting the levels of domestic and foreign output.[4]

A straightforward attempt to show that domestic prices precede domestic money while foreign money precedes foreign prices, as the causal relationships in the portfolio model suggest, is almost certain to fail. A major source of variation in domestic prices is past variation in the money supply in the world at large. Domestic money is likely to respond to unanticipated changes in the foreign money supply before either foreign or domestic prices do because of the effects of world monetary expansion on the broad range of world interest rates in the intervening period before output and prices can respond. Nevertheless, variations in Canadian relative to foreign income and prices may well precede variations in the Canadian relative to foreign money stock. Real expansions in Canada, unmatched by corresponding real changes abroad, lead to increases in domestic income and prices, also unmatched by corresponding changes abroad. Domestic residents then satisfy their demand for increased holdings of nominal money balances by selling nonmonetary assets to foreigners.

The traditional theory

The expected causal relationships between money and prices in the traditional price-specie-flow mechanism are straightforward. Monetary changes in the rest of the world lead to changes in foreign interest rates and output which ultimately influence domestic output, prices, and interest rates via changes in the trade balance. For example, an unanticipated increase in the money supply abroad causes the foreign interest rate to decline and foreign output and prices to rise. The domestic trade balance improves, leading to an increase in aggregate demand, income, interest rates, and prices in the domestic economy.[5]

---

[4] The situation is further complicated because there is no reason to believe that the parameters of price/output adjustment are the same in Canada as abroad.

[5] A fully anticipated change in the foreign money supply has the same qualitative effects on the price level and the trade balance but no effect on the real interest rate and output.

By the same argument, an unanticipated increase in the domestic money supply leads to a fall in domestic interest rates and a rise in output and prices, together with a deterioration of the domestic trade balance. This trade-balance change, however, does not have an appreciable effect on economic conditions abroad because the domestic economy is small in relation to the foreign economy.

Thus, current and past monetary changes abroad affect both domestic and foreign incomes and prices, but current and past domestic monetary changes influence only domestic income and prices.

An increase in the domestic demand for money causes domestic interest rates to rise and domestic output and prices to fall. The fall in domestic output and prices leads to an improvement in the domestic trade balance and a corresponding deterioration in the foreign trade balance. But again, the domestic economy is so small that this trade balance adjustment has no appreciable effect on foreign income and prices.

On the other hand, an increase in the demand for money in the rest of the world causes income and prices to fall both there and in Canada. The fall in foreign income and prices produces a deterioration in the domestic trade balance and a reduction in income and prices in the domestic economy. The flow of gold from the domestic to the foreign economy reduces domestic income and prices further in the long run as the gold flows affect the domestic money supply. The inflow of gold to the rest of the world, however, is too small a fraction of the foreign gold supply to influence foreign income and prices significantly. Ultimately, there is a decline in the domestic money supply and in both domestic and foreign output and prices without any significant change in the money supply abroad.

The domestic money supply change lags behind the change in foreign output. This lag is much greater than the lag that resulted from an increase in the foreign demand for money in the portfolio model. In the portfolio theory, a shift of money from the domestic to the foreign economy occurs almost as soon as output changes. In the traditional theory, money can shift between the two economies only to the extent that a domestic trade-balance deficit or surplus occurs. It would therefore be surprising to find much correlation between current values of the domestic money supply and foreign prices, holding foreign money constant, if the traditional theory were the correct one. It would not be surprising to find such a correlation if the portfolio theory were correct.[6]

---

[6] This follows even though no causal relationship is established by the portfolio theory between the two series.

This conclusion is reinforced by the effects of exogenous real changes in the rest of the world. Suppose that these forces lead to an increase in output in the rest of the world. Under the usual assumptions, this leads to an improvement of the domestic trade balance. Aggregate demand increases in the domestic economy and output and prices rise. While the domestic money supply eventually increases because of the inflow of gold, this monetary expansion lags behind the increase in foreign output. The gold flow does not affect the foreign money supply appreciably because of the small size of the domestic economy. There is thus a statistical relationship between domestic money and lagged foreign prices. Since foreign real expansion can only affect the domestic money supply through protracted trade-balance changes, however, not much correlation between the current levels of domestic money and foreign prices would be expected.

On the other hand, if the portfolio theory were true, it would not be surprising to observe a strong statistical relationship between the current levels of foreign prices and the domestic money supply since the international monetary adjustment in portfolio theory can occur almost instantaneously.

Exogenous real changes that improve domestic income raise or lower domestic prices (depending on the nature of the real forces) and deteriorate the trade balance but have very little feedback effect on the rest of the world because of the small size of the domestic economy.

Some suggested statistical tests

The above analysis suggests two statistical tests that may discriminate between the portfolio theory and the traditional one adopted and modified by Viner:

1. The rapid growth that accompanied the development of the West led to an increase in both money and prices in Canada relative to the rest of the world. The portfolio theory predicts that any unanticipated greater rise in prices in Canada than abroad precedes (or is contemporaneous with) a greater rise in Canadian relative to foreign money while the traditional theory predicts the opposite. Because of the tendency of domestic money to respond to world monetary changes before incomes and prices do, unanticipated changes in the money supply in each part of the world can precede the resulting changes in that part of the world's price level even when the portfolio theory is true; such an observation is not a confirmation of the traditional theory that money always and everywhere determines the

price level. It follows that domestic monetary changes can precede domestic price changes and monetary changes abroad precede price changes abroad, but increases in domestic relative to foreign prices should precede the increases in domestic relative to foreign money.

2. Because gold movements occur through international portfolio adjustments in the portfolio model but require protracted balance-of-trade changes in the traditional mechanism, adjustments to exogenous disturbances are faster in the portfolio theory. An implication is that domestic monetary changes may be correlated with contemporary movements in foreign prices even though there is no casual effect of domestic money on foreign prices. A contemporary correlation of this sort is unlikely if the traditional theory holds because the domestic monetary changes resulting from real factors abroad occur with a lag. This lag occurs even if the exogenous changes are fully anticipated – it is a mechanical rather than an expectational one.

The timing test

As noted above, the portfolio theory predicts that variations in Canadian income and prices relative to income and prices in the rest of the world precede, or at worst are contemporaneous with, the corresponding variations in Canadian relative to world money. These money changes result from changes in the demand for money produced by the rise in output and prices associated with the growth of the Canadian economy during the study period. A lag of prices and income behind money, by contrast, is consistent with the classical price-specie-flow mechanism as formulated by Viner (1924). In that view, the expansion of prices in the Canadian economy is due to the prior expansion of the domestic money supply that results when domestic residents convert their borrowings abroad into domestic currency.

Variations in Canadian money consequent on world monetary conditions may well precede the corresponding variations in Canadian prices. Thus, Canadian monetary changes may precede the corresponding domestic price level changes, just as foreign monetary changes precede the corresponding foreign price level changes.

Table 7.1 presents estimates of the contemporaneous relationship between foreign money, income, and prices. All the coefficients are highly significant with the expected signs. As in the case of the results for Canada, regressions for the period 1890–1913 do not exhibit serial correlation in the residuals but those for the period 1871–89 do (regressions not shown

Table 7.1. *Regressions of money, income, and prices in the rest of the world, 1871–1913*

	Nominal money supply	Real money supply	Implicit income deflator
Constant	− 185.03	− 38.98	139.41
	(− 20.4)	(− 18.2)	(36.9)
Implicit income deflator	1.24		
	(13.5)		
Real income	1.68	1.42	− 1.12
	(100.6)	(99.8)	(− 13.5)
U.K. treasury bill rate	− 4.79	− 2.22	4.25
	(− 5.3)	(− 3.7)	(8.0)
Nominal money stock			.664
			(13.54)
Number of observations	43	43	43
R-squared	.996	.996	.893
Standard error	3.760	3.204	2.748
Durbin–Watson	1.128	.942	1.196

Note: The figures in brackets are *t*-ratios.

in Table 7.1). Also, the interest rate variable is insignificant for the earlier subperiod.

A standard Granger causality procedure is appropriate to test whether the increase in domestic relative to world prices during the study period came before or after the increase in domestic relative to foreign money.[7] The test requires that the series must be covariance stationary. They must have no trend and their variances must neither increase nor decrease with time. Accordingly, all the series are differenced to eliminate their trends. An examination of the autocorrelations and partial autocorrelations indicates that first differencing is sufficient to meet the stationarity requirement.[8]

[7] Granger (1969). For a simpler discussion of Granger causality tests, see Chow (1983, p. 212).
[8] Many series also can be rendered stationary by removing the trend. This is not the case here, however, because of the fact that there is a distinct break in the trend in most of our series in the mid-1890s. Detrending in this situation is a more complex process. See Hodrick and Prescott (1981).

Meaningful Granger causality tests require identifiable lags in the data. The existence of lags and their appropriate length are investigated using likelihood ratio tests.[9] The results of these tests are shown in Table 7.2. Each of the three series, money, prices, and real output, is regressed on its own past and on current and lagged values of the other two series. Beginning with five lags, F-tests are used to determine the length of the longest lag significant at the 5 percent level for each regression and for all regressions taken together.[10] The fifth lag is tested, then dropped, and the procedure is used to test the fourth lag, and so forth until a lag significant at the 5 percent level is found. As indicated in Table 7.2, no uniformly statistically significant lagged effects can be found except that in the case of a one-year lag the overall F-tests indicate significance in all three cases at the 5 percent level and the individual F-tests indicate significance at the 5 percent level in three of the nine regressions. Unfortunately, in the case involving the ratios of domestic to foreign money, income, and prices, which is the one of special interest to our hypothesis, insufficient lagged effects are found to make testing for Granger causality worthwhile.

There are a number of possible reasons why lagged effects are not evident in the data. The changes in money and real output during the study period may have been fully anticipated, or wages and prices may have been much more flexible in the late nineteenth and early twentieth century than they are today. Some of the data, especially GNP, have been generated by

---

[9] We are indebted to Angelo Melino for his help in conducting and interpreting these tests.
[10] For the individual regressions, the relevant F-statistics are defined as $[(RSSR - USSR)/ q \div USSR/(n - k)]$ where $RSSR$ and $USSR$ are the restricted and unrestricted sums of squares, q is the number of restrictions, and $n - k$ is the number of degrees of freedom in the unrestricted regression. The overall F-tests are based on a comparison of the sums of the unrestricted sums of squares across all three regressions with the last lag included and the sums of the restricted sums of squares across all three regressions with the last lag dropped. The formula is the same but $RSSR$ and $USSR$ are now defined as the sums across all three regressions of the respective restricted and unrestricted sums of squares, q is now the total number of restrictions in the three regressions together, and $n - k$ is the sum of the degrees of freedom in the three unrestricted regressions. Since the test requires that the sums of squares in the numerators and denominators be independent, the three sums of squares added together to obtain the aggregate restricted and unrestricted sum of squares in the overall tests have to be independent of each other. Accordingly, the current values of the price and money series are included in the regression determining income, while the current value of only the money series is included in the regression determining the price level, and the current values of neither income nor prices are included in the regression determining the money supply. Inclusion of the same contemporary relationships in more than one of the three regressions would destroy the statistical independence of the residual sums of squares of the three equations. In calculating the individual equation F-tests, the current values of both independent variables are included in all cases. All variables in all regressions are first differences of the logs.

Table 7.2. *Significance of lagged values of the independent variables in the presence of lagged values of the dependent variable*

Lag tested and test regression	Canada, percent	Rest of world, percent	Ratio of Canada to rest of world, percent
Fifth of five lags			
Income on money and prices			1
Prices on money and income			
Money on prices and income			1
Overall F-test			1
Fourth of four lags			
Income on money and prices			
Prices on money and income			1
Money on prices and income			
Overall F-test			
Third of three lags			
Income on money and prices			
Prices on money and income			
Money on prices and income			
Overall F-test			
Second of two lags			
Income on money and prices			
Prices on money and income			
Money on prices and income			5
Overall F-test			1
One lag			
Income on money and prices	1	10	10
Prices on money and income	5	10	
Money on prices and income		1	
Overall F-test	1	1	5

Note: The percentages in the body of the table indicate the significance level. Blanks indicate insignificance at the 10 percent level. The sample period is 1878–1913. All variables are in logarithms with the ratios of Canadian to the rest of the world money incomes and prices being logarithms of the ratios. The tests of individual regressions involve the current as well as lagged values of all independent variables. The regressions for the overall F-tests omit current income from the price level regressions and current income and the current price level from the money regressions so the separate residual sums of squares added in making the test will be independent.

interpolative procedures that may have removed lagged effects.[11] Finally, taking first differences may magnify measurement errors in the data, especially in the ratios of Canadian to foreign money, prices, and real income, which are differences of logs to begin with. The resulting noise may obliterate any signal these data contain. In any event, the absence of lags in the processes generating these series makes it inappropriate to test for Granger causality. In this connection, it is interesting to note that some fifty years ago Viner criticized the crude attempts of Angel and Carr to conduct a timing analysis on the grounds that the data were too rough for any confidence to be placed in the conclusions.[12]

The relationship between Canadian and world money and prices

If the traditional classical theory were correct, Canadian money and income would not influence income and prices in the rest of the world. Changes in the domestic money stock, and exogenous changes in domestic investment and output would lead to domestic interest-rate changes, and in turn, to adjustments in the balance of trade. While these balance-of-trade changes are large from the point of view of the Canadian economy, they are trivial fractions of overall aggregate demand abroad. Holding foreign money and real income constant, there is no reason to observe a correlation of Canadian money and real income with foreign prices.

Changes in money and real income abroad affect Canadian prices if the traditional theory holds. Foreign expansion leads to an improvement of the Canadian trade balance and an increase in the level of aggregate demand at existing levels of domestic output and money holdings. This implies positive correlations of foreign money and real income with the domestic price level, holding Canadian money and real income constant.

Exogenous real sector and demand for money shifts in the rest of the world increase world real income and improve the domestic trade balance

---

[11] Urquhart (1986, pp. 69–70) notes that a great variety of annual series were used to interpolate their census benchmark estimates of the main components of national income. While the details of the exact procedures used still await publication, correspondence and conversation with Urquhart have convinced us that the interpolators used made excellent proxies in the sense that they were able to predict any given benchmark from the preceding one with remarkable accuracy. It appears that simple linear interpolation between census benchmarks without supporting annual data of some relevant series was minimized by the use of these annual data. There is reason to conjecture, therefore, that lagged effects from year to year in the Canadian data may not have been submerged by interpolation procedures.

[12] Viner (1937, p. 423).

when the traditional theory holds. The Canadian money stock eventually rises in response to the corresponding inflow of money. Such changes in the domestic money stock lag behind changes in the foreign price level and real income, making a contemporaneous correlation between Canadian money and foreign prices unlikely. A fall in foreign relative to Canadian real interest rates might occur if the foreign expansion results from an unanticipated exogenous decline in the demand for money. The resulting shift of capital to Canada from abroad may shorten the lag of Canadian money changes behind foreign money and income changes. On the other hand, a rise in foreign relative to Canadian real interest rates would occur if the expansion abroad results from unanticipated exogenous real forces. Then capital shifts in the other direction, lengthening the lag. If the timing results above are true, no interest-rate changes occur.

A contemporaneous correlation between Canadian money and foreign prices is more likely if the portfolio theory is true. As in the traditional theory, there is no causal relation running from exogenous Canadian monetary and real forces to foreign prices. There is a strong causal relation between foreign real and monetary factors and Canadian prices – indeed, a much stronger one than in the traditional mechanism because these exogenous foreign changes are transmitted to Canada primarily through the world capital market rather than through the traditional trade-balance mechanism.

Shifts in the demand for money and exogenous real sector shifts in the rest of the world have a direct effect on output and prices in Canada through their effects on the level of world interest rates. These effects may well be contemporaneous. The response of Canadian money holdings to Canadian and world price changes is a portfolio response which can occur quickly without necessitating balance-of-trade adjustments. A contemporaneous correlation between Canadian money and foreign income and prices may therefore be observed even though Canadian money has no causal effect in that direction. The presence of such a correlation requires significant exogenous shifts in the foreign demand function for money and real factors affecting foreign output, unmatched by similar exogenous shifts in Canada.

Although a contemporaneous correlation between Canadian money and the rest of the world's price level, holding foreign money and real income constant, is not required by the portfolio theory, the observance of such a correlation is a piece of evidence consistent with it and inconsistent with the traditional theory.

Table 7.3. *Significance of Canadian and foreign money and incomes in determining the price level in the rest of the world*[a]

	Sign and *P*-value[b]			
	Levels		First differences	
Canadian money	+ /0.000	+ /0.000	+ /0.074	+ /0.006
Canadian income	− /0.013	− /0.441	+ /0.992	− /0.591
Canadian money and income together[c]	0.000	0.000	0.183	0.021
British consol rate	+ /0.000		+ /0.045	
British treasury bill rate		+ /0.000		+ /0.002
Foreign money	+ /0.815	+ /0.942	+ /0.019	+ /0.014
Foreign income	− /0.005	− /0.000	− /0.676	− /0.076
Foreign money and income together[c]	0.06	0.000	0.035	0.038
Standard error of regression	0.025	0.025	0.018	0.017

[a]The sample period is 1871–1913 for levels and 1872–1913 for first differences. All variables except interest rates are in logs.
[b]Using the standard *t*-ratio test.
[c]*F*-ratio test that the coefficients of both variables are zero.

Tables 7.3 and 7.4 present the results of regressions of Canadian and rest of the world prices on nominal money and real income both in Canada and abroad. Since interest rates contain information about the productivity of capital and shifts in the demand functions for money, they are also included as variables in the regressions. The traditional theory requires separate interest rates for Canada and the rest of the world while the portfolio theory implies a more or less uniform world interest rate. Both Canadian and world interest rates are therefore tried in the Canadian regressions. Neufeld's long-term borrowing rate is the only Canadian interest rate available. It is used alternatively with the U.K. treasury bill rate in the regressions determining Canadian prices. The British consol rate and the British treasury bill rate are used as alternative measures of world interest rates.

Table 7.3 gives the *P*-values for the independent variables in the regressions determining the level and first difference of world prices. The regressions indicate a significant contemporaneous relationship between Canadian money and rest of the world prices, holding Canadian and foreign incomes and interest rates constant. Canadian real income is not a significant determinant of the world price level. Foreign money is insignificant in the level regressions but significant in the regressions using first differences. Foreign real income is significant in three of the four cases. Interest rates are always significant.[13] The standard errors of the regressions are lower when the short-term rather than the long-term interest rate is used. Using the treasury bill rate instead of the consol rate, moreover, increases the significance of Canadian and foreign money and foreign real income in the first-difference regressions. This suggests that short-term demand for money shifts is important in explaining year-to-year changes in foreign prices.

The strong contemporaneous relationship between Canadian money and foreign prices is consistent with the portfolio theory and inconsistent with the standard classical one. Several criticisms of this conclusion may be attempted. First, it might be argued that most of the exogenous changes abroad that lead to these correlations are demand for money changes. Contemporaneous capital movements occur in response to the effects of these monetary changes on the differentials between Canadian and foreign interest rates. These capital movements, it might be argued, provide for the classical mechanism the kind of nearly simultaneous adjustment that is the basis for the portfolio theory. This argument does not rescue the classical theory, however, if the exogenous changes abroad are, in significant part, real sector shifts. These real shifts affect the interest-rate differential in the opposite direction.

Interest differential effects arising from either source, moreover, would not occur if the timing results obtained above were valid. These issues raise the question of whether the theoretical basis for the classical argument about capital flows and interest-rate differentials is sound. In Chapter 9 we argue that it is not. Evidence is also presented in Chapter 6 that denies a relationship between short-term capital movements and the differential between Canadian and foreign interest rates.

A second criticism of the portfolio interpretation of the above evidence might claim that *full anticipation* of the changes in foreign income and money demand, rather than these changes per se, accounts for the contemporaneous correlations of foreign prices and the Canadian money supply. In reply, it can be noted that even if the shifts in the demand function for money and the movements in real output in the rest of the world were fully anticipated, the effect on the Canadian money supply still must occur through protracted trade-balance adjustments if the traditional classical balance-of-payments theory is correct. As a result, Canadian money supply changes would still lag behind foreign price level changes.

---

[13] The results do not change substantively when the interest-rate variable is omitted entirely.

Table 7.4. *Significance of Canadian and foreign money and incomes in determining the Canadian price level*[a]

	Sign and P-value[b]			
	Levels		First differences	
Canadian money	+/0.000	+/0.000	+/0.052	+/0.007
Canadian income	−/0.284	−/0.206	+/0.028	−/0.003
Canadian money and income together[c]	0.000	0.000	0.033	0.002
Canadian long-term borrowing rate	+/0.000		+/0.557	
British treasury bill rate		+/0.000		+/0.003
Foreign money	+/0.393	+/0.399	+/0.000	+/0.000
Foreign income	−/0.028	−/0.000	−/0.908	−/0.153
Foreign money and income together[c]	0.085	0.000	0.033	0.002
Standard error of regression	0.058	0.056	0.034	0.030

[a]The sample period is 1871–1913 for levels and 1872–1913 for first differences. All variables except interest rates are in logs.
[b]Using the standard t-ratio test.
[c]F-ratio test that the coefficients of both variables are zero.

Table 7.4 gives the P-values for the independent variables in the regressions determining the level of Canadian prices. Current Canadian money is significant at the 1 percent level in three of the four regressions and at the 5 percent level in the fourth. Canadian real income is significant in two of the four regressions. The traditional theory postulates a causal relationship between the Canadian money supply and Canadian prices, but the portfolio theory does not. The latter theory nevertheless suggests that a statistical relationship may be observed where no causal relationship exists. Domestic money holdings adjust very rapidly to changes in the quantity of money demanded arising from real factors affecting the equilibrium level of domestic prices. Foreign money is a significant determinant of the Canadian price level only when the regressions are run in first differences. Foreign real income is significant in only one regression. The world interest rate is significant in all regressions that use it, while the Canadian rate is significant in the level regression but not in the regression using first differences. Use of the world rather than the Canadian interest rate always improves the overall fit.[14] The fact that the world interest rate works better in the regressions than the Canadian rate is another piece of evidence supporting the portfolio theory. It implies a degree of integration

[14] Again, the results do not change substantively when the interest-rate variable is dropped.

of the capital markets in Canada and abroad that is inconsistent with the traditional theory formally stated. The level regressions in Tables 7.3 and 7.4 are also run using the Cochrane–Orcutt transformations to correct for serial correlation in the residuals. Since the values of the serial correlation coefficient are for the most part over 0.9, the results are not substantively different than the ordinary least squares (OLS) regression results when the variables are first-differenced.

It is interesting that Friedman and Schwartz find the rates of change of U.S. money and income significantly related to the rate of change of U.K. prices and vice versa during the period 1879–1914.[15] When the same regressions are run in levels rather than first differences, however, none of the variables is significant. They argue that the effect of each country's money growth on the other's rate of price change is due to the common influence of traded goods prices in the two countries' price indexes. Money in each country affects that country's own nominal income. This nominal income effect is reflected in the country's traded and nontraded goods prices and, hence in its general price level. Internationally traded goods produced and consumed have significant weights in the price indexes of both countries. A rise in one country's prices, therefore, leads to a rise in the other country's price index. Friedman and Schwartz ascribe the insignificance of their level regression results to the influence of trend.

In the Canadian case it is reasonable to suppose that domestic economic developments have little effect on traded goods prices because of the smallness of the Canadian economy. As a result, changes in the domestic price level involve movements in nontraded goods prices, holding the prices of traded goods constant. Substantial evidence of such relative price movements is reported in Chapter 5. Thus, Canadian prices cannot affect prices in the rest of the world through the traded goods component of the rest of the world's price index. Canada is too small a country with too little influence on the prices of traded goods.

[15] Friedman and Schwartz (1982, pp. 327–32).

8. "Canada's balance": Viner and his critics

Writing some years after the publication of his classic study, Viner summarizes his findings as follows:

The Canadian borrowings obtained transfer into Canada smoothly and without noticeable friction in the form of a net commodity and service import surplus, as the result of relative price changes (and shifts in demands) which were of the character indicated as to be expected by the older writers. The price and demand changes resulted from a relative increase in the amounts of Canadian bank money, deposits and notes, and these increases resulted in turn mainly from the exchange by Canadian borrowers abroad of the proceeds in foreign funds of their borrowings abroad for Canadian bank deposits or notes. The Canadian banks brought into Canada in the form of specie only such part of their newly acquired foreign funds as was required to maintain their specie reserve ratios in Canada at their customary level. The remainder of the foreign funds thus acquired by the banks, to the extent that they were not absorbed in paying for the growing Canadian import surplus, was left abroad by the Canadian banks largely in the form of call loans in New York, as additions to their "outside" or "secondary" reserves. Except toward the end of the period, when a marked credit expansion occurred in Canada, the increase in the outside reserves was not used by the Canadian banks as a basis for expansion of their loans in Canada. With the exception that fluctuations in the outside reserves operated in the Canadian mechanism in the manner attributed to specie movements in the classical doctrine, I concluded that the Canadian mechanism corresponded in all its important aspects to the mechanism as formulated in the classical doctrine. (1937, pp. 413–14)

There have been two broad types of objections to Viner's conclusions. The first is the claim that Viner's interpretation of developments in the 1900–13 period is too narrow. J. C. Ingram, for example, argues that

Viner advanced the hypothesis that the disturbing factor in the period 1900–1913 was an increase in the flow of funds into Canada, and the problem he wished to examine was the response in the Canadian economy to this initial disturbance. An alternative hypothesis, equally if not more plausible, is that the rapid expansion of the Canadian economy after 1900 created investment opportunities and attracted an inflow of funds. Of course it is true that if the foreign funds had not been forthcoming the Canadian boom would have been halted, and thus the two forces

110

are inextricably linked together over the whole period. Still, it may be argued that domestic expansion in Canada was the initial disturbance. (1957 p. 95)

Essentially the same point was recognized by Cairncross (1968). Stovel goes further:

Viner's tenet that the period is illustrative of the Mill–Taussig mechanism whereby relative price changes operate on the export-import quantities to equilibrate them to the capital inflows I find unacceptable. In the first place, the period must be set in the context of the favorable world cyclical conjuncture which commenced about 1896 – a new surge of economic growth. Many of the relative price changes which Viner was relating to capital imports got under way at that time, although, capital importations themselves did not assume very great significance until the years following 1905.

Canada rose to prominence in these prosperous years as "the last best west." Increasing demands for her exports, particularly of grains, created a favorable atmosphere for domestic and outside capital. The demand for labor and for farmer settlers rose along with the demand for capital. Population and incomes expanded. Industrialization and urbanization further stimulated investment activity. All this was combined in the one process in which prospects of increasing returns and larger profits provided a major incentive. The simultaneity of the increased demand for outside capital and for imports must be emphasized. It is not unlikely that this type of simultaneous adjustment may provide the greater part of the explanation for the equilibration effected. In my view, the process of lagged income propagation as dealt with in foreign trade multiplier analysis provides an important explanation for the remaining adjustment which took place. Once induced investment, the acceleration principle, variable time lags, and heterogeneity in the causal inter-relationships are introduced, this process of income propagation may merge logically with the simultaneous 'common cause' type of adjustment. (1959, pp. 211–12)

G. M. Meier (1953), also operating within the standard Keynesian frame-work, takes a more moderate stand. He agrees that the transfer of capital is associated with an expansion of investment in Canada that can be explained in terms of profit opportunities for capital and labor. He asserts that the increase in investment, without any shift in relative prices, creates a demand for imports and a decline in exports by diverting resources away from the export industries. He nonetheless agrees that relative price changes are an important part of the adjustment mechanism. He views the expansion of investment, the balance-of-trade deficit, and the relative price changes as integral parts of the growth process.

George Borts develops a formal model of this interdependence, treating the capital movements as induced by a disturbance to the equilibrium growth path of the economy. He notes that

A difficulty with the traditional analysis is [that] . . . a rise in the demand for country A's securities is irrational unless accompanied by a corresponding rise in earnings prospects. . . . Thus lurking in the background of the traditional analysis is a rise in the earnings of A's securities, presumably reflecting a rise in the productivity of its capital. (1964, p. 342)

In Borts's model, however, the exogenous force inducing the capital movements is a rise in the world price of Canadian exports rather than a change in technology making new land available. This oversimplification is required to make the analysis tractable. Had Borts pursued the asset side of his model further, he would doubtless have produced a model very similar to that developed here. Although he notes that the gold flows equilibrate the supply and demand for money, he does not recognize explicitly that this adjustment is a one-shot portfolio adjustment. He states, "if this condition [that the supply of money be equal to the demand] is violated, there would be a flow of international money to produce the correct supply" (p. 346). This, of course, anticipates the monetary theory of the balance of payments that emerged prominently some ten years later and is applied by McCloskey and Zecher (1976) to the nineteenth-century gold standard.

   With the exception of Stovel's argument that relative price adjustments are not a part of the adjustment process, the approach taken in the present study harmonizes completely with the substance of the above comments on Viner's analysis. The evidence clearly shows that relative price adjustments are an integral part of the process by which the trade balance is brought into line with the capital inflow. Even without formal statistical analysis, it is obvious that the inflow of capital is the result of an expansion of domestic investment that is integrally related to the growth of the Canadian economy during the period.

   It is difficult to believe that an economist of Viner's sophistication did not also understand the importance of this growth process. Viner devotes considerable space to a discussion of Coats's argument that the relative rise in Canadian prices was the result of excess demand for commodities and labor resulting from increased investment. The increased investment is associated with Canadian industrial expansion and the opening up of new territory to settlement with its attendant railway construction, road making, and town building.[1] There is no doubt that Viner was aware that the capital expansion and associated borrowing abroad were part of a growth process that had its origins in

[1] Coats (1915, vol. 2).

technological changes partly associated with the settlement of the West. Viner also takes great pains to argue that the price level in Canada only rose relative to prices abroad because of the inflow of capital.

If expansion of this sort in a given country was financed from domestic savings, it would simply mean, however, that those having purchasing power were voluntarily shifting their demand from consumers' goods to producers' goods and from labour engaged in producing consumers' goods to labour engaged in industrial development. What might be expected to happen would be that producers' goods would rise and consumers' goods would fall in price. The general price level would not much be affected by this change in the character of the demand. (1924, p. 249)

He goes on to argue that prices cannot rise because of the expansion of investment per se even when the investment is financed by borrowing abroad.

On the other hand, if the expansion was financed by borrowings from abroad, there would still be available the normal supply of consumer goods, the extra supply of goods and labour necessary for industrial development being provided directly or indirectly by the lending country. In so far as the industrial expansion *per se* was concerned, there would again be no obvious reason why prices should rise more rapidly in this than in other countries, and there would even be some reason for expecting a relative fall in prices. (1924, p. 249)

He concludes that

It is not proved, therefore, that it was the industrial expansion *per se* rather than the borrowings from abroad which made prices rise. . . . Capital borrowings and industrial expansion are not unconnected. Capital is usually borrowed for purposes of industrial expansion. There is no reason to suppose that prices would have been less buoyant in the borrowing countries if the loans made to them had been 'spendthrift loans'. (1924, pp. 249–50)

Viner appears to overlook the interest-rate effects that exogenous changes leading to the capital expansion have when borrowing from abroad is not possible. The rise in the marginal productivity of capital leads to a rise in Canadian interest rates, which in turn leads to a decline in the quantity of money demanded and a rise in prices in the absence of borrowing. The rise in interest rates then serves to limit the capital expansion to whatever savings can be coaxed out of domestic income. Once borrowing abroad can occur, the rise in interest rates is prevented, or at least moderated, by the influx of foreign savings. The channeling of these savings into domestic investment, however, represents an increase in aggregate spending in Canada that leads directly to a rise in the Canadian price level because the prices of nontraded goods rise. It is this price level increase, according to the analysis put forward here, that generates the trade-balance deficit necessary to finance the net inflow of capital.[2] The expansion of the money supply, together with the supporting inflows of gold and secondary reserves, is a consequence of the rise in prices rather than a cause of it.

Viner attempts to explain the increase in Canadian relative to foreign prices as resulting from the inflow of money produced by converting the funds borrowed abroad into domestic currency. He must therefore make the expansion of aggregate demand a consequence of the inflow of money and not a cause of it. Since the money supply only increases because borrowing occurs, and since the standard monetary theory of Viner's day does not emphasize the relationship between interest rates and the demand for money, Viner cannot explain a price rise without the inflow of funds. Later theoretical developments permit a price increase to result from a rise in interest rates in the absence of borrowing abroad, and even in the presence of it if capital is not perfectly mobile internationally. The analysis of the present study goes a step further and postulates a rise in prices from the aggregate demand effect of the capital expansion financed by borrowing. This occurs regardless of whether capital happens to be perfectly mobile internationally or whether domestic interest rates rise relative to foreign rates.

The data presented in Chapter 4 and the statistical analysis in Chapter 5 leave no doubt that the relationship between relative domestic and foreign price levels and the trade balance is as Viner reports. Relative price changes are an integral part, though not necessarily the only factor, in the adjustment of the balance of trade to the net capital inflow.

A second broad objection to Viner's conclusions is that the classical model is not really consistent with the evidence on the financial side. This attack is spearheaded by Angell.[3] He writes

[A]lthough Viner's verification of the general theory seems to me conclusive on other points, I think that it breaks down on this question of the intermediary financial mechanisms. Neither the statistical data submitted nor the reasoning based upon them show any clear sequence *from* the outside reserves *to* credit and price conditions within Canada itself. Outside reserves moved closely with bank deposits in Canada, and showed no independent relationship to prices. Rather, the sequence must have been that which Viner himself rather hesitantly suggests at another point. The Canadian borrowers, having sterling funds at their disposal, deposited them

---

[2] This process is discussed in the second section of Chapter 3.
[3] Angell (1925a, 1925b, 1925c).

with the Canadian banks (except insofar as the loans were spent in England). These funds, thus converted into Canadian currency and credit, were spent in Canada and induced a rise in prices; a rise which roughly adjusted the commodity balance of trade to the volume of new borrowings. The Canadian banks recouped themselves by selling the sterling funds in New York, the proceeds being left there or taken back to Canada as needed. It does not appear from the data, however, that these changes in the *New York* balances had any direct and independent effect upon conditions within Canada. By providing potential additional metallic reserves, their increase made a Canadian credit expansion *possible,* but there is not convincing evidence, inductive or deductive, to show that it provided the initial stimulus to expansion. The stimulus came, rather, from the original increase in bank deposits within Canada itself. With respect to gold flows, finally, Viner himself shows that they played an altogether minor and dependent part. (1925c, pp. 173–4)

I think that Professor Viner's data warrant the inference – despite the opposite conclusion which he himself draws – that the classical theory is erroneous with respect to the role of gold flows, under modern conditions. The correction of the maladjustment in trade produced by the loans did not come from the effects of gold flows, or of changes in the outside bank balances. It came from the effects of the original (and prior) increase in Canadian bank deposits. This conclusion, if it be accepted, evidently has an important bearing on the whole problem of the correction of large disturbances in trade. It deprives gold flows of any effective causal connection with price movements and shifts in the balance of trade, and makes them simply a function of exchange market conditions or of the need for metallic bank reserves. The initial and significant changes, when the disturbance is great enough to require a correction in prices and the trade balance, are rather those in bank deposits. The connection between such changes and general prices is direct and immediate. (1925c, p. 174)

Angell is clearly bothered by the fact that gold and/or outside reserves did not flow into Canada and lead to a rise in prices as the traditional price-specie-flow mechanism requires. There is no "clear sequence *from* the outside reserves *to* credit and price conditions within Canada." Instead, he argues, the increase in the money supply was strictly, or at least primarily, the increase in deposits that occurred when domestic borrowers converted the foreign currency proceeds of their borrowings into Canadian dollars. The resulting increased holdings of secondary reserves (and gold, to the extent that the banks wanted to hold it) made the monetary expansion possible, they did not *stimulate* it. Angell then states in the second paragraph quoted above that gold flows thus have no "causal connection with price movements" and are simply "a function of exchange market conditions or of the need for metallic bank reserves." The connection between changes in prices and deposits are, he goes on to say, "direct and immediate."[4]

In the resulting exchange Viner obviously tries to stake a preemptive claim to the argument that an increase in deposits leads directly to monetary expansion. He simply retorts that Angell misinterprets him.

Angell thus interprets the Canadian expansion of deposits as being solely a primary expansion [that is, one resulting from the exchange of the sterling proceeds of the loans abroad for Canadian dollars] . . . while he attributes to me the doctrine that the Canadian expansion of deposits was . . . a secondary expansion [that is, one resulting from increased loans in Canada by the banks in response to the increase in reserves in New York]. . . . He presents no evidence to support his account of the role I assigned to secondary expansion, and it has no other basis, I am convinced, than Angell's assumption that when I found similarity between the role of fluctuations in the outside reserves in Canada and the role of gold movements in the classical mechanism, I must have had in mind the use of gold reserves as a basis for expansion of deposits through loans. I had in mind, on the contrary, what I now call the primary phase of gold movements in the mechanism. Instead of stressing secondary expansion in the Canadian mechanism, I ignored it except for the last few years of the period studied. (1937, pp. 416–17)

Viner recognizes and outlines in detail the direct relationship between the conversion of the proceeds of the borrowings abroad into Canadian dollars and the increase in domestic deposits and the money supply.

A Canadian railroad corporation, let us say, borrows $100,000,000 in London. To make the hypothesis as simple as possible, assume that it wants to use the entire proceeds of the loan in making purchases and paying wages in Canada. It will thereupon apply to the London branch of a Canadian bank to transfer its London funds to Canada at the current rate of exchange. The Canadian bank will buy New York exchange with the sterling funds obtained from the railroad, and will establish a deposit for the corporation in Canada. So far the situation is as follows: the railroad has $100,000,000 on deposit in Canada; the bank has increased its deposit liabilities in Canada by $100,000,000, and has increased its funds in New York by $100,000,000. To maintain its normal cash reserve ratio, which we will assume to be 10 percent, the bank will import from New York $10,000,000 of gold, using its New York funds to obtain the gold. The remaining $90,000,000 it will lend on call in New York. (1924, pp. 178–9)

The increase in Canadian bank deposits, unaccompanied by an increase in the quantity of goods in Canada, will cause a rise in the Canadian price level. Imports will be stimulated, exports checked. To pay for the excess of imports over exports, the Canadian importers will buy foreign exchange from their banks, giving checks

---

[4] Angell (1925b, pp. 173–4).

upon their deposits in payment. If the excess of imports over exports exactly equals $100,000,000, the amount of the loan, the Canadian deposits will fall by $100,000,000, the banks will reexport $10,000,000 gold from their cash reserves, and will use this $10,000,000 plus $90,000,000 of their funds on call in New York to meet the foreign bills of exchange which they had sold to their customers. Prices, deposits, cash reserves, outside reserves, will all be back to their levels prior to the flotation of the loan, and the borrowed capital will have moved into Canada in the form of commodities. (1924, p. 179)

If the borrowing from abroad is not a single transaction but is continued indefinitely at a constant rate, deposits, cash reserves, prices, outside reserves, will be definitely maintained at their increased levels. Withdrawals from deposits and consequently from the cash reserves and outside reserves, to pay for the constant excess of imports over exports, will be simultaneously offset by new accretions resulting from the continued flow of assets. If the borrowing increases, but at an irregular rate with occasional declines in the rate of borrowing, as was the case during the period under study, there will be correspondingly irregular variations in several items. Cash reserves, outside reserves, prices, deposits, will all increase with every increase in the rate of borrowings, and will decrease with every decrease in the rate of borrowings. (1924, pp. 179–80)

It was assumed above that the rise in the Canadian price level consequent upon the increase in deposits would be just sufficient to bring about an excess of imports over exports equal to the volume of borrowings. But the unfavorable balance of trade might well be for some time either greater or less than the volume of borrowings. Assume that the unfavorable balance is less than the volume of borrowings. The usual explanation of the mechanism of adjustment would contend that this would cause a steady inflow of gold until prices rose sufficiently to stimulate imports and check exports to the extent needed to adjust the balance. In Canada, however, such a situation would simply result in a piling-up of deposits in Canada and of outside reserves. Until the unfavorable balance of trade equalled the amount of borrowings, deposits would be steadily increasing, prices rising, imports increasing, exports decreasing. To take now the opposite hypothesis, namely that the increase in deposits consequent upon foreign borrowings has resulted in a rise in prices which stimulates imports, checks exports, to such a degree that the unfavorable balance is greatly in excess of the borrowings. Canadian importers, to pay for the excess, will draw heavily on their deposits, and buy foreign exchange therewith. The banks will provide the foreign funds from their outside reserves, if these are ample. Only if the outside reserves are not adequate to the task will they withdraw funds from their cash reserves. In any case, deposits will have fallen in Canada for, unlike withdrawals from deposits on domestic account, checking on deposits for foreign account means a reduction in the total of deposits, not merely a shifting of deposits from depositor to depositor and bank to bank. The reduction in deposits will cause a fall in Canadian prices; exports will increase, imports decrease; the unfavorable balance of trade will fall until it is in equilibrium with the borrowings. (1924, pp. 180–1)

This statement seems to be equivalent in substance to Angell's statement of the role of deposits quoted above.

Angell appears to be bothered by the fact that this deposit adjustment mechanism is substantially at variance with the traditional classical specie-flow mechanism. Viner apparently recognizes this, and is somewhat bothered by it, as a careful rereading of the quotes from Viner (1924) embedded in Chapter 2 reveals. Viner concedes that he modifies the classical mechanism in significant respects and offers the defense that Canada may be a special case and that the mechanism as adapted to Canadian conditions may well work better than the traditional mechanism.

It may be objected that the Canadian process is simply the process described by Mill, as modified everywhere by the development of deposit banking. The generally accepted theory, however, if presented in the form most nearly in keeping with Mill's exposition of the theory – and moreover in the form not yet shown by anyone to be untrue for other gold standard countries than Canada – would explain the variations in the Canadian bank deposits as the effect and not the cause of the gold movements; it would contend that an inflow of gold would stimulate deposits and an outflow of gold would bring about their contraction.

Through their use of outside reserves the Canadian banks can control and regulate the movement of gold into and out of Canada, largely irrespective of the state of the balance of payments. But if the outside reserves are regarded as equivalent to gold in Canada, then the Canadian process of adjustment of international balances approaches more closely that set forth *a priori* in the generally accepted theory. It is probable, however, that the Canadian variation from the typical method, by preventing sudden inflows and withdrawals of gold, operated to bring about a steadier and smoother adjustment of price levels and trade balances in the face of huge and irregular borrowings abroad than would have been possible if gold movements into and out of Canada were as automatic and free as they are elsewhere. (1924, pp. 181–2)

Instead of arguing that the adjustment takes the form of inflows of deposits rather than gold or secondary reserves, and that Viner is therefore wrong, Angell should have argued that Viner's modified adjustment mechanism departs too much from the traditional price-specie-flow formulation. If the standard mechanism does not work for Canada, why would it work elsewhere? If it does not work for other countries whose banking institutions differ from Canada's, what type of modification of the standard mechanism is appropriate for those countries? To investigate these issues requires a reworking of the entire classical theory of adjustment, something Angell does not do. Apart from quibbling over the role of primary and secondary expansion of deposits, he appears satisfied with Viner's main results. He agrees that Viner's "verification of the general theory seems ... to be conclusive on other points."[5]

When the problem is approached from a modern perspective, modifying the classical mechanism to integrate gold and capital movements within the framework of domestic and world portfolio equilibrium, everything falls into place. The standard price-specie-flow mechanism is an appropriate analytical framework only when capital does not move internationally in response to market forces. When capital is internationally mobile, world portfolio equilibrium is achieved by an international exchange of gold for assets or assets for gold. No relative price adjustments and associated shifts in imports relative to exports are required.

Two forces determine the domestic price level, the world gold supply, which determines the general level of world prices, and the world (including domestic) demand and supply of domestically produced relative to foreign produced goods, which determines the domestic relative to the foreign price level. Money determines domestic prices only through its effect on the world price level. Real factors determine the ratio of domestic to foreign prices.

When domestic residents are out of portfolio equilibrium at the domestic price level determined by the process described above, they go to the international capital market, altering their portfolios in a one-shot transaction. For example, if money holdings are too low, they sell assets to foreigners and convert the foreign exchange proceeds to domestic money at the chartered banks.[6] In the process, the banking system creates the necessary increase in the domestic money supply. The chartered banks maintain their cash reserve ratios by adjusting their secondary reserve holdings in New York, and perhaps their gold holdings as well.

To the extent that the reserve holdings of the chartered banks are too high, they either expand their less liquid asset holdings abroad or increase their loans in Canada. Increased domestic credit expansion creates more money than the private sector wants to hold, resulting in a purchase of assets abroad and a reduction in the secondary reserve holdings of the banking system toward the desired level. If reserves are too low, the banks reduce their less liquid foreign asset holdings and/or their loans in Canada.

---

[5] Angell (1925c, p. 172).
[6] They cannot rebalance their portfolios by selling assets domestically, because in the aggregate everyone wants to sell and no one wants to buy. Behind this aggregate portfolio response are the activities of financial intermediaries, the conduit through which the purchases of assets from foreigners take place.

This leads to a sale of assets abroad and an increase in chartered bank reserve holdings. The chartered banks thus control their reserve levels by adjusting their portfolios of loans and other assets. Since secondary reserves can be converted into gold at will in the New York market, there is no need to hold many gold reserves.

It is important to emphasize that, according to the theory outlined in Chapter 3, the chartered banks exert no control over the domestic money supply. All they can control is the mix of gold, secondary reserves, and other assets in their portfolios. The general public determines the money supply by its portfolio decisions.

This description of the financial mechanism accords exactly with the observations of Viner and Angell on the process of adjustment. Deposits are the direct conduit through which the expansion of the Canadian money supply induced by output and investment expansion occurs. Gold and secondary reserves play a passive role in this transmission process. There is no observed causation from gold to money to prices for good reason – the direction of causality runs the other way. Viner's attempt to reconcile these observations with the traditional specie-flow mechanism by explaining the increase in Canadian prices as the consequence of domestic deposit expansion represents a contortion imposed on the theory to make it fit the facts, a contortion Angell appears to recognize but fails to treat effectively in his criticism.

Two further issues regarding the interpretation of this factual evidence remain to be examined. The first is Viner's argument that the chartered banks do not use expansions and contractions of their domestic loan portfolios in order to influence domestic credit. If his interpretation is correct, the argument of the present study that the banks maintain their desired reserve ratios by adjusting domestic credit – a crucial ingredient of the theory supporting the hypothesis of this study – is wrong. Viner writes

The Canadian banks kept their discount rates practically constant throughout the period under study. They repeatedly claimed that no deserving request for an extension of credit was refused. There is no evidence that, at any time during the period under study, they used their power over the volume of loans to adjust their cash reserve ratios. There is abundant evidence, on the other hand, that the first consideration of the banks was the meeting of the credit needs of their customers, and that they neither contracted nor expanded their current loans primarily because of the state of their cash reserves. (1924, p. 176)

It is difficult to believe this. Banks claim today that no deserving request for credit is refused. The issue turns on what is meant by "deserving."

A. K. Cairncross, looking at the same evidence, agrees with the interpretation of the present study, arguing cogently

[I]t has been suggested that the banks played a purely passive role, and refused 'no deserving request for an extension of credit'. . . . This is as hard to believe of a group of banks as of a single bank. No bank can maintain an inflexible conception of what is 'deserving' when its reserves are slipping away. There would be no sense in the repeated complaints of monetary stringency in 1907 and 1913 if 'deserving' borrowers were not finding it difficult to arrange credits. The builders who were reported in 1913 to be using their own savings to pay for work on dwelling-houses in the suburbs of Montreal [*Canadian Labour Gazette*, May 1913, p. 1182] were hardly less credit worthy than those who had no difficulty in raising money six months earlier. Nevertheless, it is clear that circumstances might give an appearance of passiveness to the behavior of the banks. Since a favorable balance was normally accompanied by a rise in investment, the demand for credit and the secondary reserves of the banks tended to move upward together; so that it becomes difficult to disentangle changes in credit policy from changes in the demand for loans in the recorded statistics of bank advances. (1968, p. 170)

A somewhat related issue is whether, as Goodhart contends, the chartered banks collude to control credit conditions and interest rates in Canada, using the New York market as a "sink" in which to dump the excess of their liquid asset portfolio over domestic requirements. Goodhart writes

[I]n order to maintain interest rates at the desired level, the banking cartel would need to be able to absorb considerable changes in its liquidity position without being forced to change its agreed rates. The easiest way to achieve this desired stability would be to hold a sizable volume of funds in a secondary reserve, earning some interest, which funds could be increased or run down at will so as to maintain a more constant liquidity in the home, protected market. (1969, p. 142)

After considerable discussion of the arguments against this view, Goodhart concludes

from the evidence that the major responsibility for holding interest rates in Canada at a nearly constant level must be put upon the internal agreements, most likely in the nature of 'gentlemen's agreements' – that is unwritten and unsigned – between the Canadian bankers. Their actions must be analyzed in the light of this market structure. (1969, p. 145)

One of the arguments that Goodhart uses to support his case is that interest rates in the Montreal call loan market are much more stable than interest rates in New York. The implication is that the Montreal rate is a collusive rate.

Although the possibility of collusion is acknowledged, Goodhart's reasons for the comparative stability of the Montreal call loan rate are unacceptable. As Goodhart himself recognizes, call loan rates in many other U.S. cities, such as Kansas City and Detroit, for example, are also more stable than the New York call loan rate. The institutional structure of banking in these cities suggests that collusion is unlikely. Goodhart uses another argument based on seasonal flows of money between New York and the interior to rationalize the stability of interest rates in these cities.

Contrary to Goodhart's view, the greater stability of call loan rates outside New York may be due to the nature of the markets in these cities. These markets, including the one in Montreal, may be very narrow, with loans made only to clients well known to the lending bank. As a result, the risk associated with these loans may be more stable over time. Interest rates may thus not vary much. It is difficult to rationalize differences between call loan rates in New York and other cities on grounds other than differences in risk. The capital market may not have been perfect, but funds probably moved to eliminate observed interest differentials of several percentage points.

In any event, even if Canadian banks do collude to influence deposit and loan rates and conditions, the argument that the chartered banks adjust their reserves by expanding and contracting domestic loans still holds. A monopoly bank will respond in the same way as a competitive banking system to changes in its desired reserve levels.

The second important issue that requires discussion is the question of timing. The theory of Chapter 3 states that Canadian residents increase their money holdings in response to an increase in the domestic price level while the standard specie-flow mechanism views the price level as increasing in response to an increase in the domestic money supply. It is generally believed that in situations where prices respond to monetary changes they do so with a lag. If Viner's theory is correct, therefore, prices lag behind money. According to the portfolio theory proposed in the present study, prices cause money holdings to change, and as a consequence, either the two variables vary simultaneously or money lags behind prices.

In reviewing Viner (1924), both Angell (1925b) and Carr (1931) deal with this question of timing. Angell finds that the "excess of net capital imports over the final means of payment" precedes the changes in bank deposits by up to a year and that the fluctuations in the net imports of commodities tend to lag about a year behind the changes in bank deposits.[7] He does not present any empirical arguments about the presumed lag of

---

[7] See Angell (1925b).

prices behind the changes in bank deposits. Carr (1931) looks at the evidence and concludes that the ratio of Canadian to world prices rises before bank deposits, and hence, before the "excess of capital imports over the final means of payment" and the excess of commodity imports over exports. Prices, he writes, "appear to be the active factor in the situation, all the others following with a lag, and for the most part prices maintained their lead throughout the period" (p. 713).

Carr goes on to argue that

[the] industrialization made great demands upon labour and certain local commodities. The higher wages and prices paid by the more lucrative industries raised the costs of production generally, and consequently prices. . . . And so Canada's industrial development raised . . . prices. (1931, p. 717)

Viner (1937) vigorously opposes these arguments. He notes that what Angell calls the "excess of capital imports over final means of payment" must, by definition, equal the accumulation of foreign exchange by either the private sector or the banks. He goes on to note that in calculating net imports of capital, Angell uses data that include the net private and public accumulation of foreign exchange as part of net investments by Canadians abroad. Since this is subtracted in calculating net imports of capital abroad, Angell's "excess of capital imports over final means of payment" should equal zero when correctly estimated. As a result, Angell's series represents "merely the net errors and omissions in the several series of estimates from which they are derived and [has] no other significance."[8] Finally, using the above argument and noting the frailty of data Angell uses in his arguments about timing, Viner dismisses Angell's analysis.

[W]hatever Angell's charts may appear to show, the defects both in my estimates upon which these charts are based and in Angell's use of them are such as to make the charts have little bearing on the questions of chronological sequence which he attempts to answer by them. (1937, p. 423)

Viner also dismisses Carr's arguments more or less summarily, citing the same arguments. Our analysis of timing in Chapter 7 indicates that on this point Viner was correct.

Most recently, Rich (1988) reexamines the Canadian evidence on balance-of-payments adjustment within a business cycle framework. The balance of payments, and hence the monetary base, vary countercyclically. But bank reserve ratios are sufficiently countercyclical to result in procyclical variation of the money supply itself. As a result, Rich argues,

---

[8] Viner (1937, p. 425).

The evidence is clearly inconsistent with Viner's assertion as to a close link between the Canadian money stock and the balance of payments. There is little doubt that the long-run changes in the money stock were due largely to overall balance-of-payments surpluses or deficits. Over the business cycle, however, the two magnitudes were not closely related since the procyclical movements in the money stock mirrored pronounced countercyclical fluctuations in the aggregate reserve ratio of the chartered banks. (1988, p. 86)

Clearly, Rich is looking for an explanation of the procyclical variation of the money supply in terms of reserve flows and doesn't find it. He is led to suggest that something might be wrong with Viner's theory.

Neither the original classical specie-flow mechanism nor Viner's modified version of it provide the correct explanation of this evidence. With regard to the long-term trends, the rise in the Canadian relative to the foreign price level was a direct result of the effect of the inflow of world investment on the demand for domestic resources. At this new higher level of domestic prices, Canadian residents chose to hold a larger money stock. The chartered banks were forced to supply these additional money holdings or face a reduction in their reserves to unacceptable levels. Since the chartered banks chose to maintain reserve levels that varied directly with their liabilities, the long-term increase in bank reserves was the *result* of the long-term growth of the money supply, *not* the cause of it. The long-term growth of the money supply *results* from the increase in domestic prices.

The cyclical evidence can be similarly interpreted. Domestic residents chose to adjust their money holdings directly in response to cyclical changes in nominal income because the demand for money was positively related to nominal income. If the reserve ratios of the chartered banks had remained constant, bank reserves would have varied procyclically. The chartered banks, however, chose to increase their reserve ratios in bad times and reduce them in boom periods. Since the public's ratio of coin and Dominion notes to chartered bank note and deposit liabilities did not vary cyclically, the monetary base tended to vary countercyclically along with bank reserves. The money multiplier therefore varied procyclically.

Countercyclical variability of bank reserves and base money leads, quite naturally, to countercyclical variability of the balance-of-payments surplus. The chartered banks created these countercyclical balance-of-payments adjustments by expanding domestic credit by more than the increase in the public's desired money holdings in boom times, and by less than the rise in the public's desired money holdings in recession periods. The public maintained its desired money growth by buying assets abroad in good times and selling them abroad in bad times. The chartered banks, in turn, achieved a reduction in their reserve ratios in boom periods and an increase in recessions. Had they not wanted to vary their reserves countercyclically, they would have varied domestic credit in step with the variations in the demand for money, making balance-of-payments adjustments unnecessary.

An important difference between the analysis of this study and Rich's relates to the role of the monetary base. Rich views the problem in the standard framework – changes in the money stock are determined by changes in the monetary base in conjunction with the money multiplier. This approach is appropriate for a closed economy or an open one with flexible exchange rates. Government open market operations then change the monetary base. Given the public's desired ratio of currency to deposits, and the banking system's desired reserve/deposit ratio, this leads to a change in the stock of money and, in turn, to changes in the price level and the exchange rate.

In the present context of fixed exchange rates and international capital mobility, however, the monetary base is not a useful concept. The money supply was endogenously determined as a result of private portfolio decisions. Dominion note holdings of the public plus bank reserves constituted the monetary base. If people held too many Dominion notes, they deposited them in the bank or exchanged them for bank notes. Bank reserves were determined by the profit maximizing decisions of the chartered banks. The monetary base was thus simply an endogenous outgrowth of private sector decisions and in no sense the driving force behind the money supply as it would be in other institutional settings. In the Canadian environment before 1914, the concept of base or high-powered money has no meaning.

Although it is probably somewhat more useful to define and measure the concept of the "monetary gold stock," this too is an endogenous variable in the system. The chartered banks chose the fraction of their total reserves to be held in gold. They also chose, subject to legal minimum requirements imposed by the Bank Act, the fraction of their reserves held in the form of Dominion notes. Given the stock of Dominion notes outstanding, the government must, by law, hold an appropriate gold reserve. Since it had no reason to hold gold except to back these notes, its gold stock was endogenous. The stock of money thus determined the stock of monetary gold in the country, not the other way around.

This conclusion is of particular interest in relation to Rich's comments about the government's "discretionary" monetary policy prior to the mid-1880s. He argues that the government was trying to finance its expenditure by printing money in those early years but later "apparently abandoned monetary discretion in favour of a predominantly automatic system of monetary policy."[9] The theory of gold-standard adjustment proposed in the present study suggests that "printing money" and "discretionary monetary policy" are inappropriate terms to describe this form of fiscal finance since the government had no control over the money supply and therefore could not print money. It could finance its expenditure by printing Dominion notes only if it could get someone in the community to hold them and only to the extent that the Dominion note issue did not have to be covered by gold. It induced the private sector to hold Dominion notes by making them the only permissible denominations under five dollars and by forcing the chartered banks to hold them as reserves. Since a significant part of the increase in the outstanding stock of Dominion notes was un-covered in the early years, the government in effect forced the community to make it an interest free loan backed only partially with noninterest bearing gold. This was a tax on the chartered banks and the general public that involved a change in the size and composition of the monetary base. It was not an increase in the supply of money.

Rich's evidence strengthens the case for interpreting Canadian monetary history along the lines suggested in Chapter 3 rather than in terms of the traditional classical price-specie-flow mechanism as extended by Viner. The portfolio adjustment theory explains this evidence in a clear and straightforward manner.

Rich (1988, chapter 4) touches further on the mechanism of balance-of-payments adjustment when he develops his views on business cycle transmission. In Rich's view, the mechanism of cycle transmission is based entirely on the domestic income and trade balance effects of changes in real output abroad. Neither the traditional nor the portfolio theories of balance-of-payments adjustment provide complete explanations of cycle transmission, but portfolio theory has somewhat different, and the present study contends more convincing, implications than the ones drawn by Rich from his balance-of-payments analysis.

Within the portfolio equilibrium approach to the balance-of-payments adjustment process, there are at least two avenues through which business cycles are transmitted above and beyond the effect of the foreign business

---

[9] Rich (1988, p. 73).

cycle on the trade balance. First, world business cycle activity is, at least to some extent, of monetary origin. It is the result of random gold discoveries together with expectationally driven cyclical variations in the reserve ratios of commercial banks, the desires of private individuals to hold gold rather than other forms of money, or the desires of private individuals and firms to hold money rather than other assets. In this situation, the transmission of business cycles occurs through parallel changes in expectations at home and abroad, and somewhat less directly through cyclical variations in world interest rates. Because capital is highly mobile internationally, domestic and foreign real interest rates tend to move together.

Second, the international business cycle is, at least to some extent, the result of cyclical changes in real factors – expectations about the profitability of investment and serially correlated changes in inventory investment – and the free flow of information (or misinformation) across international boundaries thus leads to the direct transmission of cyclical disturbances. That countries are linked together through their trade balances is obviously a particularly important factor, but by no means the only one, operating to transmit cyclical disturbances within the real sector.

Considering both real and monetary factors and the fact that Canada is part of a world monetary and trade system, the covariation of economic activity in Canada and the United States and Great Britain is no more surprising than the covariation of economic activity in Ontario and Quebec.

From the time that Viner first wrote about Canada's balance of payments until now, his interpretation has been in contention. Yet neither Viner nor his critics saw that the difficulties with the price-specie-flow story were of a sort that could not be resolved without abandoning its central features. Instead, all commentators on Viner (1924), including Viner himself, have made no more than cosmetic changes in the traditional view of balance-of-payments adjustment. The present study, by presenting a new theory of adjustment, recognizes the need for departing from the tradition of Viner and his critics.

9. The theoretical implications of capital mobility

This chapter develops the theoretical implications of capital mobility more fully and examines the consequences for interpreting the pre–1914 Canadian experience. The theoretical model developed in Chapter 3 and the less formal discussions in the subsequent five chapters show that the essential difference between the portfolio adjustment and traditional classical models lies in the treatment of capital mobility. The formal presentations in Chapters 3 and 7 assume that capital is perfectly mobile internationally. The question now is: Does the fact that capital was less than perfectly mobile between Canada and the rest of the world alter in any significant way the overall conclusions of this study?[1]

As noted in the last chapter, the traditional theory does not rigorously incorporate international capital mobility. Most classical monetary economists view capital movements as in part exogenous and in part a function of domestic/foreign interest rate differentials. Not until Mundell',s analysis of the 1960s, however, is this view formalized to any extent.[2] The classical theory, of course, deals with imperfect rather than perfect capital mobility – otherwise a domestic/foreign interest-rate differential could not exist.

Once it is recognized that capital mobility is the crucial difference between the portfolio adjustment theory and the traditional one, it is important to see what conclusions can be drawn from capital mobility alone. It is easily established that, during the study period, capital is mobile, albeit imperfectly, between Canada and the rest of the world in the sense that Canada is part of a world capital market. Foreign capital was instrumental in building railroads and expanding industry'and the chartered banks and

---

[1] The evidence for imperfect capital mobility is the observed differences in the interest yields at which investors at home and abroad hold internationally traded securities of similar term and coupon yield. As early as the mid-nineteenth century, the London capital market discounted Canadian securities. These were commonly underwritten with government guarantees to encourage their sale abroad (Aitken, 1952; Faucher, 1960; and Baskerville, 1985). It also appears that, despite this element of subsidy, international investors may have at times underestimated the risk (Kindleberger, 1984, pp. 259–68).

[2] Mundell (1960, 1961, 1963).

other Canadian corporations dealt freely in the New York and London money markets.[3] Using this fact alone, how far can theory take us in establishing how the Canadian economy must have operated? Can it be established that the portfolio-adjustment theory gives the correct interpretation of the evidence, and correspondingly, that the classical theory is an incorrect guide to understanding what was going on?

It has already been shown that when capital is perfectly mobile, the portfolio theory is the best vehicle for addressing the evidence. Is it possible that the traditional classical theory could be a useful window on the evidence when imperfections of capital mobility are explicitly taken into account? In other words, can the classical approach of treating capital flows as a function of domestic/foreign interest differentials provide a logically coherent theoretical framework in which the evidence can be interpreted? If, as this chapter seeks to demonstrate, the classical approach cannot provide such a framework, an additional very strong piece of evidence in favor of the approach developed here emerges. The abundant evidence as to the existence of a world wide market for capital in and of itself thus supports the portfolio theory and rejects the traditional theory.

It is maintained below that the portfolio theory of balance-of-payments adjustment is the logical consequence of the assumption of an (albeit imperfectly) integrated world market for capital and that the classical theory is not a logical consequence of this assumption. In an important sense, therefore, the choice between the two theories depends on whether or not capital was free to move internationally.

It is necessary first to review the analysis of perfect capital mobility presented in Chapter 3 and develop more rigorously some implications that are only discussed in general terms in the intervening chapters. The model is then expanded to encompass imperfect capital mobility and to investigate its consistency with the traditional price-specie-flow mechanism.

Review and refinement of the perfect capital mobility analysis

Following custom, perfect capital mobility means that individuals are free to trade domestic and foreign assets in the international market, and world

---

[3] The placement of Canadian securities in world capital markets has been documented by a number of researchers. See, for example, Paterson (1976), Hartland (1964), Fishlow (1985, p. 384, and section 2), Bloomfield (1963, pp. 62–5; 1968, pp. 24–7), Cairncross (1968), and Simon (1970).

asset holders regard domestic and foreign assets as perfect substitutes in their portfolios. Domestic and foreign interest rates are therefore equal.

The domestic price level can then be formally expressed by equation (3.19):

$$P = \frac{q(N, K, r^*, Z, \mu, \Omega)^\alpha V^* G^*}{\delta^*(q^*)^{\alpha^*} Y^*} \tag{3.19}$$

where N and K are the stocks of labor and capital employed in the domestic economy, Y^* is foreign output (and income), V^* is the income velocity of money in the rest of the world, G^* is the rest of the world's gold supply, Z is the domestic real debt service balance, α and α^* are the shares of nontraded goods in total output at home and abroad, μ is the domestic terms of trade, δ^* is the ratio of the foreign gold stock to the foreign money supply (reciprocal of the money multiplier), q^* is the exogenously determined ratio of nontraded to traded goods prices abroad and $q[\dots]$ is the function determining the ratio of nontraded to traded goods prices in the domestic economy, r^* is the domestic (and foreign) real interest rate, and Ω is a portmanteau variable capturing exogenous changes in technology and resource discovery in the domestic economy.[4] Since Canada holds a trivial fraction of the world gold stock, the rest of the world's gold stock can be approximated by the world gold supply.

Equation (3.19) is derived from the equality of the demand and supply of the domestic nontraded good. The relative price of nontraded in terms of traded goods, given by $q[\dots]$, must adjust to ensure that equilibrium occurs. The effects of the various exogenous factors on the equilibrium relative prices of nontraded in terms of traded goods can be seen intuitively. For example, increases in the quantity of labor and capital employed lead to both increases in the output of the nontraded good and increases in income and the demand for it. The direction of the effect on the relative price variable depends on the relative magnitudes of these supply and demand forces. An increase in the domestic real interest rate reduces investment in the domestic economy. The demand for the nontraded good and its price in terms of traded goods falls.[5] An improvement in the terms

---

[4] A prominent finding of Canadian economic historians, starting with Harold Innis, is that the integration of the Canadian economy into the world economy provided a channel for introducing new technologies that helped discover and develop new resources to satisfy external markets. See Berger (1986, chapter 4).

[5] This statement must be qualified. A rise in the domestic, and world, interest rate may result from an improvement in the productivity of capital in the rest of the world. If a similar improvement of productivity does not occur in the domestic economy, this rise in

of trade increases income and consumption, including consumption of the nontraded good, causing the relative price of that good to rise. An increase in the portmanteau variable Ω, representing the development of western Canada and the associated industrial expansion, also leads to an expansion of the demand for the nontraded good for investment purposes. Again this causes the relative prices of the nontraded good to rise.[6]

The prices of domestic traded goods are exogenously determined in the world market by the stock of gold, level of income, money multiplier, income velocity of money, and ratio of nontraded to traded goods prices abroad. An increase in the relative prices of domestic nontraded in terms of traded goods therefore leads to a rise in the domestic price level. Neither the domestic nominal money stock nor the demand for money enters into the equation determining the domestic price level.

The quantity of money held by Canadians is determined by equation (3.20):

$$M = P \cdot L(r^*, Y) \tag{3.20}$$

This can be extended to represent a demand for reserve money using the domestic money multiplier, $1/\delta$. Let R be the stock of reserve money, defined as chartered bank gold and secondary reserve holdings plus gold holdings of the government.[7]

$$R = \delta \cdot M \tag{9.1}$$

The domestic nominal money stock is determined endogenously. From equations (3.10) and (3.13), the level of domestic income is a function of the stocks of labor and capital employed, the terms of trade, net repatriated earnings on capital (ignored here), and the portmanteau variable Ω.

---

the interest rate is associated with a decline in domestic investment. An equivalent improvement in the productivity of capital in the domestic economy results in an appropriate increase in the portmanteau variable Ω and no net effect on domestic investment. Of course, the partial derivative of $q[\ldots]$ with respect to r is still negative.

Productivity improvement in Canada takes the form of adapting technology developed elsewhere to suit Canadian circumstances. Increased investment at higher Canadian relative to foreign real interest rates is possible because world markets favor the Canadian products of this new capital. The portmanteau variable, Ω, increases.

[6] This follows because the productivity of investment is higher in Canada than abroad. An emerging comparative advantage of resource products in world markets is the basis for this higher return.

[7] R differs slightly from what is normally defined as the monetary base. The latter equals the stocks of gold, Dominion notes and secondary reserves held by the chartered banks plus the public's holdings of Dominion notes. This difference between reserve money and base money is of neither theoretical nor empirical significance for the conclusions of this study.

$$Y = Y(X, \mu) = Y[F(N, K, \Omega), \mu] \qquad (9.2)$$

Here, X is the level of domestic output. The stock of money balances held by domestic residents is obtained by substituting (3.19) and (9.2) into (3.20).

Equilibrium in the market for the domestic nontraded good plus the constraint that total receipts equals total expenditure implies equation (3.5):

$$P_T(T - T_c - T_I) + DSB + I - S = 0 \qquad (3.5)$$

where P_T is the price of the traded good, T is the quantity of that good produced domestically, T_c and T_I are the quantities of it absorbed by consumption and investment respectively in the domestic economy, DSB is the debt service balance or net repatriated earnings, I is the level of domestic investment, and S is the level of domestic savings. Expansion of equation (3.5) by substituting in the expressions for P_T, T, T_c, T_I, I, and S yields the domestic price determination equation (3.19) above. Both (3.5) and (3.19) are alternative statements of the condition that domestic aggregate demand and supply must be equal.

Equation (3.5) says that the balance of trade plus the debt service balance plus the net capital inflow must sum to zero. But it specifies nothing about the division of the inflow of capital into net sales of securities to foreigners by the nonbanking public, net sales of gold and secondary reserves to foreigners by the chartered banks, and net gold sales abroad by the government. Aggregate savings break down into two components:

$$S = dR/dt + S' \qquad (9.3)$$

As before, dR/dt is the rate of increase of reserve money, defined as the chartered bank's gold and secondary reserves plus the gold reserves of the government. S' is total net accumulation of assets by domestic residents, both directly and through financial intermediaries and on both private and public account, minus dR/dt. Substitution of (9.3) into (3.5) yields the traditional statement of the balance-of-payments surplus:

$$dR/dt = P_T(T - T_c - T_I) + DSB + (I - S') \qquad (3.5)'$$

The balance-of-payments surplus equals the balance-of-trade surplus plus the debt service balance plus what is conventionally defined as the autonomous net capital inflow.

At the same time, it is evident from equations (3.20) and (9.1) that the accumulation of reserves is given by:

$$dR/dt = \delta \, dM/dt$$
$$= \delta \, L(r, Y) \, dP/dt$$
$$+ \delta \, P \, L_r \, dr/dt + P \, L_y \, dY/dt \qquad (9.4)$$

where L_r and L_y are the partial derivatives of the demand function for money with respect to the interest rate and real income, dP/dt and dY/dt are the derivatives of (3.19) and (9.2) with respect to time, and dr/dt is determined abroad. Equation (9.4) states that the inflow of reserves equals some fraction δ of the public's desired accumulation of money balances.[8]

Domestic savings equals domestic income minus consumption and from a rearrangement of equation (3.1) can be expressed as follows:

$$S = P_U U + P_T T + DSB - P_U U_C - P_T T_C \qquad (3.1)'$$

The prices of nontraded and traded goods and the quantities of both goods produced and consumed are unaffected by the change in the level of bank reserves, so the flow of reserves has no effect on savings. Thus, dR/dt increases dollar for dollar with declines in S'.

The balance of trade is unaffected by the flow of additions to the stock of reserves for the same reason that savings are unaffected. The level of domestic investment is determined by interest rates, domestic output, and the portmanteau variable Ω, and is therefore unaffected by the balance-of-payments surplus as well. Since the debt service balance depends on past capital flows, it too is unaffected by the balance-of-payments surplus.[9]

Changes in the balance-of-payments surplus or deficit are thus related to none of the components of (3.5)' except S'. They relate only to the proportion of savings which takes the form of gold and secondary reserve accumulations of the chartered banks and gold accumulations by the government. If domestic residents want to add to their money balances at a faster rate, they allocate a greater proportion of their savings to the accumulation of bank notes and deposits and a smaller proportion to the accumulation of other assets. The banks are forced to supply this additional money either by accumulating secondary reserves in New York and London or by expanding their domestic loan portfolios. The amount of reserves

---

[8] Nothing is gained here by formally introducing the dependence of δ on the interest rate and the scale of the financial system.

[9] In many models incorporating international capital mobility, changes in the stock of reserve holdings may have wealth effects because the general public does not view the foreign assets held by the government as part of its wealth. This is not a serious problem here because, apart from the small stock of gold held by the government, none of the reserves in question are held on public account.

accumulated depends on the banking system's desired ratio of reserves to note and deposit liabilities. In causal terms, dR/dt is caused by S', which is in turn caused by the public's desired rate of monetary growth. In contrast to the standard classical price-specie-flow mechanism, there is no direct causal relationship among the inflow of gold, secondary reserves, and the balance of trade. Changes in the balance of trade can affect the gold inflow only if they lead to changes in the private sector's desired rate of monetary growth.[10]

Extension to include imperfect capital mobility

To incorporate imperfect capital mobility, the conditions of domestic and foreign portfolio equilibrium must be developed more fully. Define the quantity of a capital asset as the stream of permanent real income yielded by it.[11] Let Y_L, Y_L^*, Y_K, and Y_K^* represent the quantities of human (L) and physical (K) capital assets employed in the domestic and foreign (*) economies. Suppose domestic residents own a fraction Q_d of domestically employed physical capital assets and foreigners own a fraction Q_f of physical capital assets employed abroad. Human capital employed in each country, by contrast, is owned exclusively by that country's residents. Then the vectors of assets in the portfolios of domestic and foreign residents can be written

---

[10] Take, for example, an increase in domestic exports resulting from a bumper wheat crop. Apart from any resulting minor change in domestic wheat consumption, the expansion of exports is coterminous with the increase in wheat output. This implies, in turn, an equivalent increase in domestic income. Part of this increase in income is channeled into domestic nontraded goods consumption, raising the relative price of nontraded goods and the domestic price level. The rise in income also increases the level of domestic savings. Barring an inflow of new investment in response to the bumper wheat crop, this leads to a decline in the net capital inflow. The rise in the equilibrium relative price of nontraded in terms of traded goods switches just enough domestic expenditure from nontraded to traded goods to increase imports by the amount of the net increase in exports minus the decrease in the net capital inflow.

Although this new equilibrium is unaffected by what happens to gold flows, the rises in the levels of domestic income and prices lead to an increase in the quantity of money demanded by domestic residents. They adjust their portfolios by accumulating cash instead of nonmonetary assets. The banking system is forced to create this additional money partly by the expansion of domestic loans and (depending on the desired reserve ratios of the chartered banks) partly by the accumulation of secondary reserves. The reserve accumulation is a one-shot affair – a higher continuous rate of money growth and resulting reserve accumulations in the future need not occur. This one-shot reserve accumulation is financed by a shift in the composition of domestic residents' portfolios and not by an adjustment of the balance of trade.

[11] A full discussion of the implications of defining the quantities of assets in this way can be found in Friedman (1962, chapter 13).

$$m, Q_d Y_K, (1 - Q_f) Y_K^*, Y_L$$

and

$$m^*, (1 - Q_d) Y_k, Q_f Y_K^*, Y_L^*$$

where m and m^* are the domestic and foreign real money stocks.

Assume that domestic and foreign residents choose the mixes of assets in their portfolios that maximize the following utility functions:

$$U[m, Q_d Y_K, (1 - Q_f) Y_K^*, Y_L]$$

$$U^*[m^*, Q_f Y_K^*, (1 - Q_d) Y_K, Y_L^*]$$

Utility also depends on the quantity of leisure enjoyed and the division of permanent income between present and future consumption. Here it is assumed that the stock and flow terms in the utility function are additively separable and the latter are ignored.[12]

Any given portfolio mix in each country generates three independent marginal rates of substitution: the marginal rate of substitution of domestic physical capital assets for money, the marginal rate of substitution of foreign physical capital assets for money, the marginal rate of substitution of domestic human capital assets for money. These three marginal rates of substitution are the reciprocals of the interest rates at which the country's residents hold that particular mix of assets in their portfolios. Of the three interest rates, only two are of concern here: the interest rate on domestic physical capital assets and the interest rate on foreign physical capital assets. Human capital assets are not traded either domestically or internationally.[13]

The vectors of domestic and foreign nominal interest rates at which the residents of the two countries hold alternative mixes of assets in their portfolios can be written as follows:

[12] A more modern theoretical approach would be to frame the analysis explicitly in terms of intertemporal maximization. This would express international portfolio equilibrium along lines of the consumption-based asset pricing literature. See Merton (1971), Lucas (1978, 1982), Kouri (1977), and Stulz (1984). Unfortunately, that literature has not developed to the point where an application to this problem useful for our purposes can be easily constructed. Nevertheless, as noted in note 19 below, preliminary indications are that an extension of the theory to utilize this literature will make the case for a portfolio interpretation of imperfect capital mobility stronger and further weaken the credibility of traditional views of the role of capital mobility and interest differentials in balance-of-payments adjustment.

[13] This means that there is no market in human capital assets, not that workers do not move from job to job within and between countries.

$$i_{dd} = i_{dd}[m, Q_d Y_K, (1 - Q_f) Y_K^*, Y_L]$$ (9.5)

$$i_{fd} = i_{fd}[m, Q_d Y_K, (1 - Q_f) Y_K^*, Y_L]$$ (9.6)

$$i_{df} = i_{df}[m^*, Q_f Y_K^*, (1 - Q_d) Y_K, Y_L^*]$$ (9.7)

$$i_{ff} = i_{ff}[m^*, Q_f Y_K^*, (1 - Q_d) Y_K, Y_L^*]$$ (9.8)

i_{ij} is the interest rate at which the ith country's physical capital asset is held by the jth country's residents.

If there are no impediments to international trade in physical capital assets,

$$i_{dd} = i_{df} = i$$ (9.9)

and

$$i_{fd} = i_{ff} = i^*$$ (9.10)

where i and i^* are the observed market interest rates at home and abroad.

The six equations, (9.5) through (9.10), solve for the six variables, i, i^*, Q_d, Q_f, m, and m^*, as functions of the four arguments Y_K, Y_K^*, Y_L, and Y_L^*.

$$i = i(Y_K, Y_K^*, Y_L, Y_L^*)$$ (9.11)

$$i^* = i^*(Y_K, Y_K^*, Y_L, Y_L^*)$$ (9.12)

$$Q_d = Q_d(Y_K, Y_K^*, Y_L, Y_L^*)$$ (9.13)

$$Q_f = Q_f(Y_K, Y_K^*, Y_L, Y_L^*)$$ (9.14)

$$m = m(Y_K, Y_K^*, Y_L, Y_L^*)$$ (9.15)

$$m^* = m^*(Y_K, Y_K^*, Y_L, Y_L^*)$$ (9.16)

Because of the small country assumption, developments in the domestic economy have no impact on the interest rate or the money supply abroad. The partial derivatives of i^* and m^* with respect to Y_K and Y_L therefore approach zero. The fraction Q_f is positive and very close to unity, but $(1 - Q_f) Y_K^*$ is still of significant size in relation to $Q_d Y_K$ and m.

Past capital accumulation, the forces of technology, and current employment and output determine the permanent income streams from labor and capital employed at home and abroad. The differential between Canadian and foreign interest rates can be expressed:

$$i - i^* = i\,(Y_K, Y_K^*, Y_L, Y_L^*) - i^*(Y_K, Y_K^*, Y_L, Y_L^*) \qquad (9.17)$$
$$= D(Y_K, Y_K^*, Y_L, Y_L^*)$$

This implies:

$$i = i^* + D(Y_K, Y_K^*, Y_L, Y_L^*) \qquad (9.18)$$

Given that the nominal interest rate in each country equals the real interest rate plus the expected rate of inflation, equation (9.18) becomes

$$r = r^* + D(Y_K, Y_K^*, Y_L, Y_L^*) - (E_p - E_p^*) \qquad (9.19)$$

where E_p and E_p^* are the domestic and foreign expected inflation rates. Since the exchange rate is fixed, $(E_p - E_p^*)$ is equal to the expected rate of change of the relative price of domestic in terms of foreign output – often referred to as the real exchange rate – as the domestic and foreign economies grow through time. The expression

$$\phi = D(Y_K, Y_K^*, Y_L, Y_L^*) - (E_p - E_p^*) \qquad (9.20)$$

is the risk premium on domestic assets in the world capital market.[14]

The domestic price level is determined in the same fashion as in Chapter 3. The relative prices of nontraded in terms of traded goods must adjust to drive the demand for the nontraded good into equality with the supply. Because the domestic economy is small, the price of traded goods is fixed abroad. The domestic price level thus depends on the equilibrium relative price of domestic nontraded in terms of traded goods and the price of traded goods. The latter is, in turn, determined by the ratio of nontraded to traded goods prices abroad and the foreign price level. From equations

---

[14] Our approach differs from many contemporary models of international portfolio equilibrium. See, for example, Dornbusch (1975), Frankel (1983), Branson and Henderson (1985), and Frenkel and Mussa (1985). These models formulate issues in terms of a wealth aggregate composed of four assets consisting of domestic money, foreign money, domestic bonds, and foreign bonds, where the quantities of all aggregates are defined as their present values. Demand functions for the respective assets are then constructed with domestic and foreign interest rates and the aggregate present value of wealth as arguments. Given exogenously determined (in the short run) supplies of the assets, the system of equations solves for the domestic and foreign interest rates and the portfolio shares. This type of formulation focuses on the effects of changes in government debt and official reserve holdings in a world of Ricardian nonequivalence. It largely ignores international exchange in real capital assets. Our purposes do not require an explicit definition of aggregate wealth. Moreover, we deal with a time period in which foreign exchange reserves were largely private assets (there being no central bank in Canada) and in which fiscal policy involving substitutions of bond for tax finance was of little consequence. The usual wealth effects that drive these contemporary models were therefore not present, and international capital transfers took the form of direct or indirect claims on real capital.

(3.16) and (3.17) in Chapter 3, with (9.19) and (9.20) above, the domestic price level can be expressed as follows:

$$P = q[N, K, r^* + \phi, Z, \mu, \Omega]^\alpha P_T = \frac{q[N, K, r^* + \phi, Z, \mu, \Omega]^\alpha}{(q^*)^{\alpha^*}} P^* \tag{9.21}$$

Utilizing (3.18) and the fact that the foreign nominal money stock is a multiple $1/\delta^*$ of the world stock of gold, (9.21) can be expressed as follows:

$$P = \frac{q[N, K, r^* (Y_K^*, Y_L^*) + \phi, Z, \mu, \Omega]^\alpha G^*}{\delta^*(q^*)^{\alpha^*} m^*(Y_K^*, Y_L^*)} \tag{9.22}$$

The small country assumption is used here to eliminate Y_K and Y_L from the functions $m^* (\ldots)$ and $r^* (\ldots)$. Equation (9.22) is the counterpart to equation (3.19) when domestic and foreign assets are imperfect substitutes in portfolios. The fact that velocity equals

$$V^* = Y^*/m^*(Y_K^*, Y_L^*) \tag{9.23}$$

can be used to eliminate the term $m^*(Y_K^*, Y_L^*)$ from (9.22). The resulting equation differs from (3.19) only in that the domestic interest rate differs from the foreign rate by the risk premium ϕ. As in the perfect capital mobility case, the domestic money supply does not appear in the equation determining the domestic price level. Domestic money does not cause domestic prices.

Consider the domestic demand function for money:

$$M = P \cdot m(Y_K, Y_K^*, Y_L, Y_L^*) \tag{9.24}$$

To convert (9.24) into the more conventional formulation, one can utilize two facts, $(Y_K + Y_L)$ equals permanent income, which is directly related to current income Y, and following the usual assumptions in the literature, foreign income affects domestic desired money holdings only through its effects on domestic and foreign interest rates, that is, on the cost of holding money. It follows that $m(Y_K, Y_K^*, Y_L, Y_L^*)$ can be equivalently represented by some function $L(r, r^*, Y)$. As in the perfect capital mobility case, the equilibrium stock of reserves can be represented by $R = \delta M$.

The rate of increase in the stock of primary and secondary bank reserves – the balance-of-payments surplus – is thus as follows:

$$dR/dt = \delta \, m(Y_K, Y_K^*, Y_L, Y_L^*) \, dP/dt + \delta \, P \, M_{YK} \, dY_K/dt$$
$$+ \; \delta \, P \, M_{YL} \, dY_L/dt + \delta \, P \, M_{YK}^* \, dY_K^*/dt + \delta \, P \, M_{YL}^* \, dY_L^*/dt$$

$$= \delta \, L(r, r^*, Y) \, dP/dt + \delta \, P \, L_r \, dr/dt +$$
$$\delta \, P \, L_r^* \, dr^*/dt + \delta \, P \, L_Y \, dY/dt \qquad (9.25)$$

The terms M_{YK} and M_{YL} are the partial derivatives of $M(Y_K, Y_K^*, Y_L, Y_L^*)$ with respect to the subscripted variables. It is reasonable to assume that $m(Y_K, Y_K^*, Y_L, Y_L^*)$ and $L(r, r^*, Y)$ are equivalent. As domestic and foreign assets become perfect substitutes in portfolios, (9.11) and (9.12) become identical, r approaches r^*, and the risk premium ϕ approaches zero. And the demand function for money becomes equivalent to equation (3.20). As in the perfect capital mobility case, the surplus in the balance of payments is equal to the rate of increase in the desired gold and secondary reserve holdings of the chartered banks plus the increase in the government's holdings of gold.

It is now obvious that the condition of balance-of-payments equilibrium is fundamentally the same under imperfect and perfect capital mobility. Restrictions on international transactions in particular types of assets drive wedges between i_{dd} and i_{df} and i_{fd} and i_{ff} in equations (9.9) and (9.10), and are likely also to shift the asset utility functions. For both reasons, the vectors of domestic and foreign interest rates and the real quantity of money demanded by domestic residents are affected. Domestic and foreign assets probably become less perfect substitutes in portfolios, but this is of little import since there is likely to be imperfect substitutability in portfolios in any event. Restrictions on international transactions in particular types of assets simply result in some reshuffling of assets in domestic residents' portfolios. By changing the domestic demand for nominal money balances, these restrictions lead to a shift in chartered bank reserve holdings and a one-shot balance-of-payments adjustment. Once this new equilibrium is achieved, the public may wish to increase its money holdings, and the chartered banks their reserve holdings, at different rates than in the old equilibrium, implying that the balance-of-payments flow surplus might differ as well.

Imperfect capital mobility, whether it results from restrictions on certain types of international asset transactions or simply from imperfect substitutability of domestic and foreign assets in portfolios, has no fundamental effect on the *process* by which balance-of-payments adjustments occur. Even if the risk premium varies through time, a change in the surplus or deficit in the balance of payments is the direct consequence of a change in the rate of desired money accumulation and a resulting change in the accumulation of domestic bank reserves and government gold holdings. Balance-of-payments deficits and surpluses are not "financed" by changes in exports relative to imports as the traditional theory holds. There is no causal relationship between international capital flows and domestic/foreign interest-rate differentials.

This latter point requires further discussion because the supposed effect of interest-rate differentials on capital flows is the cornerstone of the traditional approach to incorporating capital mobility. It is clear from the preceding analysis that the international capital flow equals the level of investment world asset holders wish to undertake in the domestic economy minus the level of domestic savings. The domestic quantity of money, being endogenous, has no effect on either of these magnitudes, regardless of whether capital is perfectly or imperfectly mobile internationally. For this reason, changes in the domestic money supply have no effect on the balance of trade.

The differential between domestic and foreign interest rates depends on the views of world asset holders as to the relative desirability of domestic and foreign assets, and on any government-imposed constraints on international capital transactions. If domestic assets become riskier, domestic interest rates rise relative to foreign rates. The result would be a shift of new investment away from the domestic economy. A rise in the domestic/foreign interest-rate differential is then associated with a decline in the net capital inflow, rather than an increase as the traditional classical paradigm requires.

Increased perceived riskiness of domestic relative to foreign assets may also arise when an enormous expansion of new domestic investment opportunities (represented by an increase in the portmanteau variable Ω) draws large quantities of capital from the rest of the world. Given the convexity of the asset utility functions, an increase in the risk premium is required to compensate world investors for holding larger fractions of their portfolios in domestic assets. In this case, an increase in the observed net inflow of capital is associated with a rise in the domestic/foreign interest differential. The relationship is in the direction postulated by the classical theory, but the capital flow is long-term rather than short-term.

It is likely that, in the period under study, a substantial risk premium on Canadian assets existed in the minds of world investors, and that government policies operated to offset it. It has been established that government, through homestead and other policies, encouraged earlier settlement of the Canadian prairies than would otherwise have been the case.[15] Much western settlement before 1900 therefore, was premature and impermanent.[16] Railroad subsidization was far in excess of that offered to American railroads to the south,[17] with the result that the system was clearly overbuilt by 1914. Much British investment in Canadian enterprises before 1914 yielded a poor return.[18]

The traditional classical mechanism emphasizes the effects of central bank policy on interest-rate differentials and, hence, on net movements of short-term capital. Although Canada did not have a central bank during the period studied, it is instructive to examine the scope that an appropriately endowed monetary authority might have to influence the balance of payments. Consider, for example, a domestic central bank that holds gold and issues reserves in the form of central bank deposits to the domestic banking system. One could argue that a reduction of commercial bank reserves by this central bank (through, say, rediscount policy) causes the banking system to contract credit and reduce its note and deposit liabilities. The public is forced to sell assets in the international market to maintain money holdings at the desired level, bringing gold into the coffers of the central bank. If domestic residents hold a larger fraction of their wealth in domestic assets than do foreign residents, the effect of a balanced reduction in the size of domestic private nonmonetary asset holdings is to create an excess supply of domestic assets in the world capital market. This would lead to a rise in domestic relative to foreign interest rates. An inflow of capital is associated with a rise in domestic relative to foreign interest rates in much the same fashion as implied by the traditional classical theory.

It should be noted, however, that the interest-rate differential is determined simultaneously with the inflow of capital and does not cause it. The inflow of gold, moreover, occurs even if domestic and foreign assets are perfect substitutes and domestic interest rates are therefore unaffected.

A crucial assumption underlying this analysis is that the private sector either cannot or will not adjust its gold holdings on private account to

[15] See Marr and Percy (1978).
[16] By encouraging settlers to move onto lands before they were privately profitable, the government stimulated and intensified competition to a degree that eroded the potential rents to be captured from these lands for some years to come. See Southey (1978).
[17] See Mercer (1982).
[18] See Paterson (1976).

compensate for the change in the amount of gold the government is forcing it to hold on public account. Were this not the case, the nation's gold holdings would be constant at some equilibrium level and independent of central bank policy.

To incorporate these considerations formally into the portfolio model, national gold stocks must be included as additional items in domestic and foreign portfolios and in the domestic and foreign asset utility functions. Two additional world portfolio equilibrium equations must be added to the group (9.11) through (9.16) to determine the quantity of gold held on combined private and public account by each country's residents. The world gold stock would appear as an argument in all eight reduced form asset equilibrium equations. If a country's residents do not regard privately and publicly held gold as equivalent, the fraction of the national gold stock held on public account must also appear as an argument in the asset utility function, and hence, in the reduced form asset equilibrium equations.

An accumulation of gold by the central bank, without any change in private gold holdings, requires a private sale of nonmonetary assets to foreigners. Domestic residents on combined public and private account are being forced to hold a greater fraction of domestic wealth in noninterest-bearing gold and a lower fraction in interest earning assets. Since portfolio mixes tend to be biased toward home assets, this reduction in the nongold asset holdings of domestic residents is composed of a higher proportion of domestic assets than foreigners are willing to acquire at the existing domestic/foreign interest-rate differential. Domestic asset prices fall and the market interest rates on domestic assets rise.[19]

Even if this line of analysis were pursued to the limit, however, the classical price-specie-flow mechanism could not be validated. Government gold holdings would appear in the domestic interest rate and the demand for money equations. Changes in these official gold holdings would have simultaneous effects on the equilibrium level of domestic money holdings

[19] A model that approached this problem in terms of modern consumption-based asset pricing theory would lead to the interpretation of domestic/foreign interest-rate differentials as resulting from the covariance structure of domestic and foreign asset returns. Central bank policies involving changes in gold reserves and attendant adjustments of private asset holdings would affect international interest-rate differentials to the extent that they change this covariance structure. Since the effects of these policies on the covariance structure are by no means obvious, there is little reason to believe that an extension of the theory in this direction would strengthen the case for central bank control over interest rates in an open economy. Indeed, in a modern stochastic intertemporal framework any nonrandom central bank policy is a process or procedure rather than a series of distinct one-period policy actions.

and, via the domestic real interest rate and investment, on the equilibrium level of domestic prices. The balance-of-payments surplus, however, remains equal to some fraction of the rate of growth of the public's desired money holdings. It is not "financed" by an increase in exports relative to imports induced by the effects of gold movements on domestic prices. Changes in official gold holdings lead to some change in the balance of trade and hence in the net international flow of capital, but the change in gold stock is a once-and-for-all stock adjustment whereas changes in the trade balance and net capital flow are a permanent adjustment of equilibrium flows. Depending on how the desired rate of money growth is affected, a change in the continuous flow of gold between the domestic and foreign economies may also occur, but the change in the balance of trade does not normally equal either the one-shot gold transfer or the change, if one occurs, in the continuous gold flow.

As long as domestic and foreign assets are not perfect substitutes in portfolios, the authorities can affect the level of prices and induce a one-shot change in the domestic stocks of money and gold by expanding and contracting domestic credit.[20] There is no one-way causal relationship, however, running from gold to money to prices as the traditional classical theory postulates. To the extent that these variables are simultaneously determined, the interrelationship between them bears no resemblance to the traditional price-specie-flow mechanism.

The above argument is not relevant to the Canadian economy in the period under study. Not only did Canada not have a central bank, but the government did not conduct monetary policy in a way that would make the argument valid. The Canadian government held stocks of gold to back its Dominion note liabilities but there is no evidence that it varied these gold holdings with a view to affecting domestic interest rates and the balance of payments. By prohibiting the chartered banks from issuing bank notes in denominations under five dollars and forcing them to hold reserves of Dominion notes, it undoubtedly had some effect on domestic interest rates, but this policy was really a tax policy and not a monetary policy.[21]

---

[20] This possibility should not be confused with the argument made by Rich (1988, chapter 3) that the government was able to exercise discretionary monetary policy before 1880. That argument was discussed in chapter 8 above, and essentially reduces to an argument about the composition of the money supply and monetary base. The argument in the present context implies only the theoretical possibility of limited discretion based on imperfect substitutability of domestic for foreign assets.

[21] Rich (1988) points out that the government did attempt on occasion to manipulate the backing of its notes to get more of them into circulation and economize on the cost of

It must be concluded that one cannot construct the classical price-specie-flow mechanism from basic assumptions of wealth maximization combined with the usual income and wealth constraints. The traditional classical theory, except where it rules out capital movements entirely, is an ad hoc construction not based on fundamental principles. Allowance for imperfect capital mobility, for which considerable historical evidence exists, in no way reduces the validity of this conclusion. Only in the case of perfect capital *immobility*, a case surely ruled out by the historical context being examined, is it possible to visualize the price-specie-flow mechanism as a logical extension of the model presented in this study.[22]

Appendix: Perfect capital immobility

In the perfect immobility case, when international movements of private capital other than gold are restricted so that aggregate capital movements cannot respond to market forces, the traditional price-specie-flow mechanism is a logical extension of the portfolio model. Under these conditions, $Q_d = Q_f = 1$, and the asset utility functions become

$$U\ (m,\ Y_K,\ Y_L) \tag{9.A.1}$$

$$U^*\ (m^*,\ Y_K^*,\ Y_L^*) \tag{9.A.2}$$

from which separate equations determining domestic and foreign interest rates can be derived:

$$i\ =\ A(m,\ Y_K,\ Y_L) \tag{9.A.3}$$

$$i^*\ =\ A^*(m^*,\ Y_K^*,\ Y_L^*) \tag{9.A.4}$$

By rearranging terms and assuming the permanent income streams from labor and capital in each country are functions of current income, these equations can be transformed into conventional demand for money functions of the form

servicing the public debt. The view taken here, however, differs from his in that he believes that the government practiced this economy by exercising a power to print money, whereas the government's behavior and potential influence on the interest rate is only the result of forcing the community to make an interest-free loan.

[22] See the Appendix following Chapter 9 for the details of this extreme case.

$$M/P = L(r + E_p, Y) \tag{9.A.5}$$

$$M^*/P^* = L^*(r^* + E_p^*, Y^*) \tag{9.A.6}$$

The usual relationship between nominal and real interest rates and the expected rate of inflation is substituted into (9A.5) and (9A.6).

The restrictions on capital mobility also impose a flow constraint. Domestic savings must equal domestic investment plus the flow of additions to the domestic gold stock. This reduces equation (3.5) to

$$dG/dt = P_T(T - T_C - T_I) \tag{9.A.7}$$

where the debt service balance is assumed equal to zero and dG/dt is the rate of growth of the domestic gold stock. The identity of total receipts and payments – equation (3.1) – becomes

$$P_U U + P_T T = P_U U_C + P_T T_C + I + dG/dt \tag{9.A.8}$$

Ignoring terms of trade changes and problems of aggregation, $(P_U U + P_T T)$ is expressed as Y and $(P_U U_C + P_T T_C)$ as the level of consumption, denoted by C and expressed as a function of Y. Within the spirit of the model in Chapter 3, the level of investment is expressed as a function of the domestic real interest rate and the portmanteau variable Ω. Using these relationships, (9A.8) becomes

$$Y = C(Y) + I(r, \Omega) + dG/dt \tag{9.A.9}$$

Using (9A.7) and expressing the balance of trade as a function of domestic income and the ratio of domestic to foreign prices, (9A.9) can be written

$$Y = C(Y) + I(r, \Omega) + B_T(Y, P/P^*) \tag{9.A.10}$$

Equation (9A.10) joins with the domestic demand for money function (9A.5) to solve for r and either P or Y, depending on whether fixed or flexible wages and prices are postulated. Exogenous changes in the level of the domestic money supply or shifts in the domestic demand function for money lead to changes in the domestic price level which in turn lead to a change in the trade balance. This causes gold to flow into or out of the domestic economy. Prices rise or fall, gradually driving the domestic price level back into line with the price level abroad. The model described is thus essentially the same as the traditional classical model.

Note that validity of the classical model requires a comprehensive restriction on private international transactions in capital, not zero substitutability of domestic and foreign assets in portfolios. Zero substitutability in portfolios means that asset holders choose to hold domestic and foreign assets in fixed proportions. It does not mean that they are unable to buy and sell domestic and foreign assets in the international market. The zero capital mobility case is not the limiting case where domestic and foreign assets become poorer and poorer substitutes in portfolios.

10. "Canada's balance of indebtedness": reinterpreting the historical evidence

Over the 1870–1913 period international trade in goods, factors of production, and assets exposed Canada to both long- and short-term external shocks. The long-term shocks were mainly real shocks associated with the inflow of long-term capital encouraged by the expected profitability of Canadian production and exports. Such shocks typically occurred during the upward phase of long swings driven by inverse changes in relative economic opportunity on opposite sides of the Atlantic (Thomas, 1973). Short-term shocks, usually associated with business cycles, were sometimes accentuated by these same real forces, but also appear to have been partly monetary in origin (Bordo, 1985; Rich, 1988). As Thomas (1973) and Chambers (1964) have demonstrated, Canada participated in an Atlantic economy and experienced the world business cycle in close association with the United States, and to a lesser extent, with Great Britain. Caves and Holton (1961, p. 77) have emphasized "the consistency between the long-run model implied by staple theory and the historic chronicle of short period income changes."

Given the widely acknowledged vulnerability of the small open economy to external shocks, the substantial economic progress of the pre-World War I period that economic historians have now documented may seem remarkable or even fortuitous. The present book makes no claim to have uncovered the mainsprings of economic growth in this context, but the smoothly functioning balance-of-payments adjustment mechanism that our research has uncovered must have contributed something to this favorable growth outcome. Without this mechanism at least some of the gains from trade would have been offset. We do not purport to provide a complete theory of the transmission of external shocks to the Canadian economy nor to have provided the only theory consistent with their transmission, but we do claim to have exposed the mechanism of adjustment in the balance of payments that smoothly accommodated some of the forces commonly thought to have been important engines of growth and/or sources of business fluctuation.

147

How then did the open Canadian economy absorb the external shocks to which it was so vulnerable during the early years of growth? In this chapter we provide an historical account of some of the main episodes of shock and show how, according to our theory and evidence, the balance of payments smoothly adjusted. In no small way, we believe, this smooth functioning helps to account for the durability of the gold standard regime in Canada before 1914 and to demonstrate its consistency with the growth priorities of this era.

Finally, as an observation on the history of economic thought, it appears that the key problem of how to address the role of prices in balance-of-payments adjustment under conditions of international capital mobility, the crux of the theory we present, was first perceived by Frank Taussig, but left curiously unresolved by his famous student, Jacob Viner.

The nineteenth century: 1871–1895

Recent statistical work by Urquhart (1986) and others indicates a turning point in Canada's economic growth around the mid-1890s (Figure 4.4). In this section we treat the early period and in the next section the 1900–13 period analyzed by Viner (1924).

In the early period, growth was based on intensive developments in the central part of the country while attempted settlement of the West was largely a failure. Territorial expansion of agriculture was limited before western settlement began and there was no acceleration in the exports of farm and forest products. Under the National Policy manufacturing growth was encouraged by tariffs and subsidies, contributing to urban growth and structural change that favored industry relative to primary activities (Bertram, 1963; McDougall, 1971, 1973; Green and Urquhart, 1987). Net capital formation included residential construction to house urban growth, industrial plant and equipment to accommodate the growing scale of industry, and railroad construction, in particular the Canadian Pacific Railway, that fed expectations of the forthcoming boom in the West (Pomfret, 1981a).

Over this nineteenth-century subperiod, the Canadian economy was connected to the rest of the world by sales of wheat and forest products to Great Britain and the United States, imports of finished goods and producer durables increasingly from the United States rather than Great Britain, and capital and labor imports mainly from Britain. As indicated in Figure 10.1, in all but a few years the trade balance was negative and a modest net

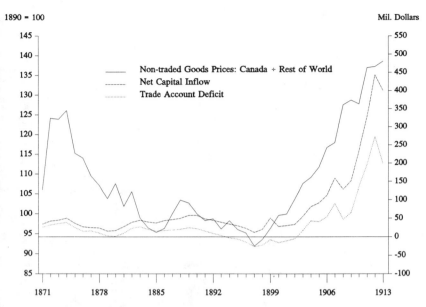

Figure 10.1. Relative nontraded goods prices and the net capital inflow, 1871–1913. Source: Appendixes A and C.

capital inflow occurred. In the early years of industrialization there were significant imports of industrial inputs to be combined with Canadian resources, but it is unlikely that these were enough to cancel the net increase in the aggregate demand for Canadian resources occasioned by capital inflow when the latter was growing.[1]

Within the 1871–95 subperiod there were two long swings involving capital and labor migration linked to domestic capital formation as well as a number of shorter business cycles (Buckley, 1952, 1963; Chambers, 1964). The first long swing rose to a peak in the early 1870s and the second peaked in the late 1880s. Both peaks coincided with reference cycle peaks in 1873 and 1887 identified by Chambers (1964, p. 406). The first peak fed expectations of the promise of Confederation. The decline that followed prompted a protective reaction within the framework of National Policy. The second peak followed United States resumption of the gold standard. In each case there was a relative decline in economic opportunity in Great Britain that helped to stimulate a movement of people and capital

---

[1] The importance of this issue to the mechanism of adjustment is recognized above in Chapter 5, as well as by Caves (1961, p. 88) and by Viner (1924, part 2).

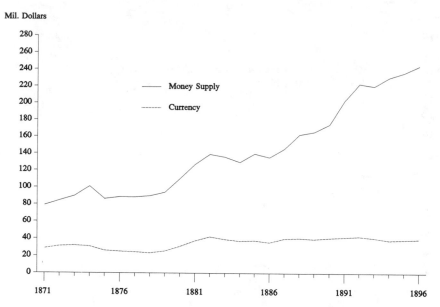

Figure 10.2. The nominal money supply and currency holdings of the public: Canada, 1871–1913. Source: Appendix A.

toward North America (Thomas, 1973, p. 256; Marr and Paterson, 1980, p. 280).

The prosperity of the early post-Confederation years was reflected in rising gross immigration, railroad building, and urban construction, substantially funded from foreign savings. As net capital inflow rose, pressure on Canadian resources was evident in the rising relative prices of nontraded goods, also shown in Figure 10.1. As the production costs of exports rose and the consumption costs of imports fell, a trade deficit resulted that matched (and financed) the capital inflow.[2]

The resulting price level changes created an excess demand for money. Part of this excess demand was met by sales of foreign assets on the world market and reflected in an increase of gold and liquid foreign assets in the banking system as portfolio holders exchanged the proceeds of their sales for domestic money. Bank notes and deposits increased (Figure 10.2) as the number of bank branches and the amount of bank capital rose. Bank note issue, limited only by paid up bank capital, was sensitive to business demand. These combined responses made it unnecessary for Canada to

---

[2] The notion of the capital account driving the current account is also supported by U.S. evidence (Thomas, 1973, p. 271).

experience the gold inflows Viner (1924) believed were needed to produce the price effects he observed after 1900. In this early expansion, reserve ratios fell (Figure 4.11) as bank notes had not expanded to the level where 100 percent gold backing was required, and no reserves were required against deposits.

The downswing to 1879 was equally marked. A vigorous upswing in Great Britain led by shipbuilding and new construction drastically reduced the Canadian trade deficit and the associated net capital inflow from Britain (Thomas, 1973, p. 268). At the same time, the relative prices of Canadian nontraded goods fell. The excess demand for money was reduced, bank expansion slowed and the rise in the money stock moderated (Figure 10.2) (Bloomfield, 1968, p. 25). Little gold was lost from Canada as banks continued to adjust their reserve ratios downward (Rich, 1988). Gross immigration, capital formation, and residential construction all declined in Canada (Thomas, 1973, p. 257).

The upswing came after the launching of the National Policy in 1879 and coincided with a dampening of activity in Britain and on the European continent (Kindleberger, 1987, p.22). Although Canada followed the United States in experiencing two minor cycles in the 1880s, there was a basic upswing in North American investment before the Baring Crisis of 1890 (Thomas, 1973, pp. 274–5; Kindleberger, 1984, pp. 224–5). Once again capital and labor migrated toward Canada from Great Britain, both before and after the completion of the Canadian Pacific Railway in 1885 (Thomas, 1973, p. 257). The completion of the railroad led to an induced demand for capital in manufacturing and agriculture (Paterson, 1976, p. 24).

Starting in the mid-1880s there are distinct price movements indicative of the resource market pressure derived from the net capital inflow that swelled aggregate demand (Figure 10.1). Canadian nontraded goods prices rose relative to traded goods prices and relative to nontraded goods prices in the rest of the world (Figure 4.3). As before, these price movements produced the trade deficit required to finance the net capital inflow and prompted banks and private wealth-holders to expand the money supply in the ways already described when the excess demand reappeared (Figure 10.2). The primary reserve ratio continued to fall in the 1880s as the limit to fractionally backed bank note issue was raised and issue expanded toward the limit (Figure 4.11).[3]

---

[3] The limit began to be exceeded by the mid-1880s and the decline in the primary reserve ratio halted. Bank note issue was henceforward 100 percent backed by gold and/or Dominion notes convertible into gold (Rich, 1988).

In Britain the bottom of the long swing came early in 1891 after the Baring Crisis in the wake of disastrous investments in Argentina. Britain's home investment then began an upswing until the late 1890s while capital formation in the periphery, including Canada, was relatively depressed (Thomas, 1973, pp. 276–80; Thorp, 1926, pp. 300–01). Construction and shipbuilding boomed in Great Britain almost until the turn of the century. Net capital flows reversed to such an extent that Canada briefly experienced a trade balance surplus in the mid–1890s (Figure 10.1).

This downturn relieved the pressure on resource markets in Canada. The prices of Canada's nontraded goods relative to the prices of traded goods and the prices of nontraded goods elsewhere declined (Figures 10.1 and 4.3). The upward trend of the terms of trade that had existed from the beginning of our study period disappeared from this point onward (Figure 4.6). Money was in excess supply rather than excess demand, and the rate of increase in the money supply fell as the expansion of banks and Dominion notes slowed and private wealth-holders purchased assets abroad (Figure 10.2). Gold inflows fell (Figure 4.13) and reserve ratios no longer declined (Figure 4.11).

An important aspect of the interaction between Great Britain and what Thomas calls the "periphery" in this story is the changing relative participation of Canada and the United States within North America before and after 1896. Whereas the United States throughout the period absorbed far more migrants than did Canada and was nearly self-sufficient in capital, Canada experienced net outmigration in the late nineteenth century and substantially greater capital inflow from Great Britain in the twentieth century than in earlier years (Green and Urquhart, 1976). Many migrants to Canadian farms before 1900 resettled somewhat later in the United States, some returning to Canada after 1900 to swell the ranks of new migrants (Buckley, 1963; Thomas, 1973, p. 280). About a third of British lending abroad went to Canada before 1914 (Edelstein, 1982, p. 287). The early twentieth century best exemplifies how the economy performed in the face of a major real shock emanating principally from the net inflow of long-term capital.

The twentieth century: 1896–1913

An important break in the Canadian accumulation pattern immediately prior to 1900 has been widely acknowledged (Buckley, 1955, p. 5; Edelstein, 1982, p. 272; Urquhart, 1986, p. 60). A conjunction of circum-

stances, including a shift in prairie settlement opportunities and a rise in
the world price of wheat, undoubtedly accounts for this (Buckley, 1955,
p. 5; Dick, 1980; Edelstein, 1982, pp. 276ff). At the same time, British
population increase peaked in the first half of the 1890s and British capital
formation peaked in the last five years of the century (Thomas, 1967,
p. 21). The Atlantic economy was about to begin another long swing
sending people and capital from Great Britain toward the periphery and
to Canada in particular (Thomas, 1973, p. 257). Real GNP per capita rose
faster in Canada than in the rest of world after 1895 (Figure 4.4).

There is little doubt that extraordinarily favorable expectations of growth
were created in early twentieth-century Canada, generating an investment
demand well in excess of domestic savings (Edelstein, 1982, p. 286).
These expectations were fed by government publicity in Great Britain and
by the flotation of large public debt at all levels of government as well as
by the growth in population and more favorable terms of trade (Buckley,
1955, chapter 5).[4] Notable results of this process were two further major
transcontinental railroad projects destined to become a public corporation,
the Canadian National Railways, in the 1920s. Virtually all public utility,
railroad, and government securities were sold abroad (Buckley, 1955,
p. 67). This optimism may have been created by the prospect of wheat
sales, and certainly coincided with extensive prairie settlement, but it was
well in advance of the major surge in wheat exports that came only after
1910 (Caves and Holton, 1961, p. 95; Ankli, 1980).

Western prospects were by no means the only ones that attracted external
funds. British direct investment went into natural resource industries such
as land, mining, timber, and oil, and into finance, distribution, utilities,
and manufacturing widely dispersed throughout the country (Paterson,
1976, chapter 3; Field, 1912). Although British firms established almost
no branch plants, British savings far exceeded American savings in meeting
Canada's investment demand. Less than half the capital invested in manufacturing was held by American interests.

About two-thirds of domestic capital formation before 1914 was supplied

---

[4] Whereas it is inconceivable that Canadian trade was sufficiently large relative to world
consumption and production of traded goods for Canada to have any effect on the terms
of trade, it may be noted that the terms of trade began to turn against Canada in 1909
before the capital inflow had peaked (Figures 4.2 and 4.6). Thomas (1967, pp. 26–9) also
notes that the terms of trade turn in favor of Britain starting in 1910 before British capital
exports have peaked. It may be that the terms of trade are here a general equilibrium
consequence of the redistribution of world savings and investment rather than a purely
exogenous factor generating expectations.

out of foreign savings. The other third, largely residential construction driven by population growth, came from domestic savings channeled through insurance companies into urban mortgage securities which the banks were prohibited from holding (Buckley, 1955, chapter 6). The domestic savings rate did show a substantial rise after 1900 (Edelstein, 1982, pp. 282–3).

The movement in relative prices that followed 1896 gives the clearest demonstration before 1914 of the pressure on Canadian resources resulting from a net increase in aggregate demand associated with net capital inflow. The relative prices of nontraded goods moved sharply upward after 1897 with the exceptions of 1904 and 1909 when there were brief interruptions in the outflow of capital from Britain (Paterson, 1976, pp. 25–7). Not only did nontraded goods' prices move up against Canadian prices as a whole, but also against nontraded goods' prices elsewhere in the world (Figure 4.3). Interest rates rose in the United States, Great Britain, and Canada after the mid-1890s, with the Canadian long-term rate maintaining a risk premium over comparable UK rates (Figure 4.14).[5]

These price movements are what created the trade deficit sufficient to finance the unprecedented inflow of capital coincident with the investment boom. At the same time, they prompted the banking system and wealth-holders to match the excess demand for money by expanding capital and selling securities abroad. Except in 1907–08, the money supply rose sharply (Figure 4.7), whereas gold inflows were sharply higher except in 1909–10 (Figure 4.13). Dominion notes and bank deposits assumed greater importance and reserve ratios rose (Figures 4.7 and 4.11). By now the limits of unsecured note issue had been reached.

The financial crisis that began in New York in 1907 illustrates another type of disturbance that affected Canada and to which the balance of payments was able to adjust smoothly (Schwartz, 1986, p. 15). It appears that there was no significant relationship between seasonal variations in the balance of trade and in the balance-of-payments surplus. A rise in world interest rates at the time led to a reduction in the demand for money balances in Canada and downward pressure on chartered bank reserves (Rich, 1989). The banks were relieved from having to reduce loans to

---

[5] From a somewhat wider Imperial perspective, Edelstein (1982, p. 281) suggests that British investors may not have been very risk averse in this case. Had it been otherwise, he concludes, Britain's capital export might have been smaller and the risk premium higher. This is consistent with Paterson's (1976) finding that many British investments in Canada were less than spectacularly profitable.

maintain reserves by a government advance of Dominion notes against the collateral of high-grade securities. The alternative, given capital mobility, would have been for banks to reduce loans during the crop moving season leading exporters to sell securities abroad and to convert the borrowed funds into Canadian dollars to provide the desired inflow of bank reserves. As it was, the government and banks worked together to avoid a massive portfolio adjustment. In fact, in this instance Canada was able to act as a lender of last resort to the New York money market (Rich, 1988, p. 178).

The evolution of economic thought

Economic thinking about balance-of-payments adjustment under the gold standard has evolved slowly. It was early recognized that events after 1870 did not fit comfortably into a price-specie-flow framework, yet a satisfying new theory of adjustment did not develop. Unable to find the proper sequence of gold flows, price changes, and trade balance adjustments in American data, Taussig (1927, p. 239) observed, "it must be confessed that here we have phenomena not fully understood. In part our information is insufficient; in part our understanding of other connected topics is in- adequate" (Flanders, 1989, pp. 233–6).

The price-specie-flow theory had emerged in the eighteenth century when there was little if any distinction between the balance of trade and the balance of payments. The large-scale overseas lending that began in the 1880s presented the theory with a challenge very unlike the world that had originally generated the theory. It is little wonder that Taussig, referring to traditional theory, complained.

The point that is less familiar, in connection with the theory of the subject, or at all events is not commonly considered, is the closeness and rapidity with which the varying balance of payments has found its expression in the varying balance of trade. The actual merchandise movements seem to have been adjusted to the shifting balance of payments with surprising exactness and speed. The process which our theory contemplates – the initial flow of specie when there is a burst of loans; the fall in prices in the lending country and rise in the borrowing country; the eventual increased movement of merchandise out of the one and into the other – all this can hardly be expected to take place smoothly and quickly. Yet no signs of disturbance are to be observed such as the theoretical analysis premises; and some recurring phenomena are of a kind not contemplated by theory at all. Most noticeable of all is the circumstance that periods of active lending have been characterized by rising prices rather than falling prices, and that the export of goods apparently has taken place not in conjunction with a cheapening of goods in the lending country, but in spite of the fact that its goods have seemed dearer at times of great capital export. (1927, p. 239)

Taussig had stumbled on the same features of the data that we have uncovered in studying the Canadian balance-of-payments data generated by the gold standard era.

As we showed in Chapter 2, neither Viner nor his critics allowed their discomfort with certain features of the evidence to persuade them to give up their adherence to the traditional price-specie-flow doctrine. Instead, they preoccupied themselves with the largely extraneous issue of whether capital flows were autonomous, as Viner said they were, or endogenous as his critics seemed bent on proving. Viner (1937, pp. 430–1) eventually conceded the point, and Kindleberger (1987, p. 11) concludes simply that it is now a settled matter that "the boom in Canada attracted the capital, rather than the capital produced the boom." Not until Caves and Holton (1961) and Ankli (1980) did it begin to be realized that the boom and the inflow were both simultaneously the consequence of a third group of factors – whatever generated favorable expectations in Canada to an extent that drove investment demand above domestic savings. As a result, the traditional theory was, for many years, simply patched up to try to cover circumstances for which it was never intended. Even Taussig (1927, p. 235) did not allow his doubts to penetrate the work of his pupil, Viner, and concluded about the Canadian case that "it is rare that the possibility of verifying the deductions of theory is found so successfully." We have shown in this book, however, that this success was only skin deep and that international capital mobility made a crucial difference to the theoretical framework necessary to explain balance-of-payments adjustment in these circumstances.

In developing what can legitimately be called a "monetary approach to the balance of payments" and applying it to the Canadian case, the present study might be interpreted by some readers as either the same in concept as early models based on a monetary approach that were equivalent to the elasticities and absorption approaches, and/or resting on some unique feature of the Canadian historical experience. They would be wrong on both counts.

Error of the first kind is committed by Friedman and Schwartz (1982, p. 28), who argue that "the monetary theory of the balance of payments ... is logically equivalent to the price-specie-flow mechanism except that it makes different assumptions about the speed of adjustment of the several variables." After describing how this works, they admit to oversimplification from failing to consider capital flows, but without realizing how fundamental a difference this omission makes to a logically coherent theory. In the discussions they cite that address this deficiency (Frenkel and Johnson, 1976) it is made clear that the role of prices in the adjustment process when capital is internationally mobile is not a simple extension of Hume's original theory, much less an elaboration "logically equivalent to the price-specie-flow mechanism." But even in this collection of essays, notwithstanding the valuable contribution of McCloskey and Zecher, the implications of international capital mobility are not fully worked out. The elasticities, absorption, and monetary approaches to balance-of-payments adjustment are only equivalent if the balance of payments and the balance of trade are one and the same thing.

The possibility that the conclusions of this book may be biased by historical circumstances unique to Canada is a task for future research in other contexts to investigate. Canada was by no means alone on the periphery that interacted with London. The United States, Argentina, and Australia were also recipients of large capital inflows from Britain under the gold standard. Some studies of these countries, notably Thomas (1973) and Ford (1962), have uncovered evidence suggesting adjustment stories similar to Canada's. Preliminary work on Australia is even now revealing a well fitting application of the adjustment model used in this book. We, like Viner, believe Canada is a well chosen historical example of the phenomena we analyze.

We believe that the present study goes some way toward finally filling the gap left open by the "insufficiency" and "inadequacy" that discomforted Taussig over a half-century ago. It does so by hypothesizing a general equilibrium determination of the price level in a world of capital mobility and fixed exchange rates. In such a world it can no longer be said of a small open economy that domestic money determines the domestic price level; Taussig's doubts were not only ignored, they were also entirely justified.

11. Conclusions: How the gold standard worked

This monograph accomplishes three things: first, it presents a rigorous analysis of some aspects of an important period in Canadian monetary history; second, it tests a modern portfolio theory of balance-of-payments adjustment in a period admirably suited to the task; and third, it improves our understanding of how the international gold standard functioned. We conclude that the portfolio approach developed here better characterizes gold standard adjustment than the traditional price-specie-flow mechanism. We believe this approach not only explains Canadian balance-of-payments adjustment, but also has general merit for analyzing balance-of-payments adjustment and price level and exchange-rate determination under a gold standard and other types of fixed exchange-rate regimes.

Our results have implications for a number of outstanding questions about the gold-standard system. What was the role of sterilization? Why could the Bank of England, as the financial center of the system, operate on so few reserves? Why could the system not be effectively reconstituted after the War? The answers explain and reconcile many anomalies that, as Bordo (1984, 1986) notes, began to appear in the classical theory around the turn of the century. These ancillary hypotheses, most of which remain to be tested, suggest directions for future work.

The results of this study also support and extend the application of the so-called "monetary approach to the balance of payments." McCloskey and Zecher (1976) present one modern statement of this approach within the gold-standard framework. Their analysis relies on the efficiency of arbitrage in both commodity and asset markets. The portfolio theory developed in this present study lays primary emphasis on well functioning asset markets in a world where capital is internationally mobile. We maintain that commodity markets and prices adjusted without preserving purchasing-power parity, and in a manner consistent with the theoretical implications of capital mobility. The essential features of the monetary approach apply notwithstanding the lack of evidence of purchasing-power parity.

158

We conclude by reviewing in summary the statistical evidence and the inferences it supports, the implications of capital mobility for balance-of-payments adjustment and determination of interest rate differentials, the place of purchasing-power parity in the monetary approach to the balance of payments, and finally, our view as to how the gold standard really worked.

Review of the statistical evidence

Our statistical results are of two sorts – those that are consistent with both the portfolio theory and the standard price-specie-flow theory, and those that support the portfolio theory and are inconsistent with the traditional classical mechanism. No evidence inconsistent with the portfolio approach is found.

Capital inflows, relative prices, and the balance of trade

A key element in the portfolio theory developed in chapter 3 predicts a strong relationship between the net capital inflow and relative prices. Such a relationship is also a prediction of the traditional classical theory. The subsequent empirical work confirms this prediction. It is unquestionably the case that the massive flows of capital into Canada during the early part of this century were smoothly transferred in real terms by adjustments of the balance of trade. These adjustments were clearly brought about by a rise in the prices of Canadian nontraded goods relative to both internationally traded goods and nontraded goods abroad. Some of this relative price adjustment fell on the ratio of Canadian nontraded to traded goods prices, and some on the ratio of traded to nontraded goods abroad. In view of Canada's size, the effect on the ratio of traded to nontraded goods prices abroad was a consequence of the simultaneous flow of investment from Europe to other newly developing countries.

Contrary to Viner, no significant positive effect of the net capital inflow on the terms of trade is found. Although the terms of trade improved after 1900, a negative relationship with the capital inflow appears once the growth of real income is taken into account. These results are consistent with the possibility that Canada, as a minor producer and consumer of most internationally traded goods, had little influence on her terms of trade. Exogenous outside developments explain the observed terms of trade movements.

Money and asset market equilibrium relationships

A second element of the theory of chapter 3 found to be consistent with empirical evidence is a group of hypotheses about asset market behavior. Our findings relate to the demand for money, the currency/deposit ratio, and the reserve ratio of banks. There is considerable evidence of a developing financial system to which our theory applies.

The demand for money function fits the data well. The quantity of money demanded responds well to U.S. and U.K. short-term interest rates, a strong confirmation of the existence of a degree of capital mobility appropriate for the application of international portfolio theory. The fit is especially good for the subperiod 1890–1913 in that the Durbin–Watson statistics indicate no first-order serial correlation in the residuals – a rare occurrence in demand for money estimates. This is consistent with the maintained hypothesis that Canadian asset-holders adjusted their portfolios by freely exchanging money and nonmonetary assets in the international capital market.

Serial correlation is present in the residuals for the subperiod 1871–89. It appears, however, that some special forces operated during this subperiod that were not present in later years. Long-term interest rates fell substantially before 1890 in Canada and the United States relative to Great Britain. The income velocity of money fell much more steeply before 1895 than after, as did the primary reserve ratios of the chartered banks. This suggests that the early years of our sample were years of rapid development of the financial system. The public increased its reliance on money holdings, particularly deposits, and the chartered banks economized on noninterest-bearing reserves. These structural changes are evident in all the regressions pertaining to asset equilibrium. Not only do the demands for money estimates exhibit serial correlation in the residuals in the earlier period, but the estimating equations for the composition of the public's money holdings and the asset holdings of the chartered banks also fit poorly in those years.

The currency component of the public's money holdings is positively related to real income and negatively related to the long-term Canadian interest rate in the 1890–1913 subperiod. During the 1871–89 subperiod, it is positively related to real income but insignificantly related to the interest rate. The fit is considerably poorer in the earlier subperiod. The interest rate and real income coefficients in the estimating equation for the deposit component of money holdings are essentially the same as those in the demand function for money. In both the currency and the deposit equations there is serial correlation in the residuals before 1890 but not after. Since the interest elasticity of demand for currency is much lower than that for deposits, a rise in the interest rate is associated with an increase in the currency/deposit ratio.

The ratio of the chartered banks' primary reserve holdings to their note and deposit liabilities shows a weak negative relationship to short-term interest rates during both subperiods. In the earlier subperiod this ratio declines as the scale of the banking system expands. In the later subperiod it increases with the scale of the banking system. The secondary reserve ratio of the chartered banks shows the same pattern, with two exceptions – interest rates are significantly negatively related to the reserve ratio in both subperiods, and no significant scale effect is evident in the period before 1890. These differences in the effects of the scale of banking on the reserve ratios of the chartered banks strongly confirm that the structural development of the financial system was different before 1890.

As in the case of the evidence on capital inflows and relative prices, these statistical results are consistent with either the traditional classical price-specie-flow mechanism or the portfolio theory, but the progressive integration of Canada into world capital markets favors the latter. Foreign short-term interest rates work well in the demand functions for money, suggesting a degree of integration of the capital markets in Canada and abroad supportive of the portfolio theory but not the classical approach. If capital markets are integrated to this degree, it is impossible to derive the classical adjustment mechanism from the basic principles of portfolio maximization subject to the usual constraints.

Balance-of-payments adjustment

The third and most important element of our theory deals with the nature of the balance-of-payments adjustment process. Our statistical analyses of balance-of-payments adjustments decisively confirm the portfolio theory and reject the traditional price-specie-flow mechanism. The traditional analysis, for all fixed exchange rate regimes including the gold standard, seeks to establish that the balance of trade is responsive to relative price and income changes. It then argues that, since the trade balance is a component of the balance of payments, the balance-of-payments surplus must also respond to these relative price and income changes. Moreover since the balance of trade, short-term and long-term real capital flows are independent additive components of the balance of payments in the traditional specie-flow mechanism, the response coefficients of the balance of payments and balance of trade to relative prices and incomes must be the same if the traditional theory is true. Our statistical tests indicate that the evidence is overwhelmingly inconsistent with this implication, and consistent with the portfolio interpretation of independence between the international reserve flow and balance of trade.

In the portfolio approach, the balance-of-payments surplus represents a portfolio adjustment – an international exchange of assets – that brings the demand for money into line with the supply. If domestic residents hold too little money, they sell assets abroad, forcing the domestic banking system to accumulate gold and foreign exchange. The total flow of capital between Canada and the rest of the world is unaffected – only its composition changes. The nonbank public sells nonmonetary assets abroad and the banking system accumulates an equivalent amount of foreign exchange reserves. The overall net capital inflow from abroad is the same, with a larger fraction of it now in the form of gold and liquid foreign reserve assets and a smaller fraction held in nonmonetary assets by the nonbank public. A balance-of-payments surplus or deficit is thus strictly a capital account phenomenon, involving no change in autonomous exports and imports. The fact that the balance of trade responds to relative price and income changes has no bearing on balance-of-payments equilibrium.

A strong statistical relationship exists between domestic and foreign relative prices and real incomes and the balance of trade. Indeed, this is implied by the relationship found between the massive inflow of capital and the ratio of nontraded goods prices in Canada to nontraded goods prices abroad. But no significant response of the balance-of-payments surplus to relative prices or the domestic/foreign interest-rate differential is found and there is a weak response to domestic and foreign incomes. Because of the alleged response of short-term capital to interest-rate differentials, a positive relationship between the excess of Canadian over foreign interest rates and the balance-of-payments surplus should also be present. No such relationship is found.

The portfolio view that the balance-of-payments surplus equals the rate of change in the demand for money, or more specifically, in the rate of change in the factors that determine the demand for money, is clearly borne out by the data. When those variables that are important in determining the balance of payments under the portfolio theory are included with the traditional classical determinants of the balance-of-payments surplus, they dominate. When the variables that the classical theory deems important in determining the real reserve flow are added to the estimating equation derived from the portfolio theory their contribution to explaining the international reserve flow is insignificant.

The classical model fails because no satisfactory relationship can be found between the factors it says determine the balance-of-payments surplus and the size of that surplus. Relative prices and incomes are related to the trade balance as expected, but that is not enough. The approach cannot explain net capital movements. No strong relationship can be found between short-term capital flows and the differential between Canadian and foreign interest rates, and, though strong relationships between long-term capital flows and interest differentials are found, these relationships do not uniformly have the correct signs.

Temporal relationships between domestic and foreign money and prices

A fourth element of our view of the adjustment process, developed in Chapter 7, deals with the temporal relationships among prices, money, and real income in Canada and the rest of the world. An important result emerges from regressions of the rest of the world's price level on the Canadian money stock and real GNP. Given Canada's size, the classical theory of adjustment cannot explain the observed positive contemporaneous relationship between Canadian money and the rest of the world's price level, holding foreign money and real income constant. Under either theory, there is no possibility that the Canadian money supply could actually affect the price level abroad. In both theories, the increase in the foreign price level would have to result from a decline in the demand for money abroad because foreign money and real income are held constant in the regression. An increase in Canadian money holdings can occur under the classical theory only through the effect of the rise in foreign prices on the trade balance and the resulting flow of gold. Since these trade balance effects take time, a contemporaneous correlation is unlikely.

The portfolio theory easily explains the correlation between Canadian money and foreign prices, holding foreign money and real income constant. A decline in the demand for money abroad leads to an increase in the price level in Canada as well as abroad because Canadian prices are tied to foreign prices as a consequence of international capital mobility and real sector equilibrium. The resulting increase in the Canadian price level leads to an immediate accumulation of money balances by domestic residents through a sale of assets abroad as they maintain their real money holdings at the desired level.

The traditional classicist might respond by arguing that the reduction in the demand for money abroad lowers foreign interest rates and causes capital to flow into Canada, making gold flow in almost immediately without much change in the trade balance. This argument, however, effectively concedes the case. Such instantaneous adjustment is implied by the portfolio theory, which can be derived from basic maximization principles while the classical theory that capital flows respond to interest-rate differentials cannot.

Evidence of Viner and his critics

We also find that the work of Viner and his critics, on careful reading, tends to support the portfolio theory rather than the classical approach. Viner cannot find much evidence that the gold and secondary reserves of the chartered banks are the driving force behind domestic money creation. In fact, he argues at a number of points that the expansion of chartered bank note and deposit liabilities appears to result from the demand for such instruments on the part of the Canadian public rather than from the expansion of bank reserves. The banks seem to adjust their reserve positions to provide protection for their current liabilities (1924, pp. 174–8). This is, of course, precisely what our portfolio theory predicts. Viner's reconciliation of the evidence with the classical theory on the asset side appears forced; the puzzle does not quite fit together. His critics, Angell and others, dwell on this but make little headway because they have no alternative theory to explain the ease with which adjustment occurs in the absence of any apparent pressure of reserves on the money supply. The portfolio adjustment approach provides this alternative.

Viner's evidence fits the portfolio theory well. The only exception is his conclusion that the chartered banks do not use domestic loan policy to bring about adjustments in their reserve ratios – a necessary condition for the portfolio theory to hold. On this point, fifty years of history since Viner's study suggest that his interpretation of the evidence, consisting almost entirely of statements by bankers, is wrong. Cairncross (1968, p. 170) uncovers evidence in the *Canada Gazette* that the chartered banks tighten their loan policies to protect their reserves when the situation requires. As he states, it is difficult to believe that banks, either past or present, meet "all deserving requests for credit" when their reserves are slipping away.

Timing and causality

Another obvious test of the portfolio theory against the traditional one is a causality or timing test. Portfolio theory maintains that an increase in the Canadian money supply is a response to an increase in demand for money resulting from the effect of an inflow of capital and expansion of domestic investment on the price level. The traditional theory, as modified by Viner, maintains that the rise in prices is due to the expansion of the money supply resulting from the net capital inflow. According to the traditional theory, changes in money precede changes in prices; according to portfolio theory, changes in prices precede or are contemporaneous with changes in money. It turns out that no significant lagged effects can be found in the data.

In summary, the combined evidence emerging from our statistical work and the controversies stimulated by Viner support the international portfolio adjustment theory. Although some of the evidence is also consistent with the traditional specie-flow theory, the behavior of the balance of payments decisively rejects that theory. This is an important conclusion because it resolves a major conflict between theory and empirical evidence that has obscured a proper understanding of the gold standard for over half a century.

The determinants of interest-rate differentials when capital is internationally mobile

The interpretation to be put on interest-rate differentials among countries depends crucially on whether or not capital is free to move in response to perceived differences in investment opportunities unmatched by local savings. When there is complete freedom, we may say there is perfect mobility of capital only if domestic and foreign assets are perfect substitutes. In that case, there would be no interest-rate differentials. There may be only imperfect mobility, however, even when there is complete freedom to trade assets internationally. In this case, interest-rate differentials emerge as part of a general equilibrium to reflect risk premiums that make domestic and foreign assets imperfect substitutes.

The pervasive practice (in both traditional classical and more recent models) of treating international capital movements as a function of the differential between domestic and foreign interest rates implicitly imposes a constraint on international trade in asset stocks, while at the same time allowing for trade in asset flows. It imposes a friction that prevents assets from moving internationally at an instant of time, but allows stocks to change through time at a rate that increases with the differential between domestic and foreign interest rates. Because asset movements are constrained, domestic and foreign interest rates are determined by local asset market conditions – asset markets in the individual countries are not directly linked in a worldwide market.

This approach cannot be sustained. Anyone who wants to purchase assets from foreigners can do so as long as international trade in assets is not prohibited by the actions of government. The situation is analogous to international trade in goods. Imports or exports of certain goods may be restricted but trade nevertheless takes place freely subject to the constraints imposed by the restrictions. When asset holders are free to hold assets in foreign countries, world market pressure establishes an interest rate on each domestic and foreign security appropriate for the perceived risk of holding it. This vector of interest rates already reflects any restrictions on trade in particular assets. Domestic/foreign interest-rate differentials are thus determined by the world market's perception of differences in risk. Interest rates are high or low in a particular country relative to the rest of the world because that country's assets are perceived as more or less risky than assets abroad. Capital does not flow between countries in response to these differences in interest rates. On the contrary, differences in interest rates reflect the market's evaluation of the assets. It is the tendency of capital to want to move that causes changes in interest-rate differentials. Models that incorporate capital movements as a function of international differentials in interest rates are thus inconsistent with the principles of wealth maximization.

Nevertheless, there are conditions under which one might possibly observe a correlation between interest-rate differentials and international gold flows. Suppose, for example, that the Bank of England tightens domestic credit by reducing its rediscounts to the banking system. The decline in bank reserves forces an incipient reduction in the money supply leading British residents to sell assets abroad to maintain their money holdings at the desired level. Gold flows in. British asset-holders undoubtedly hold a bigger fraction of their assets in British securities than foreign asset-holders do. The proportion of U.K. assets in the mix of assets that British residents are trying to sell will thus be greater than the proportion of U.K. assets in the mix that foreigners are trying to buy, leading to an excess supply of U.K. securities on the international market. Where British and foreign assets are not perfect substitutes, a rise in interest rates in the United Kingdom relative to the rest of the world is necessary to maintain world asset equilibrium.

Note that the gold inflow and the rise in British interest rates occur simultaneously as a result of the tightening of credit by the Bank of England. The rise in domestic interest rates does not "cause" the gold inflow. If British and foreign securities were perfect substitutes, gold would flow in without a change in interest rates.

There are reasons to expect that, in fact, Bank of England policy should have had little observable effect on interest-rate differentials, even if British and foreign assets were not very good substitutes. Changes in the stocks of gold and other short-term foreign exchange assets held by the Bank of England appear to have been very small in relation to the total stock of nonmonetary assets held by British residents. Perhaps 15 percent of national income represented a return of nonhuman capital. At the going long-term interest rate of around 3 percent, this implies a stock of nonhuman wealth on the order of five times national income. The average year-to-year absolute change in the British nominal money supply (M3 definition) over the whole period 1871–1913 was less than 0.3 percent of nonhuman wealth so measured. Accordingly, the average absolute change in gold and other foreign exchange reserve assets as a result of Bank of England policy must have been an even smaller percentage of nonhuman wealth. It is therefore hard to believe that changes in Bank of England rediscounting could bring about any empirically significant portfolio shift, considered in relation to nonmonetary wealth as a whole. Significant changes in British relative to foreign interest rates would therefore probably not be required to get world asset-holders to absorb this portfolio shift. Even if British and foreign assets were not good substitutes, the data would be unlikely to show any statistically significant relationship between gold and foreign exchange reserve flows and relative interest rates. Any such relationship would be swamped by the interest-rate effects of other exogenous forces – changes in investor expectations, shifts in the domestic and foreign demand for money functions, and shifts in the desired reserve ratios of the domestic and foreign banking systems.

The intuition of earlier researchers that a significant relationship between capital flows and interest-rate differentials should exist is based on the theory that short-term capital flows represent an aggregate of individual portfolio responses to a change in relative domestic and foreign interest rates, holding risk constant. This aggregation involves a fallacy of composition. Individual asset-holders might well respond vigorously to differences in interest rates that do not reflect their perceived risk differentials. Nevertheless, interest rates always reflect the risk perceptions of wealth-holders in the aggregate. Thus, there can be no "aggregate" response to differentials in interest rates.

In the Canadian case, a positive relationship between the ratio of domestic to foreign interest rates and the balance-of-payments surplus would appear only if three conditions had been met: (1) changes in the public's desired money holdings or the reserve holdings of chartered banks were large in relation to the existing stock of domestic assets; (2) Canadian and foreign assets were poor substitutes in portfolios; and (3) these interest effects were not offset by the effects on interest rates of the accelerating investment expansion after the mid–1890s. The shift of world investment to Canada from other countries may well have required a risk premium to compensate foreign investors for increasing substantially the fraction of their wealth held in Canadian assets.

The average year-to-year absolute changes in money and reserve holdings as a percent of nominal GNP over the 1871–1913 period were 3 and 1.5 percent respectively. If nonhuman wealth were also five times income in Canada, the average year-to-year absolute changes in nominal money and bank reserve holdings would have been only 0.6 and 0.3 percent, respectively, of nonhuman wealth. (These figures are higher than the corresponding ones for Britain because of the very substantial growth in Canada in both output and financial assets during the period.) It is thus not surprising that no statistical relationship between the interest-rate differential and the balance-of-payments surplus can be found.

A significant corollary of this understanding of interest-rate differentials combined with Canadian circumstances is that those differentials observed between Canadian rates and rates in the rest of the world cannot be understood outside the framework of a portfolio model of balance-of-payments adjustment. This is because capital was free to move between Canada and the rest of the world and investors demanded a risk premium. In other words, the fact of capital mobility provides a strong confirmation of the portfolio approach taken in this study.

Purchasing-power parity and the monetary approach to balance-of-payments theory

The results of this study fully support the view that balance-of-payments disequilibria are monetary phenomena. They are inconsistent, however, with the purchasing-power-parity theory sometimes associated with that view. Balance-of-payments disequilibria are monetary phenomena because they are the mechanism by which the demand and supply of money are equilibrated. This is more strictly true in the international portfolio adjustment model than in applications of the monetary theory where capital flows are ignored. In the present analysis, balance-of-payments equilibrium is established by a direct exchange of money and nonmonetary assets, whereas in the analysis that ignores international capital flows, disequilibria in the balance of payments lead to money flows financed only by adjustments of the trade balance. Gold movements are short-run equilibrium flows in the traditional monetary approach. They are one-shot stock adjustments in the portfolio approach. Gold "flows" occur in the international portfolio adjustment theory only when portfolios are adjusting continuously at some rate.

Despite its strong confirmation of the monetary approach, the analysis of this study is inconsistent with purchasing-power parity as conventionally defined. The ratios of different countries' price levels defined in a single currency are not constant, even though price levels are interdependent. Although the view that price levels differ by a constant under fixed exchange rates is rejected, price level interdependence occurs much more directly in the international portfolio approach than in the traditional specie-flow mechanism. Simultaneous equilibrium in the real goods markets of all countries implies a set of relative price levels that are largely independent of asset equilibrium.

In the traditional price-specie-flow mechanism, relative price levels are determined by the separate conditions of asset equilibrium in each country in conjunction with worldwide real goods market equilibrium. Balance-of-payments disequilibria imply opposite movements of the countries' price levels. In the portfolio model, gold flows and asset disequilibria have no effect on relative price levels. The price levels of the different countries are linked together in much the same way as they are under the purchasing power parity theory, but the linkage is not the rigid one implied by purchasing-power parity. Real exchange rates change through time as a result of differential productivity growth, reallocations of world investment among countries, changes in savings rates and changes in preferences with respect to nontraded versus traded goods. It remains true, of course, that traded goods prices, measured in a single currency and adjusted for tariffs, transport costs, and other impediments, are the same in all countries. Changes in the money supply or the demand for money, holding all real factors constant, also result in proportional changes in prices and require proportional changes in exchange rates in both models.

The law of one price holds in the model developed here as it does in any properly formulated one, but it implies one price for each commodity in each market, not one price level throughout the world. The essential difference between the formulation underlying the analysis of the present study and that underlying the traditional analysis arises not from the unity of goods markets. It arises from the unity of capital markets. The direct interdependence of price levels in the analysis developed in this study is a consequence of free international trade in capital assets. This leads to a unified world market for assets that allows the relative price levels in the different countries to be independent of local asset equilibrium conditions.

How the gold standard really worked

Although the analysis of this book focuses on a narrow problem, the operation of the gold standard in one small country, it has important implications for the functioning of the gold standard in general. Three main issues concerning how the gold standard in fact operated appear in the literature. First, there is the question of whether central banks played according to the "rules of the game." It is widely believed that the gold standard could not be reconstructed after the Great War because individual countries would not allow their domestic credit conditions to be determined by its requirements. Many scholars argue that the rules were not followed even before 1914.[1] Could the gold standard have survived so long if countries were not playing by the rules? If the rules were not being followed, why did the breakdown occur after the War and not before?

Second, there is the anomalous observation that for decades the gold standard provided a reasonably stable world monetary system with relatively little actual movement of gold between countries and, for the most part, no significant shifts in relative price levels associated with the gold

[1] For example, see Ford (1962), Bloomfield (1959), Pippenger (1974), and Dutton (1984).

movements that did occur. Although relative price adjustments appeared from time to time, there appears to be little empirical support for the traditional role of gold flows and money supply and discount changes in the adjustment process. Surely, if the gold standard were operating as the standard theory postulates, one should observe frequent movements of gold accompanied by trade balance and relative price level adjustments.[2]

Third, there is the anomalous fact that the Bank of England, reputed to have been the central stabilizing force in the gold standard system, remained on gold continuously for a hundred years, holding gold reserves which, judged in relation to its apparent responsibilities, were a minuscule fraction of the note and deposit liabilities of the British commercial banking system.

This present study has revealed a great deal about the "rules of the game." According to the theory of the adjustment mechanism proposed here, the rules were not what they are thought to have been. The money supplies in small countries like Canada are endogenous. The Canadian authorities could not have sterilized the effects of gold flows on the domestic money supply even if they had wanted to. Any attempt to counter an outflow of gold by expanding domestic credit would have led to a further gold loss, leaving the domestic money supply at its equilibrium level. In fact, a small country could maintain any stock of gold it wished at an unchanged domestic money supply by expanding or contracting domestic credit. A larger country like England or the United States could moderate the effect of gold outflows on its domestic money supply by expanding credit, but this would increase the outflow of gold and the effect on the money supply and domestic (and world) prices would depend on the fraction held of the world gold stock. Enough gold would have to be dishoarded to raise world prices, including the domestic price level, to a level sufficient to induce domestic residents to hold the target money stock. Given the sizes of their gold reserves and the further gold losses that would inevitably result from attempts to implement domestic monetary policy, it seems unlikely that even Great Britain and the United States, let alone the somewhat smaller countries, would have wanted to engage in such a policy.

Our analysis casts serious doubt on whether the Bank of England could have orchestrated the international gold standard by manipulating its discount rate, as many scholars believe it did.[3] The only way it could have

---

[2] These problems are noted very early by Taussig (1927) and his students, Williams (1920), Graham (1922), White (1933), and Beach (1935), who conduct empirical investigations of a number of countries.

[3] For a discussion of these issues, see Eichengreen (1987).

affected the differential between interest rates at home and in the rest of the world was by buying and selling reserves in the international market, an effect limited by the degree of substitutability between British and foreign assets in portfolios. And, as noted above, the fraction of British nonmonetary wealth involved in the reserve flows actually experienced was exceedingly small, making it doubtful that the process of reestablishing private portfolio equilibrium in response to these reserve flows would have involved sufficient portfolio shifts to bring about significant changes in the marginal rates of substitution between domestic and foreign assets. The Bank of England could have affected world interest rates in general by increasing or reducing British reserves, but these effects were limited by its share of the world gold stock. Since British gold reserves were somewhere between 5 and 10 percent of the world stock of monetary gold,[4] it would have taken between a 10 and 20 percent change in British gold reserves to change the world demand for gold (and hence, roughly, the equilibrium world price level) by 1 percent. At an interest elasticity of demand for money of 0.5, this would have resulted in a short-run change in world interest rates of less than one tenth of one percentage point.

The theory maintained in this study suggests that countries face "constraints," not "rules." The gold standard imposes the constraint that the domestic price level is, for practical purposes, independent of domestic control in both the short and long runs. Sterilization cannot even temporarily avoid this dependence of domestic on world prices, and must surely be, for even the largest country, an ineffective means of controlling the world price level. The constraint imposed by the gold standard is nothing more than the constraint imposed by any fixed exchange rate system in an environment in which capital is internationally mobile. This constraint cannot be avoided by sterilization. It can be avoided only by going off gold.

This suggests an interesting hypothesis. Since sterilization was not a feasible policy, it could not be responsible for the failure of the gold standard after World War I. Its absence could not be responsible for the success of the gold standard in the decades before the War. Clearly, the gold standard's demise must have resulted from an unwillingness to live with the consequences of fixed exchange rates. This could be traced either to a change in public tastes in the form of a rise in economic nationalism, or to an increase in the costs to the individual economies of maintaining

---

[4] See de Cecco (1984, Table 13, p. 244, and Table 16, p. 247).

fixed exchange rates in the inter-War as compared to the pre-War period. An obvious source of increased costs of maintaining fixed exchange rates is greater variability of *real* exchange rates in the period after the War. There is no doubt that exchange rate variability was much greater after the War than before.[5]

One must be careful here because there are two ways in which the causation can run. On the one hand, increased variability of real exchange rates could have resulted from structural shifts in the world economy, with countries choosing to let their nominal exchange rates float rather than to live with changes in their internal price levels. On the other hand, monetary instability resulting from the pursuit of independent policies may have led to a breakdown of the gold standard system. Real exchange rates may then have varied in step with nominal rates as a result of the slowness of price level adjustment in the short run.

A useful initial test would examine whether the greater variability of real exchange rates after World War I took the form of short-term year-to-year movements or of sustained movements of several years' duration. It appears that the latter is the case.[6] It also appears that sustained real exchange rate variability was much greater after the breakdown of the Bretton–Woods system in 1971 than before.

Taken as a whole, this evidence suggests that fixed exchange rate systems, gold standard or otherwise, break down in periods of structural change and are reestablished during periods of structural stability. A complete and convincing test of this hypothesis, however, would require identifying the nature of these structural changes and the factors responsible for them.

Why did the adjustments of gold stocks appear to take place so smoothly, without the wrenching relative price adjustments required by traditional theory? The theory developed in this study provides an obvious explanation. Under the circumstances of the late nineteenth and early twentieth centuries, where capital was internationally mobile, the classical specie-flow mechanism does not apply. Excess or deficient money holdings of the private sector were eliminated by one-shot international exchanges of monetary and nonmonetary assets. No relative price and balance-of-trade adjustments were necessary to bring about equilibrium.

The same theory also has little difficulty explaining how the Bank of

[5] See Floyd (1985, pp. 69–78).
[6] Floyd (1985, Table 5.2, p. 77).

England operated under the gold standard on so few gold reserves. The Bank accumulated additional reserves very easily by tightening domestic credit. When it reduced its discounts to the banking system either by direct rationing or by raising the rediscount rate, British short-term rates rose relative to short-term rates abroad only to the extent that British and foreign securities were imperfect substitutes. An effect on international interest-rate differentials would be observable in the data only if the portfolio adjustment were of significant size in relation to the total stock of British assets outstanding. The numbers presented above suggest that portfolio adjustments were, in fact, small in relation to the total asset stock. In any event, no protracted changes in the price level in Britain relative to abroad would have been necessary to transfer gold into or out of the Bank of England's coffers.

What sense does it make to view the Bank of England as the central player in the gold standard game? London's role as the world's financial center gave the Bank proximity to the action, but it did not endow it with any special mechanism of financial control. The view that the Bank of England did increase and should have increased its gold holdings in periods when world credit conditions were slack and decreased them when they were tight only makes sense if the Bank controlled a significant fraction of the world gold stock. As the discussion above makes clear, that was not the case. The Bank of England must surely have been only a bit player in the gold standard drama. The system operated beyond the influence of any country's authority. Countries stayed on gold because it ensured integrity of the domestic currency unit at little cost as long as the world gold supply and real exchange rates were relatively stable and there were no wars to be financed by inflationary means.

Appendix A: The data sources

The statistics used in this study document the annual changes in the balance of payments, money, income, prices, and interest rates in Canada and the "rest of the world." The latter is defined as the United States, the United Kingdom, France, Germany, Italy, Norway, and Sweden. These were Canada's main trading partners during the study period.

Canadian data

The years 1871–1913 represent the first period for which trade and census statistics organized on a national basis are available for Canada. These data are the basis for Canada's historical national accounts. National monetary statistics also begin in 1871 when federally chartered banks and the federal government were both issuing notes that circulated as money redeemable in gold. The development of price statistics, on the other hand, lagged behind the complication of other economic series, especially for the years before 1900.

Except for the reconstructed Canadian price series discussed in Appendix C, this study relies on existing sources of data. Some of these data represent the quite recent work of other researchers.

The balance of payments

The earliest efforts to reconstruct the balance-of-payments accounts are due to Coats (1915) and Viner (1924). Both focus mainly on the twentieth century. The first reconstructions that provide data from the time of Confederation were made by Firestone (1958, 1960) and Hartland (1954, 1964). Their work has recently been extended by Rich (1988) and Alasdair Sinclair.[1] Apart from one adjustment, the Sinclair estimates incorporated

---

[1] Sinclair is one of a number of investigators who worked under the direction of M. C. Urquhart of Queen's University to construct new estimates of national income for the 1870–1925 period. See Urquhart (1986).

in Urquhart (1986) provide the balance-of-payments data used in this study. An adjustment was made, following the definitive work by Rich (1988), to isolate clearly the magnitude of monetary gold flows.

Rich (1988) shows that the trade accounts reported by the Customs Department are seriously flawed in that they fail to make any distinction between monetary and nonmonetary gold flows. Although Canada produced gold, this apparently had no direct effect on the monetary base before 1908 when gold coins were minted in Canada for the first time. Gold exports, insofar as they reflect Canadian production, were typically nonmonetary flows that belong to the merchandise accounts. Gold imports were typically monetary flows and belong to the capital account.[2]

Canadian balance-of-payments data focus principally on the current account, but also include more tentative independent assessments of the capital account. All current account estimates agree that, except for a brief period in the 1890s, merchandise trade is consistently in deficit. Net invisibles and debt service, though more problematic, typically also show a deficit. The invisibles deficit arises from net debits on freight, noncommercial remittances, and insurance that more than outweigh the net credits from tourism and the capital of migrants.[3] The debt service deficit is consistently larger than the invisibles deficit and commonly in excess of the trade deficit as well. The debt service balance is derived from independent estimates of net capital inflow and interest and dividend costs.[4]

On the financial side of the balance of payments, attempts to isolate capital movements by direct estimation rather than infer them as a residual from the current account do not always yield convincing results. Early direct estimates were made by Hartland (1954) and Viner (1924). In criticizing these efforts, Rich (1988) concludes that direct estimation is too contentious to attempt. He does not explicitly estimate the debt service

[2] Although Viner (1924) recognizes a problem with the Customs reporting of gold flows, only Rich makes the appropriate separation between current and capital account items. Firestone (1958, p. 274) takes the Customs data to be monetary flows, and Sinclair, in Urquhart (1986), takes them to be nonmonetary, when in fact they are consistently neither.

[3] This conclusion is based on the most recent estimates provided by Urquhart (1986). Earlier efforts based on Hartland (1954) suggest that net invisibles exclusive of interest and dividends may be positive, at least before 1905, but too small to have any important effect compared to the overwhelmingly negative net trade and debt service balances.

[4] These conclusions and their implications are again based on new estimates provided in Urquhart (1986) that approximate the post-1900 estimates of Viner (1924, chapter 5). Rich (1988), on the other hand, eschews direct capital flow and service estimates, preferring instead to make these residual items. As a result, the trade balance dominates his current account estimates. Either way, a persistent current account deficit and net capital inflow is confirmed.

balance. Urquhart (1986) provides a series dominated by long-term capital inflow that comes close to matching the magnitude of the negative of the current account balance. The inflow of long-term funds, especially after 1900, appears to be by far the most important and best documented. The remainder of capital movements, apart from gold flows, is accounted for by changes in secondary reserves or short-term capital in the form of call loans abroad or net claims on foreign banks.

Short-term security placements are recorded somewhat incompletely by both government and the banking system.[5] More often than not, the movement of short-term capital was a net outflow with the gold movements representing a net accumulation of gold held in Canada. The main capital inflow appears to have been long-term, an autonomous item arising from the excess of investment prospects in Canada over domestic savings. Short-term capital movements were more likely to have been induced by people's decisions about the form in which to hold wealth. Banks, for example, presumably maximized the return on reserve assets held in New York while at the same time accommodating the demand of Canadians to hold money and standing ready to redeem notes and deposits in gold. In the absence of a short-term money market in Canada, New York was the most accessible location for short-term funds.[6]

Given the current account, long-term capital flows and net monetary movements, short-run adjustments become a residual item. Secondary reserves constitute much of this but there remains a substantial gap representing errors and omissions. Some of this gap can be attributed to shortcomings in the trade and long-term capital flow data. It is likely, however, given the state of banking data and our meager knowledge about short-term capital flows, that errors and omissions are in major part unreported short-term capital movements.

The terms of trade data are from Taylor (1931) and Firestone (1958, pp. 146–53). They are based on the official trade statistics underlying the above current account estimates. These data take account of all Canada's international trade, but the prices associated with Canada-U.S. and Canada-U.K. trade clearly dominate the series.

Canada's participation in the gold standard system meant fixed exchange rates for most of the 1871–1913 period. Convertibility of Dominion notes, bank notes, and bank deposits into gold prevailed from the passage of the

---

[5] See Viner (1924, chapter 8), and Rich (1988, appendix B). These studies draw heavily on Curtis (1931) and Taylor (1931).
[6] Goodhart (1969) investigates the rationale for this behavior.

Bank Act of 1871 to the passage of the Finance Act in 1914.[7] Only when gold convertibility was suspended in the United States during the years before 1879 did Canada experience a variable exchange rate. The tie with gold in the United States arose de facto in the 1830s and was broken only between 1862 and 1879 by the issue of greenbacks.[8] In Great Britain, gold became the monetary standard early in the eighteenth century and was confirmed by the Bank Act of 1844.[9] During the suspension in the United States the British pound fluctuated against the U.S. dollar. The dollar-pound exchange rate can be represented by the premium on gold in terms of greenbacks.[10] The data for this premium are drawn from Mitchell (1908, p. 4).

For purposes of this study, the average Canadian dollar price of foreign currency is a weighted average of the Canadian dollar prices of the U.S. dollar and the U.K. pound. The weights are the proportions of Canadian trade accounted for. By construction, this exchange rate fluctuates only before 1879. The dollar-pound rate is fixed while the dollar-greenback rate moves. From 1879 to 1913, Canada's real exchange rate and her nominal domestic to foreign price level ratio are identical.

Some variability around the gold points set by the cost of moving gold may be expected with changes in market conditions. Davis and Hughes (1960) and Paterson and Shearer (1982) find fluctuations exceeding these points during the years before 1870 and attribute them to apparent inefficiencies in arbitrage. In this study, it is assumed that markets are sufficiently well developed by 1870 to rule out substantial deviations from the implicit gold exchange rate, except for the U.S. dollar during the greenback era.[11]

Money

The available monetary statistics pose conceptual problems arising from ambiguities in the definition of the monetary base. Ultimately, the circulating medium, whether a liability of the government or of the banks, is redeemable in gold. The money supply consists of deposits as well as notes, however, and reserves include short-term assets held in New York

[7] See Shearer, Chant, and Bond (1984, pp. 622, 627–8).
[8] See Friedman and Schwartz (1963, chapter 2).
[9] See Kindleberger (1984, pp. 59–60 and 68–70).
[10] See McCullough (1983, pp. 91–3) and Friedman and Schwartz (1963, pp. 58–65).
[11] Attempts made to reconstruct exchange rate history on the basis of bill and interest rates tend to support this assumption. See, for example, McCullough (1984a, p. 25).

as well as gold. Given gold convertibility and no legally stipulated ratio of reserves to be held against bank notes or deposits, the public chooses the composition of money holdings and the banks choose the magnitude and composition of the reserves that back this money.

The definition of the money stock used in this study, following Rich (1988), corresponds in the main to a "Canadian owned" money stock. It includes Canadian dollar bank deposits held by Canadian residents, chartered bank notes held by the public and the government in Canada, and the Dominion notes held by the public in Canada.[12] Dominion government deposits ought ideally to be included but are not available. Provincial government deposits, however, are included in Rich's estimates. These data are subject to two other minor caveats: it is not known whether all deposits in Canada are owned by Canadian residents and whether some Canadian bank notes are foreign owned.

The monetary base, again following Rich (1988), is defined as Dominion note holdings of the chartered banks and the public plus gold and U.S. dollar assets (call loans and so forth) held by Canadian chartered banks both at home and abroad. In this definition of base money, bank notes are excluded. Rich departs here from earlier definitions used by Macesich and Haulman (1971) and Hay (1968) that in principle include those bank liabilities. One argument for excluding bank notes, aside from imperfections in the data, is based on the observation that there is little tendency for the public to substitute bank notes for deposits thereby affecting bank reserves.[13] Bank notes are at most about 15 percent of bank liabilities at the beginning of the period under study, dwindling to only about 7 percent by 1913.[14] A stronger argument for excluding them is a conceptual one. Bank notes are like deposits in that they are a liability of the chartered banks, rather than a liability of the government and an asset of the banks as they are today.

Given the pre-1914 institutional arrangements, it is hardly surprising that total reserve ratios are somewhat volatile over the period. Before the mid-1880s, there are significant amounts of Dominion notes outstanding beyond those permitted by the statutory gold reserve requirement. These

---

[12] Rich (1988, appendix A, Tables A.1 and A.2).

[13] See Rich (1988). Rich notes that in 1908 banks were permitted to create excess issue during the crop moving season. Also, some substitution of bank notes with an impact on reserves may occur when banks contribute to the Circulation Redemption Fund created in 1891.

[14] See Neufeld (1972, p. 118)

uncovered notes are one aspect of government fiscal policy under the early Conservative governments. Even in these early years, however, uncovered issue appears to have led to only a minor increase in the monetary base. Movements in the base are dominated by changes in the balance of payments.[15]

Income

Although national accounting begins on a formal basis in Canada only in 1926, shortly after the formation of the Dominion Bureau of Statistics, Firestone (1958, part 4) records earlier efforts to extend the data back to at least the middle of the nineteenth century.[16] The culmination of this early work is a set of national income estimates developed and revised by Firestone (1958, 1969). This is the first comprehensive reconstruction based on a value added technique. Notable among the earlier revisions of this work are unpublished estimates by Kenneth Buckley utilized in Buckley (1963). The most recent estimates, by Urquhart (1986), are used in this study. They are the product of a decade of research by M. C. Urquhart and his associates at Queen's University and are constructed using mostly the value added method, subtracting nonfactor costs from the gross value of production. They differ from the Firestone estimates mainly in the recalculation of agricultural income and residential rents.

Prices

With respect to price data, the main effort here focuses on the distinction between traded and nontraded goods. This recognizes quantitative differences in the price histories of different countries arising from variations in the prices of goods that are not traded internationally. Admittedly, the possibility of arbitrage may be as effective as arbitrage itself in establishing the law of one price. The division of output between traded and nontraded items is at best arbitrary. Yet there is ample evidence, using any reasonable criterion, that the law of one price holds more tightly for some groups of items than others.[17] Early investigators of Canadian price history note

[15] See Rich (1988, chapter 3, section 3.2), and (1977, p. 449).
[16] See also Urquhart and Buckley (1965, pp. 128–9).
[17] There is a vast literature on this topic that leaves little doubt as to the scope for this empirical distinction. McCloskey and Zecher (1976) are among the most recent to quantify it.

differences in the movement of wholesale prices of raw materials vis-à-vis food items.[18] In this study, food and clothing items are treated as internationally traded goods. Services such as fuel, utilities, transportation, housing, and medical care are viewed as nontraded. The Canadian prices of traded goods are assumed to be the same as those abroad.

Much of the existing documentation of Canadian price history for the 1870–1914 period consists of wholesale prices extracted from newspaper reports and, toward the end of the period, collected by the Department of Labour. For the years before 1890, there are two wholesale price indexes based on unweighted geometric means of price relatives.[19] For the years after 1890, these series are augmented by a Department of Labour wholesale index based on an arithmetic average of price relatives.[20] More recently, Barnett (1966) refined these efforts by applying geometric weights based on the gross value of output in 1900 to a combination of wholesale and retail prices, and Altman (1984) constructed an index based on unit values derived from trade statistics. From the point of view of providing a price index for the output of Canadian goods and services, these wholesale indexes are incomplete. They include primarily the prices of traded goods, mostly observed in Toronto and Montreal and assumed to be world prices.

The first systematic efforts to measure the prices of nontraded goods and services for Canada are those of the Department of Labour. The department begins price collections in 1900 to measure the cost of living of a typical urban working class family. Unlike the wholesale indexes, the coverage of the cost of living indexes based on these new data includes the prices of services like housing, utilities, and later, personal care at towns and cities across Canada.[21] Unfortunately, the weighting pattern used is obscure and some of the data are open to question. These problems are partially overcome in recalculations made by Bertram and Percy (1979) and by Bartlett (1981). Dick (1986a, 1986b) is engaged in further work along these lines.

Some reworking of the Canadian price data is therefore necessary to

---

[18] See Coats (1915), covering the years 1890–1914, reported in Viner (1924, chapters 9 and 10) covering the years 1900–13.

[19] One is constructed by Michell (1931, pp. 47–88), and the other by D.B.S. as recorded in Urquhart and Buckley (1965, Series J34–44, pp. 283–4, 293–4).

[20] See Coats (1910, pp. 433ff, and 1915).

[21] The prices entering these new indexes appeared first in the *Labour Gazette*, which began publication in 1900. For the period under study, these prices are summarized in Coats (1915). The only nineteenth-century cost-of-living index is one constructed by Barnett (1963) for Kingston, Ontario. It is limited to food, fuel, and light items.

clarify the movement of nontraded relative to traded goods prices. The requirements of the present study are for measures of the movement in the prices of Canadian output – that is, for a GNP deflator that can be decomposed to show the separate movement of traded and nontraded goods prices. The Urquhart (1986) deflator instead attempts a separation between capital formation and all other output.[22] Consumption is the largest part of noncapital spending, accounting in the period under study for about two-thirds of output according to Urquhart (1986). Unfortunately, consumption here includes both traded and nontraded goods. The difficulty arises from the fact that there is no comprehensive and detailed expenditure information in the accounts for this period. This is the principal reason why the value added approach is instrumental in making national income estimates before 1926.[23]

Accordingly, the Canadian price series used in this study are new aggregations. They are based partly on elements of existing series and partly on price relatives produced for the construction of new cost-of-living indexes.[24] As explained in Appendix C, these estimates capture the main movement of the prices of nontraded relative to traded goods, and represent a significant improvement over the older wholesale price series used by Coats (1915) and Viner (1924). The procedures used to adapt existing series for the present study are described in Appendix C.

Interest rates

Given capital mobility, the interest rates on Canadian investments are expected to equal world interest rates adjusted for risk. For purposes of this study, the ideal world interest rate would be one on Canadian securities denominated in Canadian dollars and marketed in Great Britain, by far the dominant source of long-term capital before 1914.

Most early long-term investment is portfolio investment taking the form of fixed income securities, predominantly government and railroad bonds. Direct investment, mainly from the United States, is significant only after

---

[22] Although this is now the best available deflator, Urquhart (1986, p. 86) acknowledges a number of shortcomings that make it less than definitive. The only other GNP deflator on record is one developed by Firestone (1969).

[23] See Urquhart (1986, appendix 2).

[24] In part, the approach taken follows the lead of Urquhart (1986, appendix 5). In attempting to convert his nominal estimates into real estimates, Urquhart employs an ad hoc cost-of-living index based on splicing together earlier work by D.B.S. (Series K-1 in Urquhart and Buckley, 1965), Bertram and Percy (1979), Barnett (1963), and Steele (1977).

1895.[25] The average yield on long-term foreign investments in Canada implicit in the Urquhart (1986) capital flow and debt service estimates is not immediately available.[26] Instead, the average rate on Canada sterling bonds maturing in 1903 and 1938 from Neufeld (1972) is used.[27]

At the short end of market, Goodhart (1969) provides monthly rates for the years 1902–13 at Montreal, New York, and other U.S. financial centers. It is generally understood that Canadian banks participated in making substantial call loans in New York. There appears to be no systematic relationship between these call loans and the differential between the Montreal and New York rates. The Canadian market was undeveloped and controversy exists over the nature of the Montreal call loan rate (Goodhart, 1969; Rich, 1988).

Foreign country data

For purposes of comparing nontraded goods prices in Chapter 5, it is adequate to consider only the United States and the United Kingdom, Canada's two principal trading partners, as the "rest of the world." In the statistical tests in Chapters 6 and 7, however, France, Germany, Italy, Norway, and Sweden are included to obtain the relevant "rest of the world" aggregates for money, income, and prices. The sources of the components of these aggregates and the methods of aggregation are now described.

Balance of payments

This study does not directly concern the balance of payments for countries other than Canada. The exchange rates prevailing under the gold standard for the countries included in the "rest of the world" are of concern, however, in developing the "rest of the world" aggregates. Indexes of home currency values for money, income, and prices for the selected countries must be weighted together to obtain "rest of the world" series. The procedure used involves bringing all home currency values in a base period, 1894–97, to a common denominator, set in this case by the gold values of domestic currencies or gold-standard exchange rates prevailing

---

[25] Some direct investments were also made by Great Britian. See Paterson (1976).

[26] Alternative yield data, similar in principle but applicable only to alternative balance-of-payments estimates, are provided by Hartland (1964, chapter 7, Table 28), Viner (1924, chapter 5, Table 27), and Rich (1988).

[27] Table 15.5, pp. 562–3. This series has been analyzed by Milne and Torous (1984).

at the end of the period (Board of Governors, Federal Reserve System, United States, 1943). The rates used express the U.S. dollar prices of units of foreign currency as follows:

1913	United Kingdom	pound	4.868917	U.S. dollars
1915	Norway	kroner	0.258794	U.S. dollars
1915	Sweden	kroner	0.258942	U.S. dollars
1913	France	franc	0.192897	U.S. dollars
1913	Germany	mark	0.237936	U.S. dollars
1913	Italy	lire	0.189977	U.S. dollars

At the time the Canadian dollar was at parity with the U.S. dollar.

Money

The world money stock is composed of the weighted sum of the nominal money stocks in the United States, the United Kingdom, France, Germany, Italy, Norway, and Sweden. The nominal money stock in each of these countries is typically the sum of government or central bank notes and currency and both demand and time deposits at the commercial banks as well as savings bank deposits. For the United States, the M2 definition of money used is taken from Friedman and Schwartz (1982, Table 4.8). For the United Kingdom, the Capie and Webber (1985) series, a broadly defined aggregate, is used. The broad aggregates in Mitchell (1975, pp. 705–32) are used for Germany, France, Norway, and Sweden. The series for France includes only bank notes and savings deposits. For Italy, the money supply series are from Fratianni and Spinelli (1984, Table 9.A.1).

These nominal money stock series are indexed on 1894–97, weighted, and aggregated. The weights are the shares of the individual countries in the total of their GNP for the 1894–97 base period. They are as follows:

United States	0.363
United Kingdom	0.222
France	0.129
Germany	0.192
Italy	0.072
Norway	0.007
Sweden	0.014

The weight for France is obtained as 0.67 of the weight for Germany, based on the French income figures given by Crafts (1984).

Income

Real income for the rest of the world is an index of income in the United States, the United Kingdom, Germany, Italy, Norway, and Sweden. France is excluded since the French data are sparse, and appear suspect. The U.S. series is from Friedman and Schwartz (1982, Table 4.8), the U.K. series from Capie and Webber (1985). The real GNP series from Fratianni and Spinelli (1984, Table 9.A.1) are used for Italy. The series for Germany, Norway, and Sweden are from Mitchell (1975, pp. 815–39).

To obtain a series for world real income, these six single country series in index form are combined using the following weights:

United States	0.383
United Kingdom	0.255
Germany	0.221
Italy	0.083
Norway	0.008
Sweden	0.016

Prices

The index of prices (traded and nontraded goods combined) in the rest of the world uses the implicit GNP price deflators for the seven countries included in the world nominal money series. The U.S. index uses the series from Friedman and Schwartz (1982, Table 4.8), the U.K. index, the series from Capie and Webber (1985), the Italian index, the series from Fratianni and Spinelli (1984, Table 9.A.1), and the German, Norwegian, and Swedish indexes, the implicit income deflators from Mitchell (1975, pp. 815–39). The cost-of-living series, also from Mitchell (1975), has to be used for France. These series are combined using the same weights as for the world nominal money stock.

Nontraded goods prices in the rest of the world concentrate on the United States and the United Kingdom. Although both British and American sources provide implicit price indexes for total output corresponding to total GNP, these data are not always easily disaggregated, especially before 1900, in a manner that permits the separation of traded from nontraded output.[28] New aggregates are therefore constructed from the underlying series.

---

[28] See U.S. Department of Commerce (1975, Part 1, p. 216), Kendrick (1961, p. 40), Brady (1966), and Feinstein (1972, pp. 2, 210)

1890 = 100

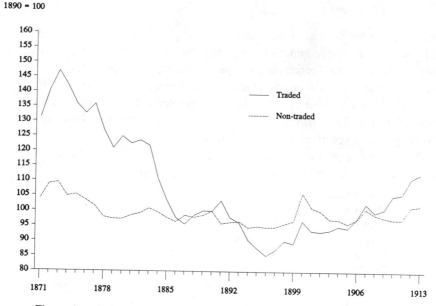

Figure A.1. Price indexes, United Kingdom: traded and nontraded goods, 1871–1913.

As noted above and again in Appendix C, in the discussion of Canadian price data, the distinction between traded and nontraded goods made by Coats (1915) and Viner (1924) is unconvincing. To measure the movement of nontraded goods prices in the United States and the United Kingdom, the present study uses the movement of house rents and fuel and light prices. Figures A.1, A.2, and A.3 show, for both countries, a marked flatness of this price movement compared to the movement of the overall wholesale price indexes, which are dominated by the movement of traded goods prices. The flatness of the time path of nontraded goods prices is in marked contrast to the upward movement of Canadian nontraded goods prices after the 1890s noted in Appendix C. The general wholesale price movements in all three countries are quite similar (see Appendix C), reflecting the operation of the world markets for traded goods.

The U.K. nontraded goods price index combines a rental index taken from Wood (1909, pp. 102–03) with a fuel and light index produced by Brown and Hopkins (1981, chapter 2). The weights used are proportional to 11.3 for rents and 4.4 for fuel and light, taken from the survey of consumer expenditure reported in Stone and Rowe (1966) for the years

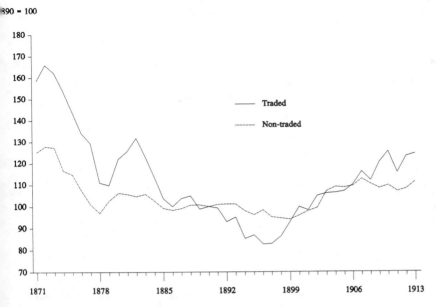

890 = 100

Figure A.2. Price indexes, United States: traded and nontraded goods, 1871–1913.

1900–04. The overall index of wholesale prices of traded goods used as a basis of comparison in Figure A.1 is the Board of Trade index reported in Mitchell (1962, Table 5).

The U.S. nontraded goods price index combines a splicing of rental indexes produced by Lebergott (1964), Snyder (1927), and Rees (1961) with a splicing of fuel and light indexes from Lebergott (1964), Aldrich (1892), and Rees (1961). The weights are proportional to 16.7 for rent and 5.4 for fuel and light, as used by Rees (1961). The overall index of wholesale prices of traded goods used for comparison in Figure A.2 is a combination of the Warren and Pearson and BLS series reported in U.S. Department of Commerce (1975).

These traded and nontraded goods price indexes for the United States and the United Kingdom are combined using population weights to yield traded and nontraded goods price indexes for the "rest of the world" displayed in Figure A.3.

Interest rates

Given capital market conditions at the time and Canada's participation in the world market for capital, the most important interest rates outside

1890 = 100

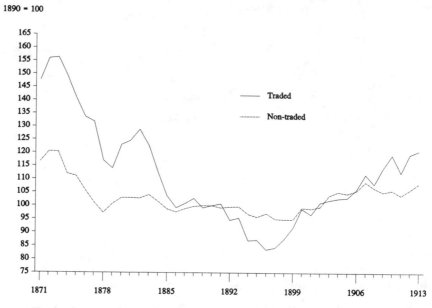

Figure A.3. Price indexes, U.S. and U.K. average: traded and nontraded goods, 1871–1913.

Canada are those prevailing in New York and London. Friedman and Schwartz (1982, Tables 4.8 and 4.9) provide long-term rates for U.S. high-grade corporate bonds, for U.S. high-grade industrial bonds, and for U.K. consols. Long-term rates on government bonds are available for France and Italy from Fratianni and Spinelli (1984, Table 9.A.1). Friedman and Schwartz (1982, Tables 4.8 and 4.9) also provide two short-term rates for the United States, a commercial paper rate and a call money rate, as well as the rate on three-month bankers' bills in the United Kingdom. When comparisons of Canadian with rest of the world interest rates are required, we compare Neufeld's rate for Canada (the only available rate) with the rate on U.K. consols since Britain was the main source of Canadian borrowing.

Appendix B: The data

This appendix contains all the data used in the statistical work of this study and in the figures incorporated in the text. The sources of these data are described in Appendix A. The only data tabulated that are newly constructed for this study are the Canadian price series; these constructions are described in Appendix C.

Table B.1. *The Canadian balance of payments, 1871–1913*

Year	Long-term net capital inflow	Short-term net capital inflow	Net monetary movements	Net capital inflow	Errors and omissions	Debt service balance	Net capital inflow plus debt service	Minus the trade account balance
1871	13289.8	7349	3000	23638.8	10818.5	−8471.9	15.2	26.0
1872	8019.4	−2431	3600	9188.4	33198.5	−10507.0	−1.3	31.9
1873	22741.6	289	−1200	21830.6	23342.6	−9112.6	12.7	36.1
1874	38509.0	−5580	−400	32529.0	17754.3	−12028.8	20.5	38.3
1875	14709.7	3303	1000	19012.7	17667.2	−11482.2	7.5	25.2
1876	16302.5	36	800	17138.5	9640.7	−11852.3	5.3	14.9
1877	10899.7	1913	−300	12512.7	12200.3	−8908.4	3.6	15.8
1878	11413.9	−2532	1100	9981.9	13901.2	−13918.6	−3.9	10.0
1879	14262.1	−1762	−2200	10300.1	4918.8	−12590.6	−2.3	2.6
1880	12357.8	−2409	1300	11248.8	5745.7	−15570.2	−4.3	1.4
1881	25774.8	−1918	−300	23556.8	3809.8	−17629.4	5.9	9.7
1882	10310.4	−584	400	10126.4	29350.2	−16705.9	−6.6	22.8
1883	18704.1	−5763	−800	12141.1	33109.2	−18075.0	−5.9	27.2
1884	23927.1	5052	−200	28779.1	11053.8	−19947.0	8.8	19.9
1885	46869.6	−533	100	46436.6	−8976.9	−21941.0	24.5	15.5
1886	35200.1	−2409	1200	33991.1	9954.0	−26730.5	7.3	17.2
1887	15631.7	−9745	−1900	3986.7	42587.2	−28073.3	−24.1	18.5
1888	66518.8	−11900	−2900	51718.8	−1980.3	−29318.7	22.4	20.4
1889	21334.2	569	3500	25403.2	32407.1	−33326.6	−7.9	24.5
1890	22471.7	−2345	−1900	18226.7	39974.6	−36342.7	−18.1	21.9
1891	15047.7	−8753	500	6794.7	41937.6	−33285.8	−26.5	15.4
1892	28625.1	−9953	−4100	14572.1	30107.0	−35786.0	−21.2	8.9

1893	15920.6	−9624	−2700	3596.6	35952.7	−36380.1	−32.8	3.2
1894	31100.6	−4855	−1600	24645.6	9970.8	−37263.9	−12.6	−2.6
1895	6567.6	−5636	−2300	−1368.4	31527.0	−36341.6	−37.7	−6.2
1896	10558.5	−11208	30	−619.5	23716.1	−37146.8	−37.8	−14.1
1897	28035.8	−6741	−3100	18194.8	−6313.3	−38301.8	−20.1	−26.4
1898	16722.0	−5312	−1000	10410.0	9488.1	−42551.6	−32.1	−22.7
1899	20000.0	−12262	800	−11461.9	42253.8	−38748.6	−50.2	−7.9
1900	25350.3	2860	−2800	25410.3	2591.8	−38542.0	−13.1	−15.7
1901	33161.4	−28699	−1900	2562.4	27736.7	−40779.0	−38.2	−10.5
1902	20366.6	−3266	−6500	10600.6	22700.3	−38649.7	−28.0	−5.3
1903	30289.6	16723	−11200	35812.6	19914.3	−38393.2	−2.6	17.3
1904	79091.0	−21150	−8600	49341.0	32421.7	−38594.9	10.7	43.2
1905	108438.0	−15785	−700	91953.2	−79.4	−50676.3	41.3	41.2
1906	81305.5	12514	−6600	87219.5	25214.4	−58526.3	28.7	53.9
1907	69846.5	21824	−4400	87270.5	71842.4	−69184.5	18.1	89.9
1908	177045.0	−92459	−27500	57086.4	71576.6	−81671.6	−24.6	47.0
1909	185176.0	−33602	−5200	146374.0	5287.6	−86360.5	60.0	65.3
1910	222072.0	25886	−11800	236158.0	−2343.5	−97464.1	138.7	136.4
1911	172535.0	−3450	−29600	139485.0	189348.0	−131976.0	7.5	196.9
1912	277868.0	182	1000	279050.0	164151.0	−170046.0	109.0	273.2
1913	326413.0	−18762	−20500	287151.0	113384.0	−202434.0	84.7	198.1

Source: See Appendix A.

Table B.2. *Price indexes: Canada and rest of world, 1871–1913*[a]

Year	Canada			Rest of world		Ratio of prices	
	All	Nontraded	Traded	Nontraded	Canadian nontraded ÷ R.O.W.[b] nontraded	Canadian nontraded ÷ Canadian traded	R.O.W. nontraded ÷ R.O.W. traded[c]
1871	120	118	121	111	111	91	82
1872	138	142	135	115	130	98	76
1873	138	142	136	115	130	98	75
1874	131	135	129	107	132	98	74
1875	123	121	123	105	121	91	76
1876	115	115	116	101	120	93	77
1877	109	108	109	99	115	92	80
1878	102	104	101	97	112	96	85
1879	99	104	98	101	109	100	92
1880	108	111	107	103	113	97	86
1881	107	105	108	103	107	91	85
1882	108	108	108	103	111	94	85
1883	104	103	105	104	104	92	88
1884	99	98	100	102	101	91	90
1885	94	94	94	99	100	93	93
1886	93	94	93	98	101	95	94
1887	96	99	95	99	105	97	93
1888	100	103	99	100	108	97	90
1889	100	103	99	100	108	97	90
1890	100	100	100	100	105	93	89

Year							
1891	99	98	100	99	103	91	88
1892	95	98	93	100	104	99	95
1893	95	96	94	100	101	95	94
1894	90	95	88	97	103	101	98
1895	88	92	86	96	101	99	99
1896	86	92	83	97	100	104	104
1897	86	87	85	95	96	96	100
1898	89	89	89	95	98	94	95
1899	91	91	90	95	101	94	93
1900	95	99	93	99	104	99	95
1901	97	99	95	99	105	97	93
1902	101	103	99	100	109	97	89
1903	106	112	101	104	113	104	92
1904	108	115	102	105	114	105	92
1905	111	117	105	105	117	104	89
1906	115	123	105	106	122	109	89
1907	122	129	114	109	124	105	85
1908	126	136	114	107	134	112	84
1909	127	135	116	105	135	109	81
1910	128	135	117	106	134	108	81
1911	135	143	121	104	144	110	77
1912	139	146	128	106	144	106	74
1913	141	150	124	109	145	113	78

[a] Rest of the world consists of the United States and United Kingdom.
[b] R.O.W. is an abbreviation for rest of the world.
[c] The rest of the world's index of traded goods prices is the same as the Canadian index.

Source: See Appendixes A and C.

Table B.3. *Real income and the terms of trade, 1871–1913*

Year	Canadian real GNP	Canadian per capita real GNP	Rest of world real income	Canada's terms of trade
	1890 = 100	1890 dollars	1890 = 100	1890 = 100
1871	52	89	58	67
1872	49	83	63	65
1873	54	90	65	75
1874	57	92	66	75
1875	56	89	67	77
1876	55	88	68	81
1877	60	93	70	81
1878	61	94	72	88
1879	66	100	75	87
1880	65	99	79	85
1881	78	115	81	85
1882	84	121	83	90
1883	86	125	83	92
1884	86	122	85	91
1885	86	121	86	92
1886	87	121	89	94
1887	92	127	91	98
1888	91	123	92	105
1889	95	129	95	98
1890	100	133	100	100
1891	104	137	101	99
1892	108	140	105	104
1893	105	136	106	104
1894	105	133	104	107
1895	104	133	112	112
1896	107	134	113	105
1897	121	152	119	107
1898	126	154	123	108
1899	132	161	131	105
1900	138	166	132	99
1901	149	176	139	100
1902	161	187	140	105
1903	162	184	146	106
1904	162	178	146	104
1905	179	190	153	101
1906	193	201	166	104
1907	206	205	171	103
1908	192	185	160	105
1909	212	198	173	113
1910	230	209	175	113
1911	240	212	180	111
1912	257	221	187	111
1913	270	226	192	110

Source: See Appendix A.

Table B.4. *Canadian money supply and income velocity, 1871–1913*[a]

Year	Nominal money stock	Real money stock[b]	Velocity
1871	0.08	0.07	5.03
1872	0.08	0.06	5.14
1873	0.09	0.07	5.25
1874	0.10	0.08	4.65
1875	0.09	0.07	5.05
1876	0.09	0.08	4.57
1877	0.09	0.08	4.73
1878	0.09	0.09	4.37
1879	0.09	0.09	4.42
1880	0.11	0.10	4.07
1881	0.13	0.12	4.16
1882	0.14	0.13	4.16
1883	0.14	0.13	4.21
1884	0.13	0.13	4.20
1885	0.14	0.15	3.68
1886	0.14	0.15	3.81
1887	0.15	0.15	3.87
1888	0.16	0.16	3.57
1889	0.17	0.17	3.66
1890	0.17	0.17	3.64
1891	0.20	0.21	3.21
1892	0.22	0.24	2.91
1893	0.22	0.23	2.87
1894	0.23	0.26	2.61
1895	0.24	0.27	2.47
1896	0.24	0.28	2.41
1897	0.28	0.32	2.38
1898	0.30	0.34	2.33
1899	0.34	0.37	2.25
1900	0.37	0.39	2.29
1901	0.41	0.43	2.23
1902	0.45	0.45	2.29
1903	0.48	0.46	2.25
1904	0.55	0.51	2.04
1905	0.61	0.55	2.08
1906	0.70	0.61	2.02
1907	0.68	0.55	2.38
1908	0.75	0.60	2.05
1909	0.89	0.70	1.92
1910	0.96	0.75	1.94
1911	1.09	0.81	1.89
1912	1.19	0.85	1.91
1913	1.17	0.83	2.07

[a] In billions.
[b] The real money stock is in billions of 1890 dollars.
Source: See Appendix A.

Table B.5. *Gold holdings and selected monetary ratios: Canada, 1871–1913*

Year	Ratio of public's Dominion note to currency holdings	Ratio of chartered bank deposits to money stock	Chartered bank's primary reserve ratio	Chartered bank's secondary reserve ratio	Gold to primary reserves: chartered banks	Gold reserves: government and chartered banks	
						Level	Change
1871	0.14	0.64	0.21	0.18	0.56	12.9	3.0
1872	0.11	0.63	0.18	0.11	0.43	9.3	−3.6
1873	0.09	0.64	0.19	0.10	0.44	10.5	1.2
1874	0.08	0.69	0.17	0.08	0.44	10.9	0.4
1875	0.11	0.70	0.18	0.09	0.45	9.9	−1.0
1876	0.11	0.72	0.17	0.06	0.43	9.1	−0.8
1877	0.11	0.72	0.18	0.08	0.41	9.3	0.2
1878	0.09	0.74	0.16	0.07	0.41	8.2	−1.1
1879	0.13	0.73	0.18	0.27	0.43	10.4	2.2
1880	0.12	0.72	0.15	0.30	0.36	9.1	−1.3
1881	0.14	0.70	0.14	0.20	0.40	9.4	0.3
1882	0.13	0.70	0.13	0.08	0.39	9.1	−0.3
1883	0.14	0.71	0.14	0.16	0.39	9.8	0.7
1884	0.14	0.71	0.15	0.14	0.41	10.0	0.2
1885	0.14	0.73	0.14	0.15	0.35	9.9	−0.1
1886	0.17	0.74	0.12	0.13	0.39	8.7	−1.2
1887	0.14	0.72	0.13	0.15	0.43	10.6	1.9
1888	0.14	0.75	0.13	0.25	0.47	13.6	3.0
1889	0.15	0.76	0.10	0.11	0.45	10.1	−3.5

Year						
1890	0.14	0.77	0.11	0.06	0.47	12.0	1.9
1891	0.15	0.79	0.09	0.14	0.44	11.5	-0.5
1892	0.15	0.81	0.10	0.12	0.42	15.7	4.2
1893	0.16	0.81	0.11	0.09	0.44	18.3	2.6
1894	0.16	0.83	0.11	0.14	0.41	20.0	1.7
1895	0.16	0.83	0.12	0.10	0.42	22.4	2.4
1896	0.16	0.84	0.12	0.10	0.45	22.3	-0.1
1897	0.15	0.84	0.11	0.12	0.41	25.4	3.1
1898	0.16	0.84	0.10	0.10	0.43	26.3	0.9
1899	0.16	0.84	0.09	0.09	0.42	25.5	-0.8
1900	0.14	0.84	0.09	0.11	0.40	28.3	2.8
1901	0.14	0.85	0.09	0.15	0.40	30.2	1.9
1902	0.14	0.84	0.09	0.13	0.39	36.8	6.6
1903	0.14	0.85	0.11	0.11	0.38	48.0	11.2
1904	0.13	0.86	0.11	0.14	0.35	56.8	8.8
1905	0.13	0.87	0.10	0.13	0.38	57.4	0.6
1906	0.13	0.87	0.10	0.10	0.36	64.0	6.6
1907	0.14	0.87	0.12	0.08	0.36	68.4	4.4
1908	0.15	0.88	0.14	0.19	0.34	95.9	27.5
1909	0.13	0.88	0.12	0.19	0.30	101.1	5.2
1910	0.14	0.89	0.12	0.13	0.33	112.9	11.8
1911	0.15	0.89	0.13	0.12	0.30	142.5	29.6
1912	0.16	0.89	0.11	0.11	0.28	141.5	-1.0
1913	0.16	0.89	0.14	0.11	0.30	162.0	20.5

Source: See Appendix A.

Table B.6. *Canadian and foreign interest rates: percent per year, 1871–1913*

Year	Canada long-term	France long-term gov't	Italy long-term gov't	United States Long-term Corp.	United States Long-term Indust.	United States Short-term Paper	United States Short-term Call	United Kingdom Consol	United Kingdom T-bill
1871	5	6	7	6	8	7	5	3	3
1872	5	5	6	6	8	9	8	3	4
1873	5	5	6	6	8	10	14	3	5
1874	5	5	6	6	7	6	3	3	4
1875	5	5	6	6	7	5	3	3	3
1876	5	4	6	5	7	5	3	3	2
1877	5	4	6	5	7	5	4	3	3
1878	5	4	6	5	7	5	4	3	4
1879	4	4	5	5	6	5	6	3	2
1880	4	4	5	5	6	5	5	3	3
1881	4	4	5	4	6	5	6	3	3
1882	4	4	5	4	6	6	5	3	4
1883	4	4	5	4	6	6	4	3	3
1884	4	4	5	4	6	5	3	3	3
1885	4	4	5	4	6	4	2	3	2
1886	4	4	4	4	5	5	4	3	2
1887	4	4	4	4	5	6	5	3	3
1888	4	4	5	4	5	5	3	3	3
1889	4	4	5	4	5	5	4	3	3
1890	4	3	5	4	5	6	6	3	4
1891	4	3	5	4	5	5	3	3	3
1892	4	3	5	4	5	4	3	3	2
1893	4	3	5	4	5	7	5	3	2
1894	3	3	5	4	5	3	1	3	1
1895	3	3	4	4	5	4	2	2	1
1896	3	3	4	4	5	6	4	2	2
1897	3	3	4	3	5	4	2	2	2
1898	3	3	4	3	5	4	2	2	3
1899	3	3	4	3	5	4	5	2	3
1900	3	3	4	3	5	4	3	3	4
1901	3	3	4	3	5	4	4	3	3
1902	3	3	4	3	5	5	5	3	3
1903	3	3	4	3	5	5	4	3	3
1904	3	3	4	4	5	4	2	3	3
1905	3	3	4	4	5	4	4	3	3
1906	3	3	4	4	5	6	6	3	4
1907	3	3	4	4	5	6	7	3	4
1908	3	3	4	4	5	4	2	3	2
1909	4	3	4	4	5	4	3	3	2
1910	4	3	4	4	5	5	3	3	3
1911	4	3	4	4	5	4	3	3	3
1912	4	3	4	4	5	5	4	3	4
1913	4	3	4	4	5	6	3	3	4

Source: See Appendix A.

Appendix C. Price indexes for Canada

This appendix describes price indexes constructed primarily from readily available existing series. Particular attention is paid in compiling these data to remedying deficiencies of the existing series that may distort the movement of nontraded relative to traded goods prices. There are several alternative ways of measuring this relative price movement based on the pertinent recent literature that are fortunately in substantial agreement with one another. Major refinements of existing series are unlikely to be critical to the balance-of-payments analyses we undertake.

The principal shortcoming of existing price series is their neglect of nontraded goods prices, a deficiency resulting mainly from omitting the rental prices of housing in indexes applied to the household spending component of GNP. Many existing series are dominated by the prices of food items and to a lesser extent clothing items at the wholesale level – items that are, with few exceptions, traded goods. Some series include fuel and light, but few have any rental component, especially before 1900. Despite minor exceptions, often of regional origin, it seems reasonable to view traded goods at the national level of aggregation throughout the period studied as mainly food and clothing items and nontraded goods as best represented by housing costs, including fuel and light. This view is a significant departure from the division of categories used by Coats (1913) and Viner (1924) to reveal the movement of nontraded relative to traded goods prices.[1]

Coats (1915) and Viner (1924) disagree over both the substance and the causes of relative price movement. Coats argues that the price movement of foods as a whole represents the movement of nontraded goods prices and compares this movement with the price movement of raw materials assumed to represent traded goods. Viner splits food into traded and non-traded items, but appears to rely mostly on house rents and other services to represent nontraded goods price movement. Like Coats, Viner includes

[1] The views of both Coats and Viner are elaborated in detail in Viner (1924, chapter 10).

1890 = 100

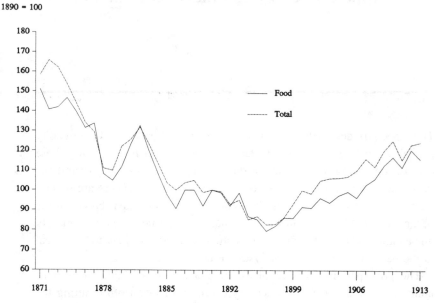

Figure C.1. Wholesale prices, United States: food and total index, 1871–1913.

certain raw materials among traded goods. Coats views price level changes that incorporate increases in the relative prices of nontraded goods as a phenomenon associated with industrialization alone while Viner argues that such price effects do not occur unless there is capital borrowing. Neither Coats nor Viner appears to select the best series for documenting the relevant price changes.[2] Their price series, moreover, are limited to the 1900–13 period.

In Figures C.1, C.2, and C.3 the movements of wholesale food prices and of all prices at wholesale are compared for the United States, the United Kingdom, and Canada from 1870 to 1914 using the best available

---

[2] Viner (1924, pp. 238–9) acknowledges that even perishable and bulky foods sometimes find their way into trade so that it becomes problematic whether any foods constitute purely domestic nontraded goods. Accordingly, he goes on (p. 252) to define domestic goods quite differently from food items by including very few such items with services and house rents. Yet when Coats argues that the price movement of foods as a whole represents the movement of nontraded goods prices, Viner (pp. 248ff) objects only on the relatively weak ground that food includes both traded and nontraded goods whose prices moved differently rather than by taking the more general and stronger position, argued earlier in the same chapter, that nontraded goods include services and rents. The distinction Viner makes between traded and nontraded items does not appear to be consistently worked out.

890 = 100

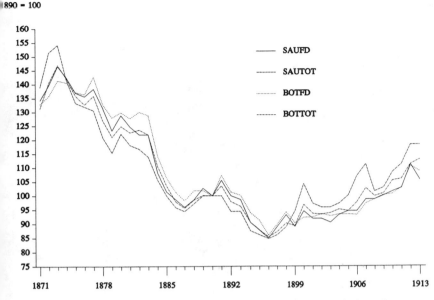

Figure C.2. Wholesale prices, United Kingdom: food and total index, 1871–1913.

series.[3] In each country, the two price movements follow remarkably similar paths. The difference between the food and total indexes is principally
what Coats refers to as raw materials or international commodities. It is
thus fair to assume that the prices of both food and nonfood items measured
by these indexes displayed similar movement. It seems probable, therefore,
that this common pairwise price movement country by country is for the
most part the movement of traded goods prices. Many of what Viner regards
as domestic or nontraded goods are unrepresented.

In Figures C.4 and C.5, the food and total wholesale price indexes of

[3] For the United States, the Warren and Pearson indexes cover the years to 1890 and the
BLS indexes are spliced in 1890 to continue the story to 1914. The resulting indexes are
tabulated in U.S. Department of Commerce (1975): series E-3 and E-16 for food (FOOD),
and series E-1 and E-13 for the total index (TOTAL).

For the United Kingdom, there are two pairs of series, one compiled by Sauerbeck
(SAUFD, SAUTOT) and the other collected by the Board of Trade (BOTFD, BOTTOT)
as found in tables Prices 4 and Prices 5 of Mitchell (1962).

For Canada, the DBS indexes are used: for food (FOOD) an average of vegetable products
(J-36) and animals and their products (J–37); for the total the general index excluding gold
(J-34) as found in Urquhart and Buckley (1965).

1890 = 100

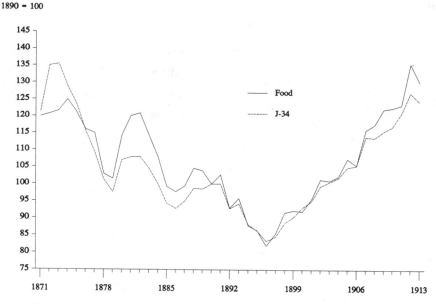

Figure C.3. Canadian wholesale prices (DBS): food and total index, 1871–1913.

the three countries are compared.[4] There are some discrepancies among the series for these countries, but they all tend to follow similar paths, downward toward the mid–1890s and upward thereafter. The only systematic differences among individual country experiences are the tendencies for Canadian prices to fall below U.K. and U.S. prices before 1895 and to rise faster after 1895, and for Canadian and U.S. prices to follow each other more closely than Canadian and U.K. prices in the post–1895 upswing. To the extent that these movements are the movements of traded goods prices, taken as given by all three countries, they largely reflect changes in the terms of trade arising from differences in the composition of exports and imports from one country to another.

Turning to the story of nontraded goods prices, it is easy to see why previous researchers have not pursued the movement of housing rentals very far. Although advertised rentals and official statistics provide a few observations of rental price, the information is too incomplete and discontinuous to provide the comprehensive measure required. Such data

---

[4] For the United States and Canada, the series used are the same as used in Figures C.1 and C.3. For the United Kingdom, the Board of Trade series used in Figure C.2 is employed. For sources, see note 3.

1890 = 100

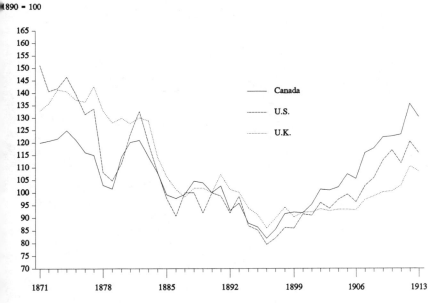

Figure C.4. Food price indexes: Canada, United States, and United Kingdom, 1871–1913.

usually omit rural dwellers and provide no systematic treatment of quality change. The Department of Labour began to collect rental prices for six-to-eight-room houses only in 1900 and a rental price index starting in 1890 covers only Toronto and uses advertised asking prices.[5] A more promising source is the work done by Marion Steele in preparing estimates of residential rent to be incorporated into the new Canadian national income estimates.[6] Using a variety of sources, Steele manages to piece together fragmentary prices and more continuous construction cost data to produce an average rent index at the national level. The alternatives described below for discriminating between traded and nontraded goods price movement make use of aspects of this study to build series measuring the movement of nontraded goods prices.

The principal shortcoming of the Steele average rent series for purposes of this study is its focus on average rent paid rather than pure price change. Average rent is an attempt to capture the actual rents paid and incorporates an allowance for changes in housing quality such as changes in the number

[5] See Coats (1915) and Chambers (1984).
[6] See Urquhart (1986) and Steele (1977).

1890 = 100

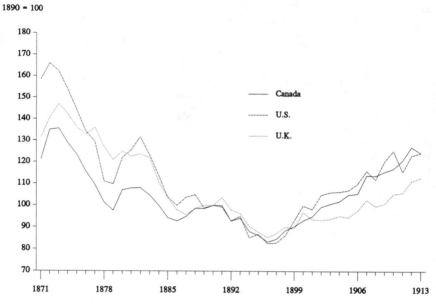

Figure C.5. Wholesale price indexes: Canada, United States, and United Kingdom, 1871–1913.

of rooms per dwelling unit and in the provision of sanitary conveniences.[7] The relevant accommodation to be priced clearly changes with time, but for price index purposes any quality improvement is best reflected in increased expenditure that increases the weight given to housing in the price index and not in the price movement associated with the various dimensions of housing itself.[8] An alternative to the average rent index, therefore, is an index of construction costs that from time to time incorporates new construction material prices that pick up at least some changes in housing quality. Such an index is a compromise between pure price change and price change that includes some quality change.[9]

[7] Steele uses benchmark information to compute average rents paid in benchmark years and then interpolates with construction cost and other data implicitly including quality change.

[8] Ideally, a price index would apply not to the housing units themselves, but to the various elements of housing that produce utility. Changes in the combination of these elements then define quality change and are reflected in the price index by changes in the weights given to these elements. Such an elaborate decomposition of price change, the objective of hedonic price indexing, is not attempted here. For the setup required in such an analysis, see Bailey, Muth, and Nourse (1963).

[9] Steele's average rent index is, of course, another compromise but is somewhat less conservative in what it implies for the relative price movement of nontraded goods prices. By

The use of construction costs as a proxy for housing price, of course, raises issues of capital theory and market performance. Housing flows consumed in any one year are derived from a stock of housing, only a fraction of which may be constructed in that year, and the fraction representing new construction may change from year to year. To the extent that construction costs reflect only the price of new housing, they may appear to ignore the value of the existing stock of housing of varying vintages, especially in years when construction is minimal. To argue that existing housing is valued differently from its replacement cost, however, requires an assumption that changes in demand for housing are only imperfectly transmitted to the demand for construction materials and workers. Lack of evidence to support this assumption encourages the use of construction costs data.[10]

In preparing historical estimates of residential rents, Steele (1977, Table 5) develops a national index of construction costs that may be viewed as an index of housing stock price. It may be converted into a series for the flow of housing services by applying the appropriate depreciation, mortgage, and tax rates.[11] The resulting series (CCP) is displayed in Figure C.6. In other work also using construction cost data, James Pickett derives a housing price series that corresponds very closely to the derivation based on Steele's data.[12] All these series show a moderate decline from the early 1870s to the latter half of the 1890s followed by a sharper rise to 1914.

The integration of rental price series with other existing series provides three alternative ways of measuring comprehensive price change that is potentially decomposable into traded and nontraded goods price movements. As can be seen from Figure C.7, the three alternative published national series correspond fairly closely to each other though they differ

choosing an index that moves somewhat less dramatically than average rents, we have selected a resulting price series biased somewhat against the movement of nontraded goods prices that would support the portfolio theory of balance-of-payments adjustment.

[10] Some have observed that construction costs bear a close relationship with housing rents. See, for example, Muth (1960, p. 68) and Steele (1977, p. 6).

[11] The mortgage rate used in this application is the Canadian rate reported by Neufeld (1972, Table 15.2, pp. 562–3). An annual depreciation rate of 0.05 is assumed, following Firestone (1951, p. 356). The tax rates are based on the city tax revenues and assessed property values for the years immediately prior to 1914 reported by Perry (1955, pp. 668–71). These rates and the relevant prices are related as follows:

$$P^* = P \cdot (r + d + t(1 + r))/(1 + r)$$

where P^* is the rental price of housing, P is the investment good price, r is the mortgage rate, d is the depreciation rate, and t is the property tax rate. These adjustments, though required in principle, produce negligible change in the underlying series.

[12] See Pickett (1963, Table 5, p. 51).

1890 = 100

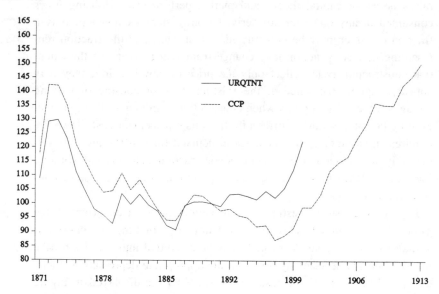

Figure C.6. Canadian nontraded goods prices: Urquhart, Steele adjusted, 1871–1913.

quite sharply in concept. The first of these (J-1) uses Michell's price index of seventy wholesale items, forty-five of which are food or clothing items.[13] The second (J-34) uses a DBS index of wholesale prices.[14] The third (URQT) is a new combination of series used by Urquhart to help interpret his new national income estimates.[15] In each case the published series are intended to offer a comprehensive measure of output price movement. It is not immediately clear, however, how much these series differ from series measuring purely traded goods prices. The first two, in the light of arguments made above, are dominated by the movement of traded goods prices, while only the latter contains a component for house rentals. Figure C.8 compares the first two with Kingston food (traded goods) prices in URQT to provide alternative views of traded goods price movement.

To decompose these data more carefully into nontraded and traded goods price movements requires information on the share of nontraded goods in the total. Although the ratios of exports and imports to GNP remain almost

[13] This series is recorded in Urquhart and Buckley (1965) as series J–1 and is described in detail in Michell (1931).

[14] This series is recorded in Urquhart and Buckley (1965) as series J–34 and described in detail on page 284.

[15] See Urquhart (1986, appendix 5, pp. 85–7).

0 = 100

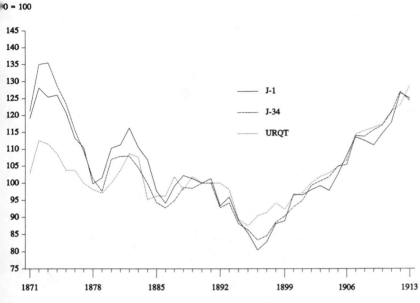

Figure C.7. Canadian price deflators: Michell, DBS, and Urquhart, 1871–1913.

unchanged over the period studied, the ratios of the value of nontraded to traded goods in consumption or production need not have remained unchanged.[16] Food and clothing that dominate the traded goods category, for example, become a less important fraction of the household budget as income and income per capita grow over the period under study.[17] The appropriate weights given to traded and nontraded goods in the total indexes constructed for this study give more weight to nontraded relative to traded goods in the later than the earlier years of the period. Urquhart (1986) is followed in using the 1880s as a weighting-pattern benchmark based on the household surveys conducted by the Ontario Bureau of Industries. Dick (1986a) has developed an historical projection of these survey results to provide a time series of the aggregate expenditure share for food. On the grounds that food and clothing are both traded goods that typically follow Engel's Law according to most budget studies, percentage changes over

[16] For evidence of constant trade ratios, see Urquhart (1986, p. 33) and Firestone (1958, p. 152).
[17] Food absorbed about 50 percent of the household budget in the nineteenth century, but the fraction falls, starting in 1900, to only about 25 percent by 1914. See Dick (1986a, p. 487).

1890 = 100

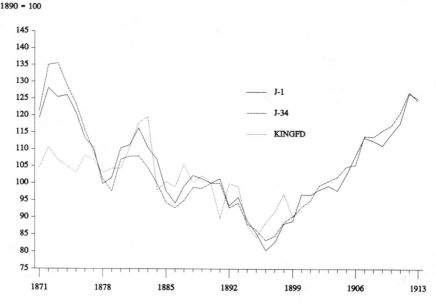

Figure C.8. Canadian traded goods prices: Michell, DBS, and Barnett, 1871–1913.

time in the historical food share are used to extrapolate forward and backward the clothing expenditure share of 0.20 for the late 1880s. The sum of food and clothing expenditure shares is used to compute the share of traded goods in the total index. The remainder of the weight is given to the movement of nontraded goods prices, principally housing, fuel, and light.

The Michell index

Although this index is sometimes regarded as a reasonable measure of comprehensive price movement, virtually all of the items therein can be found in the trade statistics. It is therefore regarded here as one possible measure of traded goods price movement. The fact that it lacks a weighting pattern, draws mainly on Toronto prices, and uses wholesale rather than retail prices limits its application in this study far less than the omission of any good indicator of nontraded goods price movement. This series (J–1) is included in Figure C.8, which compares the three alternative indexes as measures of traded goods price movement.

1890 = 100

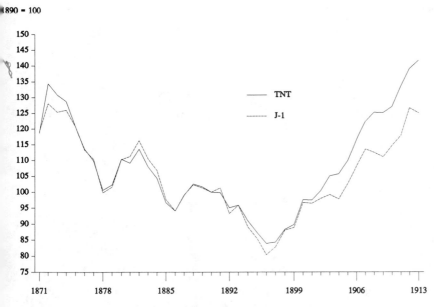

Figure C.9. The Michell deflator: combined traded and nontraded, Michell (J-1), 1871–1913.

Michell's index is combined with the national housing price index (CCP) derived from the Steele series described above, using the weights extrapolated from the Ontario Bureau of Industries surveys. The resulting total index (TNT) inclusive of both traded and nontraded goods prices is displayed in Figure C.9 along with the original Michell series (J-1). It is clear that nontraded goods prices must have advanced more rapidly starting in the 1890s to account for the more rapid rise in TNT relative to J-1 after 1895. Figure C.12 tells the same story by showing the movement in the ratio of nontraded to traded goods price movement (CCP/J-1).

The DBS index

The DBS index covers a wider variety of items than the Michell index, especially after 1900, but half the weight is assigned to food and clothing items. Many of the remaining items are also clearly traded goods, leaving only a few construction materials with minor weight as probable nontraded items. Like the Michell series (J-1), the DBS index (J-34) appears to be mainly a traded goods price index. The two correspond closely with one another in Figures C.7 and C.8.

1890 = 100

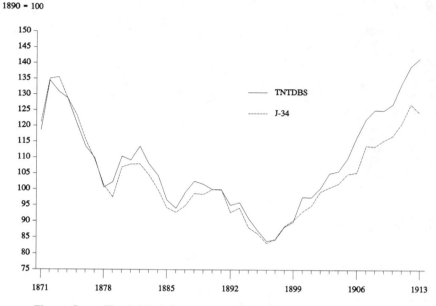

Figure C.10. The DBS deflator: combined traded and nontraded, DBS (J-34), 1871–1913.

Aggregating the DBS series with the housing price series (CCP), again using the weights derived from the Ontario Bureau of Industries surveys, yields TNTDBS in Figure C.10. The result is much the same as shown in Figure C.9. The two series follow one another somewhat more closely than in Figure C.9, with an unmistakable rise in the relative prices of nontraded goods starting in the 1890s. This is also evident in Figure C.12, where CCP/J-34 follows virtually the same pattern as CCP/J-1.

The Urquhart index

Unlike the Michell and DBS indexes, Urquhart attempts to proxy a GNP deflator with a combination of a cost-of-living index prepared for household expenditures and other price series prepared by Statistics Canada to apply to fixed capital formation. Primarily retail price movement is measured by the cost-of-living index and is derived from a splicing together of Kingston retail prices of food, fuel, and light for all of the years prior to 1900,[18]

---

[18] The Kingston series are the only existing series that attempt to measure retail price change back to 1870. They were compiled by Barnett (1963).

and a revised Department of Labour index for all Canada, interpolating a few gaps in the early twentieth century with wholesale price movement.[19] For the noncapital goods part of the deflator, therefore, Urquhart included both traded and nontraded goods prices. Using fixed Ontario Bureau of Industry weights, Urquhart combines the average rent index constructed by Steele with the Kingston cost-of-living index to provide a total index for the years before 1900. For the twentieth century, the revised Department of Labour cost-of-living index includes both clothing and rent components and uses the 1913 DBS weights – 40 percent to food, 18 percent to clothing, 20 percent to rent, and 6 percent to fuel and lighting. When the capital stock price indexes are combined with these cost-of-living components, the resulting series (URQT), as Figure C.7 shows, corresponds more closely to the Michell and DBS series than one might have expected, given that the latter two reflect traded goods price movement alone. The less dramatic fall in the Urquhart series before 1900 is undoubtedly due to the use of retail rather than wholesale prices, but the close correspondence of the different series thereafter gives little indication of the relative price movement noted in Figures C.9 and C.10. Perhaps the relative price movement we wish to isolate has been submerged by the aggregation that includes price series for capital formation. Certainly Canada was a substantial importer of durable capital goods and their prices ought to be regarded as traded goods prices. As predominantly intermediate goods, their prices may have moved in much the same way as some of the wholesale price series included in J-34 and J-1.

Without knowing the details of the weighting pattern used in the Urquhart deflator, it is difficult to derive an appropriate decomposition of the aggregate index to reveal what it may say about the movement of nontraded good prices relative to traded good prices. It may nonetheless be worthwhile to probe the Urquhart reconstruction further along the same lines explored with the alternative Michell and DBS series to see whether it can provide any useful new information about relative price movements. Since we have no information that would allow us to decompose the capital goods price series into traded and nontraded goods price movement, we examine the cost-of-living component only. We also concentrate on the years prior to 1900, since the authors of the Bertram and Percy (1979) index used by Urquhart for the post-1900 years provide no decomposition of their index

---

[19] See Bertram and Percy (1979). The missing years of 1901–04 and 1906–08 are filled in by interpolation using the DBS index J-34 as reported in Urquhart and Buckley (1965).

1890 = 100

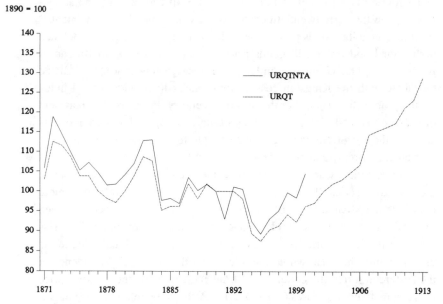

Figure C.11. The Urquhart deflator: traded and nontraded, Urquhart (NBER), 1871–1913.

to help us delineate the relative price movement of interest here. Following Urquhart's lead, the Kingston food index (KINGFD in Figure C.8) is taken as a measure of traded goods price movement, and a combination of Kingston fuel and light and the Steele average rental index is taken as a measure of nontraded goods price movement (URQTNT in Figure C.6). As Figure C.11 shows, weighting these together with the extrapolated Ontario Bureau of Industry weights yields a total index from 1870 to 1900 (URQTNTA) that tracks fairly well the total Urquhart index (URQT) for these years. The onset of the increase in the relative prices of nontraded goods (URQKINGF), however, is somewhat ambiguous according to Figure C.12 and might even be as early as the first half of the 1880s. Unless a decomposition of the movement of capital goods prices were substantially different from the decomposition just made for the cost-of-living component, there would appear to be little more we can learn about relative price movement from the Urquhart series than we already know from the other series.

The similarity of results based on wholesale and retail price data with the exception of the early 1870s deserves further comment. Markups are

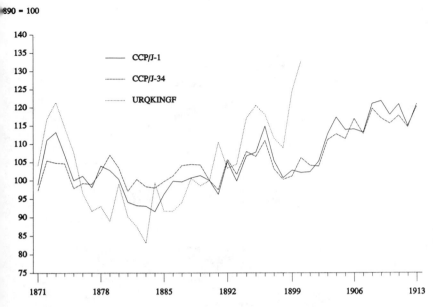

890 = 100

Figure C.12. The ratio of nontraded to traded goods prices, 1871–1913: with Michell, DBS, and Urquhart.

implicitly included in most of the series entering into the Urquhart cost-of-living index and omitted from the J-1 and J-34 wholesale price series. It is also known that markups showed a relative increase after 1900.[20] Markups represent services, in effect nontraded goods. When wholesale and retail indexes move together, it could mean that markups show the same price movement as wholesale prices, or that markups move differently, say in line with housing prices, and the weighting pattern of total indexes like TNT, TNTDBS, or URQTNT combining wholesale and housing prices gives more weight to housing than the retail index where the same price movement is partly incorporated in retail prices inclusive of markups. The issue is of some importance since the relative price movement the present study requires may be biased unless the measure used implicitly lumps markups with nontraded goods.[21]

[20] See Coats (1913). In preliminary analysis with Toronto prices it also appears that retail prices do advance somewhat more rapidly than wholesale prices after 1900.
[21] One disadvantage of the Urquhart index from the point of view of observing our sought-after relative price movement is that retail food prices include markups. Food prices are mostly traded good prices while markups are nontraded goods. This smudges the distinction that the present study wants to make. Also, Urquhart's interpolation of retail with wholesale price series confounds the same distinction.

1890 = 100

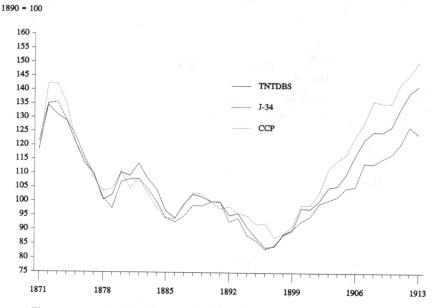

Figure C.13. Traded and nontraded goods prices: Canada, 1871–1913.

The following conclusions appear to be warranted from this price history evidence:

1. All prices follow a fluctuating downward path from 1870 to about 1895–98 and a more sharply upward and fluctuating movement thereafter.

2. Although the DBS index is more complete and more accurately weighted than the Michell series and both are conceptually poorer GNP deflators than the Urquhart index, all three appear to provide similar stories about the path of nontraded relative to traded goods prices.

3. The turning point in the relative movement of nontraded goods prices appears to be no later than the 1890s.

The reconstruction using the DBS series is chosen because it possesses several advantages for documenting the required relative price movement. First, wholesale prices of foods are purely traded output prices. Second, rents represented by construction costs are nontraded output prices. Construction costs are wholesale prices of significant inputs into housing. Third, the weights used in this reconstruction result in a conservative estimate of relative price movement.[22]

---

[22] The weights used are derived from expenditure and income data ignoring the influence of price change on expenditure. In a cost-of-living context this would mean that substitution

To summarize the provisional conclusions on the relevant Canadian price history, three series are shown together in Figure C.13: a total price index (TNTDBS from Figure C.10), an index of traded goods prices (J-34 from Figure C.10), and an index of nontraded goods prices (CCP from Figure C.6). The corresponding data series can be found in Appendix B.

based on relative price change inclusive of markups would be missed. When the relative price of food falls, for example, near the end of the period, a price inelastic food demand implies that expenditure on food should fall and a smaller weight be given to traded goods in a retail price index as a result. When this occurs, the relative price of nontraded goods rises and their weight in a retail price index should increase. The effect on the overall index of using weights that do not reflect this price effect is to understate the upward price level movement attributable to a rise in the relative prices of nontraded goods. Correcting for the substitution effect at the retail level is, however, not really proper in the present context even if it were possible since ideally what is required is the change in weights applicable to traded and nontraded goods where markups are included in nontraded goods alone, and not the change in weights among traded and nontraded commodities whose prices are all measured inclusive of markups. Since the weighting pattern actually ignores any weighting correction for relative price changes, any rise in the domestic price level due to a relative rise in the prices of nontraded goods will be understated. In other words, the relative price changes in the data used in this study are smaller than in principle such changes actually were, thus biasing our statistical results against the hypothesis we wish to confirm.

References

Aitken, H. G. J., 1952. "A Note on the Capital Resources of Upper Canada." *Canadian Journal of Economics and Political Science* 18 (November): 525–32.

1961. *American Capital and Canadian Resources*. Cambridge, Mass.: Harvard University Press.

Aldrich, N. W., 1892. *Report on Retail Prices and Wages*. Senate Report No. 986. 52nd Congress, 1st session.

Altman, M., 1984. "New Price Indexes for Canada, Quebec, Ontario 1850–1910 and Their Application to Canadian Manufacturing Output." Unpublished paper. McGill University, Montreal.

Angell, J. W., 1925a. "The Effects of International Payments in the Past." In *The Inter-ally Debts and the United States*, National Industrial Conference Board, 138–89. New York: NICB.

1925b. "Review of Canada's Balance of International Indebtedness 1900–1913." *Political Science Quarterly* 40 (June): 320–2.

1925c. *The Theory of International Prices: History, Criticism and Restatement*. Cambridge, Mass.: Harvard University Press.

Ankli, Robert E., 1980. "The Growth of the Canadian Economy, 1896–1920. Export Led And/or Neoclassical Growth." *Explorations in Economic History* 17 (July): 251–74.

Bailey, Martin J., Richard F. Muth, and Hugh O. Nourse, 1963. "A Regression Method for Real Estate Price Index Construction." *Journal of the American Statistical Association* 56 (December): 933–42.

Barnett, R. F. J., 1963. *A Study of Price Movements and the Cost of Living in Kingston, Ontario*. Mimeo. Master's thesis. Queen's University, Kingston.

1966. *Canadian Manufacturing Development and Foreign Trade 1870–1915*. Mimeo. Ph.D. dissertation. Cambridge, England.

Barskey, Robert B., and Lawrence Summers, H., 1988. "Gibson's Paradox and the Gold Standard." *Journal of Political Economy* 96 (June): 528–50.

Bartlett, E. A., 1981. "Real Wages and the Standard of Living in Vancouver 1901–1929." *BC Studies* 51: 3–62.

Baskerville, P. A., 1985. "The Pet Bank, the Local State and the Imperial Centre, 1850–1864." *Journal of Canadian Studies* 20 (3): 22–46.

Beach, W., 1935. *British International Gold Movements and Banking Policy, 1881–1913*. Cambridge, Mass.: Harvard University Press.

Beckhart, Benjamin Haggott, 1929. *The Banking System of Canada*. New York: Henry Holt.

Berger, Carl, 1986. *The Writing of Canadian History*. Toronto: Oxford University Press.

Bertram, Gordon, 1963. "Economic Growth in Canadian Industry, 1870–1915:

217

The Staple Model and the Take-Off Hypothesis.'' *Canadian Journal of Economics and Political Science* 29 (May): 159–84.

Bertram, Gordon, and Michael Percy, 1979. ''Real Wage Trends in Canada, 1900–26: Some Provisional Estimates.'' *Canadian Journal of Economics* 12 (May): 300–12.

Bloomfield, Arthur I., 1959. *Monetary Policy Under the International Gold Standard*. New York: Federal Reserve Bank of New York.

   1963. *Short-term Capital Movements Under the Pre-1914 Gold Standard*. Princeton Studies in International Finance, no. 11. Princeton: Department of Economics, Princeton University.

   1968. *Patterns of Fluctuation in International Investment Before 1914*. Princeton Studies in International Finance, no. 21. Princeton: Department of Economics, Princeton University.

Board of Governors, Federal Reserve System (U.S.), 1943. *Banking and Monetary Statistics*. Washington: Board of Governors of the Federal Reserve System.

Bordo, Michael D., 1984. ''The Gold Standard: The Traditional Approach.'' In *A Retrospective on the Classical Gold Standard, 1821–1931*, ed. Michael D. Bordo and Anna J. Schwartz, pp. 23–119. Chicago: University of Chicago Press.

   1985. ''The Impact and International Transmission of Financial Crises: Some Historical Evidence, 1870–1933.'' *Rivista Di Storia Economica* 2 (International issue): 41–78.

   1986. ''Explorations in Monetary History: A Survey of the Literature.'' *Explorations in Economic History* 23 (October): 339–415.

Bordo, Michael D., and Lars Jonung, 1981. ''The Long-run Behavior of the Income Velocity of Money in Five Countries, 1870–1975: An Institutional Approach.'' *Economic Inquiry* 19 (1): 96–116.

   1987. *The Long-run Behavior of the Velocity of Circulation*. Cambridge, England: Cambridge University Press.

Borts, George, 1964. ''A Theory of Long-run International Capital Movements.'' *Journal of Political Economy* 72 (August): 341–59.

Bowley, A. L., 1937. *Wages and Income Since 1860*. Cambridge, England: Cambridge University Press.

Brady, D. S., 1966. ''Price Deflators for Final Product Estimates.'' In *Output, Employment and Productivity in the U.S. After 1800*. NBER Studies in income and wealth, pp. 91–115. New York: Columbia University Press.

Branson, William H., and Dale W. Henderson, 1985. ''The Specification and Influence of Asset Markets.'' In *Handbook of International Economics*, vol. 2. ed. Ronald W. Jones and Peter B. Kenen, pp. 749–805. Amsterdam: North Holland.

Britnell, G. E., 1939. *The Wheat Economy*. Toronto: University of Toronto Press.

Brown, E. H. Phelps, and S. V. Hopkins, 1981. *A Perspective of Wages and Prices*. London: Methuen.

Buckley, K. A. H., 1952. ''Urban Building and Real Estate Fluctuations in Canada.'' *Canadian Journal of Economics and Political Science* 18 (February): 41–62.

   1955. *Capital Formation in Canada 1896–1930*. Canadian Studies in Economics. Toronto: University of Toronto Press.

   1963. ''Working Paper on Population, Labour Force and Economic Growth.''

Banff Business Policies Conference on Canadian Economic Survival, vol. 2. Banff School of Advanced Management and the Universities of Alberta, Manitoba, and Saskatchewan.

Buiter, Willem H., and Douglas D. Purvis, 1983. "Oil, Disinflation, and Export Competitiveness: A Model of the Dutch Disease." In *Economic Interdependence and Flexible Exchange Rates*, ed. J. Bhandari and B. Putnam, pp. 221–47. Cambridge, Mass.: MIT Press.

Cairncross, A. K., 1953. *Home and Foreign Investment 1890–1913*. Cambridge, England: Cambridge University Press.

1968 (first published, 1953). "Investment in Canada." In *The Export of Capital from Great Britain, 1870–1914*, ed. and introduction by A. R. Hall, pp. 153–86. Debates in economic history. London: Methuen.

Capie, Forrest, and Alan Webber, 1985. *A Monetary History of the United Kingdom, 1870–1982*, vol. 1. *Data, Sources and Methods*. London: Allen & Unwin.

Carr, Jack, 1972. "A Suggestion for the Treatment of Serial Correlation: A Case in Point." *Canadian Journal of Economics* 5 (May): 301–06.

1983. "The Demand for Money: A Re-interpretation." Mimeo. Toronto: Department of Economics, University of Toronto.

Carr, Jack, and Michael Darby, 1981. "The Role of Money Supply Shocks in the Short-run Demand for Money." *Journal of Monetary Economics* 8 (September): 183–99.

Carr, R. M., 1931. "The Role of the International Trade Mechanism." *Quarterly Journal of Economics* 45 (August): 710–19.

Caves, Richard E., and Richard H. Holton, 1961. *The Canadian Economy: Prospect and Retrospect*. Harvard economic studies. Cambridge, Mass.: Harvard University Press.

Chambers, E. J., 1964. "Late Nineteenth Century Business Cycles in Canada." *Canadian Journal of Economics and Political Science* 30 (August): 391–412.

1984. "A New Measure of the Rental Cost of Housing in the Toronto Market, 1890–1914." *Histoire Sociale/Social History* 17 (May): 165–74.

Chambers, E. J., and D. F. Gordon, 1966. "Primary Products and Economic Growth: An Empirical Measurement." *Journal of Political Economy* 74 (August): 315–32.

Chow, Gregory C., 1983. *Econometrics*. New York: McGraw-Hill.

Clinton, Kevin, 1973. "The Demand Function for Money in Canada, 1955–70: Some Single Equation Estimates and Stability Tests." *Canadian Journal of Economics* 6 (February): 53–61.

Coats, R. H., 1910. *Wholesale Prices in Canada 1890–1909*. Special report. Ottawa: Department of Labour.

1913. "The Role of the Middleman." *Papers and Proceedings of the Annual Meeting of the Canadian Political Science Association* 1: 1–28.

1915. *Report of the Board of Inquiry into the Cost of Living*. 2 vols. Ottawa: Department of Labour.

Cochrane, D., and G. H. Orcutt, 1949. "Application of Least-squares Regression to Relationships Containing Autocorrelated Error Terms." *Journal of the American Statistical Association* 44 (1): 32–61.

Crafts, N. F. R., 1984. "Economic Growth in France and Britain, 1830–1910: A Review of the Evidence." *Journal of Economic History* 45 (March): 49–68.

Curtis, C. A., 1931. *Statistical Contributions to Canadian Economic History*, vol. 1. *Statistics of Banking*. Toronto: Macmillan.

Dales, John H., 1964. "Estimates of Canadian Manufacturing Output by Markets, 1870–1915." In *Canadian Political Science Association Conferences on Statistics, 1962 and 1963*, ed. J. Henripin and A. Asimakopulos, pp. 61–91. Toronto: University of Toronto Press.

Davidson, R., and J. G. MacKinnon, 1981. "Several Tests for Model Specification in the Presence of Alternative Hypotheses." *Econometrica* 49 (May): 781–93.

Davis, L. E., and J. R. T. Hughes, 1960. "A Dollar-sterling Exchange, 1803–95." *Economic History Review* 8 (August): 52–78.

de Cecco, Marcello, 1984. *The International Gold Standard: Money and Empire*. London: Francis Pinter.

Dick, T. J. O., 1980. "Canadian Wheat Production and Trade, 1896–1930." *Explorations in Economic History* 17 (September): 275–302.

1986a. "Consumer Behavior in the Nineteenth Century: Ontario Workers 1885–1889." *Journal of Economic History* 46 (June): 477–88.

1986b. "Canadian Prices, Price Movements and the Cost-of-Living 1870–1914." Paper presented at the Ninth Congress of the International Economic History Association, Bern, 1986. Mimeo. Lethbridge: Department of Economics, University of Lethbridge.

Dick, Trevor J. O., and John E. Floyd, 1991. "Balance of Payments Adjustment Under the International Gold Standard: Canada, 1871–1913." *Explorations in Economic History* 28 (April): 209–38.

Dornbusch, R., 1975. "A Portfolio Balance Model of the Open Economy." *Journal of Monetary Economics* 5 (February): 3–20

Dutton, John, 1984. "The Bank of England and the Rules of the Game Under the Gold Standard: New Evidence." In *A Retrospective on the Classical Gold Standard, 1821–1931*, ed. Michael D. Bordo and Anna J. Schwartz, pp. 173–203. Chicago: University of Chicago Press.

Easterbrook, W. T., and H. G. J. Aitken, 1958. *Canadian Economic History*. Toronto: Macmillan.

Edelstein, Michael, 1981. "Foreign Investment and Empire 1860–1914." In *The Economic History of Britain Since 1700*, ed. R. Floud and D. N. McCloskey, pp. 70–98. Cambridge, England: Cambridge University Press.

1982. *Overseas Investment in the Age of High Imperialism: The United Kingdom 1850–1914*. New York: Columbia University Press.

Eichengreen, Barry, 1985. *The Gold Standard in Theory and History*. New York: Methuen.

1987. "Conducting the International Orchestra: Bank of England Leadership Under the Gold Standard." *Journal of International Money and Finance* 6 (March): 5–29.

Evans, L. T., and N. C. Quigley, 1990. "Discrimination in Bank Lending Policies: A Test Using Data from the Bank of Nova Scotia." *Canadian Journal of Economics* 23 (February): 210–25.

Faucher, Albert, 1960. "Some Aspects of the Financial Difficulties of the Province of Canada." *Canadian Journal of Economics and Political Science* 26 (November): 617–24.

Feinstein, C. H., 1972. *National Income, Expenditure, and Output of the United Kingdom, 1885–1965*. Cambridge, England: Cambridge University Press.

Field, Fred W., 1912. *Capital Investments in Canada*. Toronto: Monetary Times of Canada.

Firestone, O. J., 1951. *Residential Real Estate in Canada*. Toronto: University of Toronto Press.

1958. *Canada's Economic Development 1867–1953*. Income and Wealth Series 7. London: Bowes & Bowes.

1960. "The Development of Canada's Economy 1850–1900." In *Trends in the American Economy in the Nineteenth Century*, pp. 217–52. NBER Studies in income and wealth, vol. 24. Princeton: Princeton University Press.

1969. *Industry and Education, A Century of Canadian Development*. Ottawa: University of Ottawa Press.

Fishlow, Albert, 1985. "Lessons from the Past: Capital Markets During the Nineteenth Century and the Interwar Period." *International Organization* 39 (3): 383–439.

Flanders, M. June, 1989. *International Monetary Economics, 1870–1960*. Cambridge, England: Cambridge University Press.

Fleming, J. M., 1962. "Domestic Financial Policies Under Fixed and Flexible Exchange Rates." *International Monetary Fund Staff Papers* 9 (November): 369–79.

Floyd, J. E., 1969a. "International Capital Movements and Monetary Equilibrium." *American Economic Review* 49 (December): 472–92.

1969b. "Monetary and Fiscal Policy in a World of Capital Mobility." *Review of Economic Studies* 36 (4): 503–17.

1985. *World Monetary Equilibrium*. Philadelphia: University of Pennsylvania Press.

Ford, A. G., 1962. *The Gold Standard, 1880–1914: Britain and Argentina*. Oxford: Clarendon Press.

Frankel, Jeffrey, 1983. "Monetary and Portfolio Balance Models of Exchange Rate Determination." In *Economic Interdependence and Flexible Exchange Rates*, ed. J. Bhandari and B. Putnam, pp. 84–115. Cambridge, Mass.: MIT Press.

Fratianni, M., and F. Spinelli, 1984. "Italy and the Gold Standard Period, 1861–1914." In *A Retrospective on the Classical Gold Standard, 1821–1931*, ed. Michael D. Bordo and Anna J. Schwartz, pp. 405–41. Chicago: University of Chicago Press.

Frenkel, Jacob, and H. G. Johnson, eds., 1976. *Monetary Approach to the Balance of Payments*. London: Allen and Unwin.

Frenkel, Jacob, and Michael Mussa, 1985. "Asset Markets, Exchange Rates, and the Balance of Payments." In *Handbook of International Economics*, ed. R. W. Jones and Peter B. Kenen, vol. 2, pp. 679–747. Amsterdam: North Holland.

Frenkel, Jacob, and Carlos Rodriguez, 1975. "Portfolio Equilibrium and the Balance of Payments: A Monetary Approach." *American Economic Review* 65 (September): 674–88.

Friedman, Milton, 1962. *Price Theory: A Provisional Text*. Chicago: Aldine-Atherton.

Friedman, M., and A. J. Schwartz, 1963. *A Monetary History of the United States, 1867–1960*. Princeton: Princeton University Press.

1982. *Monetary Trends in the United States and the United Kingdom*. Chicago: University of Chicago Press.

Godfrey, L. G., 1985. "On the Use of Misspecification Checks and Tests of Non-nested Hypotheses in Empirical Econometrics." In *Conference Papers: Selected Papers of the Royal Economic Society and the Association of University Teachers of Economics*, pp. 69–81. Cambridge, England: Cambridge University Press.

Goodhart, C. A. E., 1969. *The New York Money Market and the Finance of Trade, 1900–1913*. Cambridge, Mass.: Harvard University Press.

Gordon, Robert J., 1990. "What Is New-Keynesian Economics?" *Journal of Economic Literature* 28 (September): 1115–71.

Graham, Frank D., 1922. "International Trade Under Depreciated Paper: The United States 1862–1879." *Quarterly Journal of Economics* 36 (November): 220–7.

Granger, C. W. C., 1969. "Investigating Causal Relations by Econometric Models and Cross-spectral Methods." *Econometrica* 37 (July): 424–38.

Green, Alan, and M. C. Urquhart, 1976. "Factor and Commodity Flows in the International Economy of 1870–1914: A Multi-country View." *Journal of Economic History* 36 (March): 217–52.

1987. "New Estimates of Output Growth in Canada: Measurement and Interpretation." In *Perspectives on Canadian Economic History*, ed. Douglas McCalla, pp. 182–99. Toronto: Copp, Clark, Pitman.

Griliches, Zvi, 1957. "Specification Bias in Estimates of Production Functions." *Journal of Farm Economics* 39 (February): 8–20.

1966. "Specification Analysis in Econometrics." Unpublished paper. Department of Economics, University of Chicago.

Harkness, Jon, 1969. *Monetary and Fiscal Policies in Closed and Open Economies: The Portfolio Approach*. Ph.D. dissertation Queen's University Kingston.

Harley, C. Knick, 1980. "Transportation, the World Wheat Trade, and the Kuznets Cycle, 1850–1913." *Explorations in Economic History* 17 (July): 218–50.

Hartland, P., 1954. "The Canadian Balance of Payments Since 1868." NBER unpublished paper. New York.

1964. "Canadian Balance of Payments Since 1868." In *Trends in the American Economy in the Nineteenth Century*, pp. 715–55. NBER series in income and wealth, vol. 24. Princeton: Princeton University Press.

Hay, K. A. J., 1966. "Early Twentieth Century Business Cycles in Canada." *Canadian Journal of Economics and Political Science* 32 (August): 354–65.

1968. "Determinants of the Canadian Money Supply 1875–1958." Mimeo. Unpublished paper 68–02. Carleton University, Ottawa.

Hildreth, C., and J. Y. Lu, 1960. *Demand Analysis with Autocorrelated Disturbances*. Technical bulletin 276. East Lansing, Mich.: Agricultural Experiment Station.

Hodrick, Robert J., and Edward C. Prescott, 1981. "Post-War U.S. Business Cycles: An Empirical Investigation." Working paper no. 451. Department of Economics, Carnegie-Mellon University, Pittsburgh, Pa.

Hume, D., 1898 (first published, 1752). "Of the Balance of Trade." In *Essays, Moral, Political and Literary*, pp. 330–45. London: Longmans Green.

Ingram, J. C., 1957. "Growth and Capacity in Canada's Balance of Payments." *American Economic Review* 48: 93–104.

Johnson, H. G., 1958a. "Toward a General Theory of the Balance of Payments." Chap. 6 in *International Trade and Economic Growth*, pp. 153–68. Cambridge, Mass.: Harvard University Press.

1958b. "The Transfer Problem and Exchange Stability." Chap. 7 in *International Trade and Economic Growth*, pp. 169–95. Cambridge, Mass.: Harvard University Press.

1976. "The Monetary Approach to Balance of Payments Theory." Chap. 6 in *The Monetary Approach to the Balance of Payments*, ed. J. A. Frenkel and H. G. Johnson, pp. 147–67. London: Allen and Unwin.

Kendrick, J. W., 1961. *Productivity Trends in the United States*. Princeton: Princeton University Press.

Kindleberger, C. P., 1984. *A Financial History of Western Europe*. London: Allen and Unwin.

1987. *International Capital Movements*. Cambridge, England: Cambridge University Press.

Kouri, Penti J. K., 1977. "International Investment and Interest Rate Linkages Under Flexible Exchange Rates." In *The Political Economy of Monetary Reform*, ed. R. Z. Aliber, pp. 74–96. London: Macmillan.

Leamer, Edward E., 1978. *Specification Searches: Ad Hoc Inferences with Nonexperimental Data*. New York: Wiley.

Lebergott, S., 1964. *Manpower in Economic Growth: The American Record Since 1800*. New York: McGraw-Hill.

Lewis, J. P., 1965. *Building Cycles and Britain's Economic Growth*. New York: St. Martin's Press.

Lucas, R. E., Jr., 1973. "Some International Evidence on Output-inflation Trade-offs." *American Economic Review* 68 (June): 326–34.

1976. "Econometric Policy Evaluation: A Critique." In *The Phillips Curve and Labour Markets*, ed. Karl Brunner and Allan H. Meltzer, pp. 19–46. Carnegie-Rochester Conference Series on Public Policy. Amsterdam: North-Holland.

1978. "Asset Prices in an Exchange Economy." *Econometrica* 46(6): 1426–45.

1982. "Interest Rates and Currency Prices in a Two Country World." *Journal of Monetary Economics* 10 (November): 335–60.

McCloskey, D. N., 1985. "The Loss Function Has Been Mislaid: The Rhetoric of Significance Tests." *American Economic Review* 75 (May): 201–05.

McCloskey, D. N., and J. R. Zecher, 1976. "How the Gold Standard Worked, 1880–1913." In *The Monetary Approach to the Balance of Payments*, ed. J. A. Frenkel and H. G. Johnson, pp. 357–85. London: Allen and Unwin.

1984. "The Success of Purchasing Power Parity: Historical Evidence and Implications for Macroeconomics." In *A Retrospective on the Classical Gold Standard, 1821–1931*, ed. Michael D. Bordo and Anna J. Schwartz, pp. 121–70. Chicago: University of Chicago Press.

McCullough, A. B., 1983. "Currency Conversion in British North America 1760–1900." *Archivaria* (16): 83–94.

1984a. "Canadian Sterling Bill of Exchange Rates 1760–1899." Mimeo. Unpublished paper. Parks Canada, Ottawa.

1984b. *Money and Exchange in Canada*. Toronto: Dundurn Press.

McDougall, D., 1971. "Canadian Manufacturing Commodity Output, 1870–1915." *Canadian Journal of Economics* 4 (February): 21–36.

1973. "The Domestic Availability of Manufactured Commodity Output, Canada 1870–1915." *Canadian Journal of Economics* 6 (May): 189–206.

MacKenzie, W. A., 1921. "Changes in the Standard of Living in the United Kingdom, 1860–1914." *Economica* 3 (October): 211–30.

McKinnon, R. I., and W. E. Oates, 1966. *The Implications of International Economic Integration for Monetary, Fiscal, and Exchange Rate Policy.* Princeton Studies in International Finance. Princeton: Princeton University Press.

Macesich, G., and C. A. Haulman, 1971. "Determinants of the Canadian Money Stock 1875–1964." *Rivista Internazionale Di Scienze Economiche e Commerciali* 18 (March): 249–57.

Mackintosh W. A. 1964 (first published, 1939). *The Economic Background of Dominion-Provincial Relations.* Appendix 3 of the Royal Commission Report on Dominion-Provincial Relations. Carleton Library no. 13. Toronto: McClelland and Stewart.

Marr, William L., and Donald G. Paterson, 1980. *Canada: An Economic History.* Toronto: Gage.

Marr, W., and M. Percy, 1978. "Government and the Rate of Canadian Prairie Settlement." *Canadian Journal of Economics* 11 (4): 757–67.

Meier, G. M., 1953. "Economic Development and the Transfer Mechanism." *Canadian Journal of Economics and Political Science* 19 (February): 1–19.

Mercer, Lloyd, 1982. *Railroads and Land Grant Policy, A Study in Government Intervention.* New York: Academic Press.

Merton, Robert C., 1971. "Optimum Consumption and Portfolio Rules in a Continuous-Time Model." *Journal of Economic Theory* 3 (December): 373–413.

Michell, H., 1931. "Statistics of Prices." In *Statistical Contributions to Canadian Economic History,* K. W. Taylor and H. Michell, vol. 2, pp. 47–88. Toronto: Macmillan.

Miller, Norman C., and Marina von N. Whitman, 1970. "A Mean-variance Analysis of United States Long-term Portfolio Foreign Investment." *Quarterly Journal of Economics* 44 (2): 175–96.

Milne, William J., and Walter N. Torous, 1984. "Long-term Interest Rates and the Price Level: The Canadian Evidence on the Gibson Paradox." *Canadian Journal of Economics* 17 (2): 327–39.

Mitchell, B. R., 1962. *Abstract of British Historical Statistics.* Cambridge, England: Cambridge University Press.

    1975. *European Historical Statistics 1750–1970.* London: Macmillan.

Mitchell, W. C., 1908. *Gold, Prices and Wages Under the Greenback Standard.* Berkeley: University of California Press.

Mizon, G. E., and J. F. Richard, 1986. "The Encompassing Principle and Its Application to Non-nested Hypotheses." *Econometrica* 54 (May): 657–78.

Mundell, Robert, 1960. "Monetary Dynamics of International Adjustment Under Fixed and Flexible Exchange Rates." *Quarterly Journal of Economics* 74 (2): 227–57.

    1961. "Flexible Exchange Rates and Employment Policy." *Canadian Journal of Economics and Political Science* 27 (November): 509–17.

    1963. "Capital Mobility and Stabilization Under Fixed and Flexible Exchange Rates." *Canadian Journal of Economics and Political Science* 29 (November): 475–85.

    1968. *International Economics.* New York: Macmillan.

Mussa, Michael, 1982. "A Model of Exchange Rate Dynamics." *Journal of Political Economy* 90 (February): 74–104.

Muth, J. F., 1960. "Rational Expectations and the Theory of Price Movements." *Econometrica* 98 (May): 315–35.

Nelson, C. R., and C. I. Plosser, 1982. "Trends and Random Walks in Macroeconomic Time Series." *Journal of Monetary Economics* 10 (September): 139–62.

Neufeld, E. P., 1972. *The Financial System in Canada*. New York: St. Martin's Press.

Paterson, D. G., 1976. *British Direct Investment in Canada 1890–1914: Estimates and Determinants*. Toronto: University of Toronto Press.

Paterson, D. G., and R. A. Shearer, 1982. "Canada and the U.S. Greenback Inflation." Unpublished paper. Department of Economics, University of British Columbia.

Perry, J. H., 1955. *Tariffs, Taxes and Subsidies,* 2 vols. Toronto: University of Toronto Press.

Pickett, James, 1963. "Residential Capital Formation in Canada 1871–1921." *Canadian Journal of Economics and Political Science* 19 (May): 403–10.

Pippenger, John, 1984. "Bank of England Operations, 1893–1913." In *A Retrospective on the Classical Gold Standard, 1821–1931,* ed. Michael D. Bordo and Anna J. Schwartz, pp. 203–32. Chicago: University of Chicago Press.

Pomfret, Richard, 1981a. "Capital Formation in Canada 1870–1900." *Explorations in Economic History* 36 (January): 84–96.

1981b. *The Economic Development of Canada*. Toronto: Methuen.

Rees, Albert, 1961. *Real Wages in Manufacturing 1890–1914*. Princeton: Princeton University Press.

Rich, G., 1977. "The Gold-reserve Requirements Under the Dominion Notes Act of 1870: How to Deceive Parliament." *Canadian Journal of Economics* 10 (August): 447–53.

1984. "Canada Without a Central Bank: Operation of the Price-specie-flow Mechanism, 1872–1913." In *A Retrospective on the Classical Gold Standard, 1821–1931,* ed. Michael D. Bordo and Anna J. Schwartz, pp. 547–75. Chicago: University of Chicago Press.

1988. *The Cross of Gold: Money and the Canadian Business Cycle, 1867–1913*. Ottawa: Carleton University Press.

1989. "Canadian Banks, Gold and the Crises of 1907." *Explorations in Economic History* 26 (April): 135–60.

Sargent, T. J., 1973. "Interest Rates and Prices in the Long Run." *Journal of Money Credit and Banking* 5 (February): 385–449.

Schwartz, Anna J., 1986. "Real and Pseudo-financial Crises." In *Financial Crises and the World Banking System,* ed. Forrest Capie and Geoffrey E. Wood, pp. 11–31. New York: St. Martin's Press.

Shearer, R. A., 1965. "The Foreign Currency Business of Canadian Chartered Banks." *Canadian Journal of Economics* 31 (August): 328–57.

Shearer, R. A., J. F. Chant, and D. Bond, 1984. *The Economics of the Canadian Financial System*. 2d ed. Scarborough: Prentice-Hall Canada.

Simon, M., 1970. "New British Investments in Canada, 1865–1914." *Canadian Journal of Economics* 3 (May): 238–54.

Snyder, Carl, 1927. *Business Cycle and Business Measurements*. New York: Macmillan.

Southey, Clive, 1978. "The Staples Thesis, Common Property, and Homestead-ing." *Canadian Journal of Economics* 9 (August): 547–58.

Steele, M. L., 1977. "Estimation of Residential Rent, 1871–1925." Mimeo. Unpublished paper. Department of Economics, University of Guelph.

Stone, Richard, and D. A. Rowe, 1966. *The Measurement of Consumers' Expenditures and Behavior in the U.K., 1920–38.* Cambridge, England: Cambridge University Press.

Stovel, John A., 1959. *Canada in the World Economy.* Cambridge, Mass.: Harvard University Press.

Stulz, Rene, 1984. "Currency Preferences, Purchasing Power Risks and the Determination of Exchange Rates in an Optimizing Model." *Journal of Money Credit and Banking* 16 (August): 302–16.

Taussig, F. W., 1966 (first published, 1927). *International Trade.* New York: Kelly.

Taylor, K. W., 1931. "Statistics of Foreign Trade." In *Statistical Contributions to Canadian Economic History,* K. W. Taylor and H. Michell, vol. 2, pp. 1–45. Toronto: Macmillan.

Thomas, Brinley, 1967. "The Historical Record of International Capital Movements to 1913." In *Capital Movements and Economic Development,* ed. John H. Adler and Paul W. Kuznets, pp. 3–32. London: Macmillan.

1973. *Migration and Economic Growth.* 2d ed. Cambridge, England: Cambridge University Press.

Thorp, Willard Long, 1926. *Business Annals.* New York: National Bureau of Economic Research.

Triffin, Robert, 1964. *The Evolution of the International Monetary System, Historical Reappraisal and Future Perspectives.* Princeton Studies in International Finance. Princeton: Princeton University Press.

United Kingdom Board of Trade, 1913. *Cost of Living of the Working Classes.* Cd 6955. In *Report of an Enquiry by the Board of Trade into Working Class Rents and Retail Prices Together with Certain Rates of Wages in Towns of the U.K. in 1912,* pp. 299–318.

United States Department of Commerce, 1975. *Historical Statistics of the United States.* 2 vols. Washington, DC: GPO.

Urquhart, M. C., 1986. "New Estimates of Gross National Product, Canada, 1870–1926: Some Implications for Canadian Development." In *Long-term Factors in American Economic Growth,* ed. Robert E. Gallman and Stanley L. Engerman, pp. 9–94. NBER Studies in Income and Wealth. Chicago: University of Chicago Press.

Urquhart, M. C., and K. H. A. Buckley, eds., 1965. *Historical Statistics of Canada.* Cambridge, England: Cambridge University Press.

Viner, J., 1924. *Canada's Balance of International Indebtedness 1900–1913.* Cambridge, Mass.: Harvard University Press.

1926. "Angell's Theory of International Prices." *Journal of Political Economy* 34 (August): 597–623.

1937. *Studies in the Theory of International Trade.* New York: Harper.

Whale, P. B., 1937. "The Working of the Pre-war Gold Standard." *Economica* 4(1): 18–32.

White, Harry D., 1933. *The French International Accounts, 1880–1913.* Cambridge, Mass.: Harvard University Press.

Willett, T. D., and F. Forte, 1969. "Interest Rate Policy and the External Balance." *Quarterly Journal of Economics* 83 (May): 242–62.

Williams, John H., 1920. *Argentine International Trade Under Inconvertible Paper Money, 1880–1913*. Cambridge, Mass.: Harvard University Press.

Williamson, J. G., 1961. "International Trade and U.S. Economic Development 1827–1843." *Journal of Economic History* 21 (September): 372–83.

1963. "Real Growth, Monetary Disturbances and the Transfer Process: The United States, 1879–1900." *Southern Economic Journal* 29 (January): 167–80.

Wood, G. H., 1909. "Real Wages and the Standard of Comfort since 1850." *Journal of the Royal Statistical Society* 72 (Part 1): 91–103.

Index

aggregate demand, 20, 149, 151
aggregate output, 22
Aitken, H. G. J., 34n, 128n
Aldrich, M., 187
Altman, M., 181
Angel, J. W., 104, 114–16, 118, 119n,
   120, 122–3, 164
Ankli, R., 34n, 57n, 153, 156
arbitrage, 30
Argentina, 50, 152, 157
asset markets, 3; asset substitutability, 17,
   29, 90; historical development, 61;
   market integration, 31, 129, 161;
   portfolio adjustment, 57, 161–3
Atlantic economy, 34, 147, 153
Australia, 1n, 50, 157

Bailey, Martin J., 204n
balance of payments:
   history, 9, 148–55
balance-of-payments adjustment:
   autonomous saving and, 133–4; capital
   flows and, 11, 28, 31, 47, 91–2, 133–
   4, 161–2; causal mechanism, 14, 18,
   28, 59, 89, 94–9, 120, 122–3, 139–40,
   161–3; data and their sources, 35, 37–
   42f, 175–8, 181–4, 190–1; evidence,
   75; gold flows and, 4, 28, 34, 75–85,
   92, 139–44, 161–3; history of thought
   about, 148, 155–7; monetary approach
   to, 2, 3, 28–31, 156–7, 158, 161–3,
   169–70; over business cycles, 123–7;
   process of, 139–44n; real balance
   effects and, 11; real factors affecting,
   17–18, 34, 47; secondary reserves and,
   13, 75, 92, 119–20, 133–4; smooth
   functioning mechanism of, 147–55;
   tests of causal mechanism, 99–109,
   122–3
balance-of-payments surplus: behavior over

the business cycle, 123–7; determinants
of, under classical theory, 76–82, 91;
determinants of, under portfolio theory,
76–83, 91, 162; equality with rate of
growth of reserve money, 76, 91, 132–
4, 138–9; gold and secondary reserves
as part of, 92; seasonal movements in,
154
balance of trade, 2, 54; data and their
sources, 35, 37f; determinants of, 77–
9, 132–4; exchange-rate movements
and, 10; gold flows and, 17–18, 31,
98, 163; history, Canada, 151–5;
linking economies, 97–100; net capital
flow and, 7, 31, 50, 54–5, 78, 159,
163; price/income effects on, 28, 36–7,
54–5; seasonal movements in, 154
Bank Act: first Dominion Bank Act, 7, 27
Bank of England, 1, 167, 171, 174
bank reserves (*see also* international
reserves): adjustment by banks of, 119–
20, 161–2; bank's control over, 58;
composition of, 57, 70, 72–3;
countercyclical variability of, 123–7,
154; determinants of, 58, 70, 72–3;
effect of debt service balance on, 76;
effects of exogenous monetary and
output changes on, 91–2; gold holdings
of banks, 42, 43f, 57; held in New
York, 12–13, 19, 26, 27; interest rate
effects on, 8, 58; legal requirements
concerning, 27; quantity of money
demanded and, 7; relationship to
prices, 114
bank-deposit liabilities, 58
banking system: adjustment of loans, 119–
21, 164–5; adjustment of reserve ratios,
120–1, 133–4, 151–2, 161–2; changes
in deposits of, 154–5; control over the
money supply, 57–8, 120, 133–4, 161–